Edited Clean Version

Edited Clean Version

Technology and
the Culture of Control

Raiford Guins

University of Minnesota Press   Minneapolis / London

Portions of chapter 2 were published as "The V-Chip: Seeing Eugenically," *West Coast Line* 34/1 (August 2000): 48–59. Revised portions of chapter 4 have been published as "Now You're Living: The Promise of Home Theater and Deleuze's New Freedoms," *Television and New Media* 2/4 (2001): 351–65. An early draft of chapter 5 was published as "From Senseless Acts of Violence to Seamless Acts of Visibility: 'Film Censorship' in the Age of Digital Compositing," *New Formations* 46 (Spring 2002): 23–33.

Published by the University of Minnesota Press
111 Third Avenue South, Suite 290
Minneapolis, MN 55401-2520
http://www.upress.umn.edu

Library of Congress Cataloging-in-Publication Data

Guins, Raiford.
    Edited clean version : technology and the culture of control / Raiford Guins.
        p.   cm.
    Includes bibliographical references and index.
    ISBN 978-0-8166-4814-6 (hc : alk. paper) — ISBN 978-0-8166-4815-3 (pb : alk. paper)
        1. Mass media—Censorship—United States.   2. Television—Censorship—United States.   3. V-chips.   4. Motion pictures—Censorship—United States.   5. Internet—Access control—United States. I. Title.
    P96.C42U655 2009
    363.3'1—dc22

                                                                        2008034460

Printed in the United States of America on acid-free paper

The University of Minnesota is an equal-opportunity educator and employer.

15 14 13 12 11 10 09   10 9 8 7 6 5 4 3 2 1

For Joseph "Uncle Joe" Olson, Farväl

Contents

Introduction

Michael, Marshall, and Me

On the evening of November 20, 2001, one body was deemed optically correct. The body in question belonged to Britney Spears, a body highly visible at the time through music videos, films, televised appearances, video games (*Britney's Dance Beat*, 2002), and magazine covers, as well as scores of Web pages promising uninhibited glimpses of her "celebrity skin." Spears's pre-"meltdown" performance on CBS's *Michael Jackson: 30th Anniversary Celebration* aired to an estimated 25.7 million viewers. Hers was not the only body showcased, however. Other bodies performed during the telecast. Their bodies were not deemed fit for prime-time viewing and underwent substantial correction prior to reaching the eyes of millions. On account of her "skeletal figure," diva-in-crisis Whitney Houston had pixelated flesh digitally graphed onto her broadcast image to render her body fuller and presumably healthier than its off-camera dimensions. Not even the guest of honor, himself no stranger to the scalpel, was spared from the evening's digital cosmetic procedures: the televised image of Michael Jackson was darkened digitally. The *Entertainment News* (*E!*) presenter who reported the use of digital effects to manage the presentation of bodies informed viewers that CBS's "procedure" was carried out to make Michael appear more "black" when performing alongside his brothers for the first time since the Victory Tour in 1984. Half a century ago on January 6, 1957, Elvis Presley was presented to U.S. audiences framed from the waist up on *The Ed Sullivan Show*. As is well known, manually operated television cameras denied home audiences a shot of his lower regions seemingly possessed by "lewd dancing." In 2001 Jackson performs alongside his brothers in full frame while digital compositing techniques, like those used to hide the apparatus of production in spectacular Hollywood computer-generated action films, make Jackson's televised image more "appropriate" for mass transmission according to CBS's "policy." Have digital aesthetics come to replace the overt visible mechanisms of film and television censorship? Can we even consider such actions censorship? Did the 25.7 million even notice? And what if they had?

Eminem's highly anticipated follow-up to *The Slim Shady LP, The Marshall Mathers LP,* debuted on May 23, 2000. By June 10 the dark comedy of a ruptured psyche took the number one position on the Billboard 200. A word slinger who is no stranger to controversy for lyrical content regarded as homophobic, misogynist, and replete with expletives, Eminem's self-reflexive wise-guy tales cum hip-hop social commentary were not exempted from the "cleaning" process that the music industry deployed to produce a non-stickered, "clean version" CD. The bravado of Eminem's various aliases on the album did little to intimidate Interscope Records executives' decision to secure markets by introducing the now standard edited version within which certain words or phrases are omitted or "bleeped" over by assorted sound effects. On the clean-version track "Kill You" the word *kill* is replaced by "**** You" on the back cover of the CD. Words dropped out from the song include *coke, slut, shit, bullet, fuckin, fuckin kill, Vicodin, guns, weed, choke, machete, faggots, sodomize, whore, motherfucker, knives,* and *killer. Bitches, acid, balls,* and *blood* remain. Not even the major verse of the chorus is exempt from this cleaning process: "Cause Shady, will ~~fuckin kill~~ you" goes the chorus of the clean version. The listener is subjected to a chorus that sounds incontestably impaired. In the case of "Kill You," references to drugs (even legal ones like Vicodin), violence, and sexual activities are dropped out, or certain words that executives feel most connote these actions are expelled. With this many edits (I estimate thirty-seven total) enacted on one song heard over the airwaves and on Viacom's music video monopoly, the clean version of *The Marshall Mathers LP* resembles a cross between a cell phone chat with terrible reception (we used to say a skipping record) and a noted hip-hop lyricist suffering from an incurable case of hiccups. Can the "clean version" of Eminem's *The Marshall Mathers LP,* or any clean version for that matter, be considered censored media? The album was not ruled legally obscene like 2 Live Crew's *As Nasty as They Wanna Be* in 1990. It is widely played and readily available. Listeners need simply choose: dirty or clean. The "dirty version" (the manufactured delinquent of normalizing discourses) is obtainable in CD and MP3 formats, while the "clean version" circulates on both formats and on the radio and television.

Every time I attempt to play a new DVD in my Sony PlayStation 2 (PS2) (I have only recently upgraded to PS3), a screen informs me that "The Parental Settings of This Player Prohibit Play." Programmed to interpellate me as a neophyte, or perhaps a delinquent in need of remote techno-parental supervision, my machine's default settings persist in infantilizing me regardless of my adult status. My PS2 DVD player "asks" whether I would like to allow the disc to play according to a predetermined numerical-level option (a lower level signals a stricter restriction). I select "Yes" rather than "No" as those are my options, and I certainly would not have bothered to place a disc in the machine had I not intended to use it. I then input my top secret four-digit password. It's "0000." Voila! The parental function grants access. Having enjoyed John Waters's schlock tale of sex addicts, *A Dirty Shame* (2005), in the cinema, I wanted to "go sexin'" again at home.[1] In accordance with my machine's paternalist directive, I selected "Yes" when prompted by a screen asking whether or not to allow the disc to play. I then decided to dissent and not agree to change the parental control levels to "8." The message "This movie will not play due to the parental setting of the player" dominated my television screen. I frantically tried pressing the various PS2 controller buttons (even L 1,2 and R 1,2 that allow for scanning and next scene commands) and the analog controls. Nothing. I could not access the contents of the DVD. My machine simply refused. I was locked out, placed in the strictest form of viewer time-out. A master of circumvention, I turned my PS2 off and on again to watch in conjunction with the "8" level. This action does not modify the content of the DVD but does determine whether or not one can watch the DVD inserted into the PS2. "Let's Go Sexin," *A Dirty Shame*'s theme music fills the DVD's interface as users select their "dirty" options by use of a gold halo cursor. In an age of clean media Waters's little interface satire is a sardonic touch. Few will see it, however, on account of its NC-17 rating. Is "choice" simply a matter of complying with pre-inscribed settings or levels of access: a restricted decision consisting of either clean or dirty? Are "parental controls" and "parental settings" a softer, "family-friendly" technology for censorial practices? In another constellation in Waters's universe known as *Cecil B. DeMented* (2000), "Honey Whitlock" (Melanie Griffith) exclaims, "family is just another word for censorship!"

To attend to these processes of cultural regulation and to familiarize readers with the characteristics of what I designate as *control technologies,* I would like to raise a general question that helps frame the book's subject matter: Where precisely are "the censor," the "institution of censorship," and "policy" in the practices of media regulation recounted above?[2] Today's DVD player, game console, television, and computer can block out, monitor, disable, and filter online information, digital television transmissions, and prerecorded media according to a "parental function" *designed in* the hardware or available as software. In the case of retail, consumers are outfitted with a "choice" of content type when a clean-version CD, MP3, or copyrighted Hollywood DVD, like those reedited by "film sanitizers" at Utah's CleanFlicks, are as readily available as their presumably sullied counterparts (or at least were at one time). In film production/postproduction editors can digitally "correct" an image or sound to obtain an R rating as opposed to an NC-17, as was the case when nude and clothed computer-generated actors were superimposed over scenes of simulated sex in Stanley Kubrick's *Eyes Wide Shut* (1999).

New digital media technology premised upon notions of choice, user-centered control, personal responsibility, self-regulation, security, empowerment, and consumer freedom is flooding the contemporary electronic media market. With it comes the emergence of a significant division between how we actively manage and regulate our own relations to media content and technology today and the older incarnations of institutional media censorship. To wit, how the censorial "cut" has been understood in the history of film censorship is undergoing radical changes as, in the well-documented case of *Eyes Wide Shut,* certain scenes are completely "filled up" with information; no frames are eradicated to achieve a rating or "improve" an older print. The same applies to clean versions of music as audio special effects mask words or phrases that otherwise would require a parental advisory sticker for retail sales. Consumers, in particular, have entered into new relationships with their everyday technology that enable them to personally "inscribe" and claim responsibility for their own experience with media with self-prescribed values and morals, distinct from but also a reinforcement of the "family entertainment" policies of long-standing institutions commonly associated with film censorship and classificatory practices. Moreover, institutions historically responsible for standards or media ratings are being supplanted by the development of technologies driven by media industries, retail policy, and consumer initiatives that allow for self-governance, self-regulation, and the paradoxically greater freedom of control at the touch of a button, jog of a dial, click of a mouse, or even more effortlessly and, perhaps, insidiously by default settings.

Censorial practices and procedures are generalized and multiplied at innumerable sites and experiences with the management of culture. While, for example, the Motion Picture Association of America (MPAA) and its affiliate the Code and Rating Administration (CARA) will remain and their policies will continue to broaden to cover new threats to the film and television industry, the latest being piracy, and the Internet Content Rating Association (ICRA) will continue to "encourage" Webmasters to rate and label their Web content according to their criteria for online "safety" and "protection," these policies and regulatory practices constitute a larger process of governance. Practices once reserved for industries (because of sender or broadcast models of regulation[3]) are increasingly rationalized in the everyday; they are distributed across and throughout culture and individualized as a range of practices with consumer technology. Censorial processes, as each chapter argues, are *in* our media technology as functions of choice to protect and serve users, not solely enacted *on* media as an imposing, external oppressive force. The action of regulation is relocated into the hands of users (positioned in a prescriptive discourse of empowerment, security, and choice), and their private relations with control technologies are regarded as user-centered and self-governing. Both conditions are constant, reliant on the cultural formation of what I will regard as enabled subjects who actively manage and define their own experience with media. The television equipped with a V-chip, for example, transforms our televisions into a monitoring device for televisual content; it "watches" our watching of television. Long accused of contributing to (if not causing) "moral decay" or functioning as a "corrupting influence," television is recast as a technological solution to aid parents in the policing of the mediascape of their homes. Familial digits, interfacing with a keyboard, game "controller," or television remote control device (RCD), reassign, redesign, and relocate the censor's long-imagined scissors, blindfold, and gag of regulation.

This is not to claim that the practices and institutions briefly mentioned above no longer influence how we understand and participate in censorial actions. Instead, as Nikolas Rose advises in his work on governmentality, we are at a critical juncture in the history of the strategies of rule where the "multiplication of possibilities" overrides any investment in a single monolithic institution credited with the assurance of discipline:

> There appears, then, to be no overarching "post-disciplinary" logic, but rather a multiplication of the possibilities and strategies deployed around different problematizations in different sites and with different objectives. And this problem is made more complicated when one accepts that the penal complex represents only one facet of strategies of control: school, family, factory, public architecture and urban planning, leisure facilities, *the mass media and much more* have been mobilized and instrumentalized governmentally in the name of good citizenship, public order and the control or elimination of criminality, delinquency and anti-social conduct.[4] (emphasis added)

Contemporary censorial practices require that we venture beyond the archetypes of the institution of censorship to seek new openings for thinking about "the censorial" that counteract a view that fails to come to terms with the modulations of control that relocate, redesign, reconfigure, and multiply the power effects of these practices and the means by which power is exercised in new cultural assemblages and technologies. Thus, *Edited Clean Version* does not study an era of "post-media censorship" nor declare the end of media censorship, but attempts to grasp a new beginning in its intensification.

Specifically, a firmer explanation is required of how censorial practices operate at present when newer media and our social relations to them undo habitual understandings of the phenomenon as a repressive force and centralized entity with distinct practices emanating "down" from "the State" or situated in recognizable industry and legal institutions. This, it must be stressed, is not to infer that in the not-too-distant past censorship was confined and solely identified within the domain of specific institutions. Writing on film censorship in the United Kingdom, Annette Kuhn persuasively contends that many studies on censorship "start out . . . with assumptions about where censorship takes place and with what outcomes."[5] These assumptions are often grounded in what she refers to as the "prohibition/institutions" model that "constructs censorship as an activity guided by practices of exclusion, and locates those practices in organizations such as boards of film censors, or institutions whose activities impinge directly upon those of censorship bodies."[6] Studies, in this case of film censorship, retell institutional histories in their contribution to an "official" annual for the history of film censorship: an extensive summation of organizational and governmental policies that impose restrictions *on* films.[7]

Despite Kuhn's intervention, the study of film censorship in the early twenty-first century remains overdetermined by the recounting of histories of the Production Code and the Blacklist, continued critiques of the MPAA rating system, and the incessant asking of what went wrong with the NC-17 rating.[8] A problem that Kuhn's text cannot account for, which is by no fault of her own, is the increasing difficulty of maintaining a medium-specific approach for the study of media censorship and working within the disciplinary borders that claim a medium. When cinema studies includes a discussion of television censorship, it usually appears as a lone chapter in a larger study of film censorship. The study of television censorship, to quote Heather Hendershot's excellent intervention, "has been largely unexamined" and, we could add, mostly dedicated to news coverage in journalism.[9] Music censorship has its own books, which include histories of music on television, cover art, and music video, and authors have recently turned their sights to debates around open source and the legality of downloading music.[10] In addition, scholarly work on the regulation of digital media often exists outside of the purview of film, television, and music, and this concentration has produced a substantial body of work under the auspices of cyber law studies and its investment in First Amendment law and copyright.[11] The point that I am making is that in the humanities we have preferred that our studies of censorship not cross institutions, practices, or media while, more often than not, appearing in the form of a historical study (i.e., bookmarked in the past). An intervention within the study of censorship initiated through a concentration on digital techniques and applications in the service of censorial actions on popular media is necessary in order to account for a present that increasingly looks radically different from film studio self-regulation, debates over ratings, radio bans, standards and division guidelines, and boycotts.

When clean-version music is downloadable on Apple's iTunes and consumed as CDs, when clean-version DVDs are rented online and then watched on television or a computer, when Internet filters block access to mixed media Web pages and MPEGs, when digital special effects and editing combine to darken a performer or erase and replace an object, and when our televisions and DVD players filter transmitted and prerecorded media content, we must attend to the history of the present as it appears and operates.[12]

Agreeing that the prohibitive/institutions model is counterproductive and that medium-specific models for the study of media censorship ignore the process of media convergence (or, if maintained, will proceed to be reductive and only capable of producing claims of historicity), it becomes necessary to regard censorial practices as circulating in excess of the political, historical, and social institutions through which they used to crystallize, concentrate, and execute their procedures of power. We need to move from the histories that Kuhn has problematized as predetermined and limiting and seek out different registers from which to consider the "censorial"—a more ambiguous adjective that relates to *a* censor's (in whatever form) operations and practices—as opposed to an official or institution. It is not the case that media "censorship" ceases to be effective in the present, but rather that the conditions and power relations that structure understandings and operations of censorial effects are manifest *in* new assemblages, technologies, practices, and processes. This book commences here and studies only a few such assemblages that have appeared on the U.S. market since the Telecommunications Act of 1996.

As the changing practices and processes of the censorial attest in the brief guises that I have discussed in these opening pages, we have entered into a new era of media regulation that operates (looks, sounds, and feels) differently from "censorship" that helped constitute electronic media throughout much of the twentieth century, and this emergent formation of power as well as our own conceptual uncertainty in articulating these power relations bears immediate attention in order to excogitate the governing of culture within the United States and in our digital present. Moving away from medium-specific, institutional, and broadcast models of censorship to account effectively for this technological transition on its own terms and understandings of regulation, *Edited Clean Version* identifies consumer media, digital techniques and practices in the production of film and music, and retail services that promise to empower users through choice as "control technologies" designed to advance an ethos of neoliberal governance through the very media technologies long presumed to warrant management, legislation, and policing. Our media technology becomes both a means and object of censorial actions.

To assess and understand the range of practices constitutive of media regulation, this book shares in the intellectual project that Jack Z. Bratich, Jeremy Packer, and Cameron McCarthy regard as "governmentality studies," a pursuit that expounds on Michel Foucault's essay "Governmentality" (English translation, 1991) and related lectures. Scholarship in cultural studies, politics, and sociology is engaged in a disparate inquiry into the problematization of government understood as the "arts and rationalities of governing," an analytics of thinking about government as a "conduct of conduct," a mentality for governing. Of key importance to governmentality studies is that government is articulated as a series of heterogeneous procedures in the shaping of human conduct and behavior that are not restricted to an appraisal of "the State" as a source of sovereign power. Bratich, Packer, and McCarthy make this point well when they write, "It [governmentality] is an attempt to reformulate the governor-governed relationship, one that does not make the relation dependent upon the administrative machines, juridical institutions, or other apparatuses that usually get grouped under the rubric of the State."[13] Within the context of governmentality studies the problematic of the censorial can be broadened beyond the study of censorship's medium specificity, institutions, and historicity. Here emergent cultural practices can be assessed as they circulate and engineer cultural formations with media technology as processes of control without reducing these practices to mere extensions of policy, or treating them only as a means to an institutional history, or dismissing them entirely from an analysis of the disparate components that form power relations. This reformulation of the "governor-governed relationship" expands on the study of the censorial by identifying cultural practices that, while not necessarily directly expressive of policy or legislation, persist to structure an equally viable component of governance and mark an expansion in how governing functions through culture. Turning to the innumerable practices afforded by digital media technology foregoes the assumptions that Kuhn recognizes as limiting to studies on censorship. Namely, it is impossible to predict any outcome as, in fact, the censorial is a daily practice and technique of control not necessarily recognized and practiced as "censorship" when we channel surf, google, play DVDs, game, download music, or watch films.

For Bratich, Packer, and McCarthy and the essays that comprise their edited collection *Foucault, Cultural Studies, and Government,* the exercise of examining the technologies of governing ought to be approached through an analysis of power that is understood as cultural in its diverse manifestations of both macro and micro processes of governance. Drawing from the work of Tony Bennett and Foucault, the editors situate culture within the discourse of governmentality, as a "set of reflections, techniques, and practices that seek to regulate conduct."[14] While the culture and government relation are the larger context within which I endeavor to locate this book, and, as I will discuss, control technologies are a means of governing culture as well as "culturally," I attend to an imperative component in the study of governmentality: media technology. Foucault did us no favors when he eschewed any analysis of electronic media in his corpus.[15] And it seems, given the explicit debt to Foucault, that contemporary studies of the technologies of governing, despite their overall richness, are still struggling to situate media technologies squarely in the heterogeneous ensemble of power relations for explaining how we govern and are governed in the twenty-first century. More often than not media technology as part of the study of governmentality is identified as "important" and is claimed to have massive repercussions for understanding government, but little else is said, or the engagement is managed in broad terms of examples expressive of "media." An entry point that others have taken (most notably Alexander R. Galloway, Wendy Hui Kyong Chun, and Mark Poster[16]) for positioning media technology within the study of culture and governance is Gilles Deleuze's all-too-brief work on "control." While Deleuze gives us no analysis of media technology beyond naming "information technologies and computers" as characteristic of the emergent forms of power after disciplinary *dispositifs,* and while the term *control* itself remains undefined and elusive throughout his writings on societies of control, we can turn to this slim body of work for various reasons that together allow for a sustained consideration of the governing of culture through media technology. Prolonged consideration will occur in chapter 1, so I will limit my discussion here to a few immediate reasons only.

First, the word *control* is common in discourses that enable user abilities through an engagement with media technology. By employing the V-chip, activating Internet filters, or on account of the various "versions" that circulate on the market, control is hailed as a by-product of newer media. Rather than regard these new technologies as "controlling" in a sense of domination, we are put *in control,* able to exert control over our media and those bodies attending to its screens through their acquisition and presence. Concepts like "freedom," "empowerment," "family," "parent," "choice," as well as "control" itself will prove vital for understanding the ethos of neoliberal politics and procedures of control technology. Second, Deleuze's vagueness, while no doubt frustrating if one seeks a theory, offers resourceful hints and subtle probes for tracking the "free-floating control"[17] that is multiplied and generalized in our televisions, DVD players, computers and in the digital technologies that allow the industry to sidestep any allocations of censorship when their products proceed to be accessible, available, and viewable. For this reason, I employ *control* as a prefix to technology in order to articulate and describe a range of cultural practices with media technology that function within a process of control that attempts to instill a sense of security over the immediate technology and the information transmitted and displayed upon its screen or resonating through speakers.

To clarify, everyday practices with media technology embody and intensify the processes of control that manage, circumscribe, demarcate, and regulate our "new freedoms." Practices are synecdochical to the processes of control. As both practice and process, control technologies are active instead of static and determined. Our individual, autonomous, and idiosyncratic practices are always part of a larger process in the regulation of conduct that will be discussed as "governing at a distance." Through an examination of control as a technology of governing, we can catch a glimpse of the logic and practices of censorial operations in an era that functions beyond broadcast models of media as well as the presumed centrality and inclusive governance of the institution of media censorship. That said, gauging how censorial practices function as control technologies requires an articulation of the quotidian dynamic between neoliberal social relations and control: control technologies and their subjects need to be positioned as expressive of how governing can be comprehended in regard to the study of media censorship practiced through digital culture. The concept of control is better suited, it can and will be argued, to the deregulatory mechanisms of neoliberal forms of governing explicit in governmentality studies. Therefore, control technology will function as one among many technologies of governing in our present to make sense of Michael, Marshall, and Me as well as other characters in this study of governmentality.

Edited Clean Version

This book structures its argument according to the active practices and procedures indicative of control. How control is carried out on, through, and by different media technologies is my central object of study. Chapters are organized according to operations of control practices expressed through the mechanisms, technologies, practices, and techniques of "blocking," "filtering," "sanitizing," "cleaning," and "patching." The subjects of each chapter, of course, are not designed to be considered in complete isolation from one another, as "blocking" is a type of "filtering," and "sanitizing" and "cleaning" are often used interchangeably. I have organized the book through such practices because each is identified with media technologies that are responsible for enacting the said effect. For example, chapter 2, "Blocking," identifies this process with the V-chip; chapter 3, titled "Filtering," furthers this discussion by engaging with the Internet and networked computers. In this instance the mixed and multimedia of Internet content demonstrate the difficulties and problems of maintaining medium-specific approaches to the study of media censorship. By shifting our attention to censorial practices instead of organizing a book by categories such as "film," "television," or "computer," we see how control courses through consumer media technology in a ubiquitous manner and come to realize that many media technologies are in a process of becoming control technologies or at least sharing control applications. Chapter 4, "Sanitizing," locates this process in the videocassette, DVD, and DVD player, as well as the technology of the video store, while chapter 5, "Cleaning," concentrates on digital special effects in the service of censorial practices in film and music. For as I contend, only a study that identifies and works through control procedures themselves will allow us to move beyond the institutional concentration that persists in stunting how media regulation, policing, and governance can be examined. To remain here is to ignore how the censorial operates and is practiced in the digital age. By centering censorial procedures and positing questions directed at actions rather than institutions, I hope to draw the argument away from debates overdetermined by why censorship occurs, questions of content and audience, and pronouncements on constitutionality, to an account of control technologies that redefines relations to media as a network of forces expressed through and on media objects and their subjects.

The main task of chapter 1, "Control," is to familiarize readers with Deleuze's notion of *control* and writing on governing that extends Foucault's work on governmentality. An understanding of both is crucial in order to ascertain how "the censorial" is intensified and practiced as a control technology within neoliberal configurations of rule and governance. The first section, "Control and Governmentality," examines Deleuze's claim of a shift from disciplinary society to one of control encapsulated in his metaphor of the "highway" as a means to conceptualize the generalization control. I pair Deleuze's "highway" with Nikolas Rose's understanding of governing "at a distance" to articulate how emergent technology promises ideas of securitization, choice, and disciplined freedoms through its pervasive and self-regulatory policing of conduct. The next section, "Control Technologies," outlines the key characteristics of what I define as *control technologies*. They are as follows: (1) Instrumentalized protocols delimit a social relation to emerging devices of control; (2) Control is "designed in" our media technology; and (3) Control technology is devices, applications, techniques, and practices that enable choice for disciplined freedoms.

Chapter 2, "Blocking," opens the book's study of select practices by reintroducing the V-chip as a control technology resultant from the Telecommunications Act of 1996. I say, "reintroduce," on account of the V-chip—a technological "solution" for policing television content seemingly forgotten after the Clinton-Gore administration, if not sooner—being emphatically reinvigorated by the networks, politicians, and media watchdog groups after Janet Jackson's botched half-time performance at Super Bowl XXXVIII in 2004. Instead of readdressing debates on the technology's constitutionality, considering whether or not it is censorious, and evaluating whether or not it succeeds in its performative mission to make "our living rooms safer," as scholarly work on the V-chip has discerned, I position the device as a control technology that redesigns the cultural technology of the television and reconfigures the relationship of the viewer to the television medium. Turning to William Uricchio's work on the expanding logic of television as well as Raymond Williams's notion of "reactive" technology, I consider the V-chip as part of this expansion and argue that it must be considered alongside, for example, the remote control device and digital video recorder as yet another index of viewer-centered control, one "designed in" to enable a parental function for all. In arguing for the V-chip as an expansive element to television as well as how we experience television as control technology, I also ask a question that has not been raised in relation to the V-chip: how does it govern vision and visuality. The V-chip's original conceptualization targeted vision as its object for regulation as explicated in the meaning of "V": "Vyou Control," that is, view-you control. I introduce Paul Virilio's concept of "sightless vision" to assist in making sense of the production, proliferation, and display of the visual enabled by the V-chip.

Chapter 3, "Filtering," continues our engagement with blocking by turning our attention to computer software that blocks, filters, and monitors both Web content and our actions online. Internet filtering software appears in the form of "parental controls" provided by Internet Service Providers (ISP) and third-party software that enables parents, again the targeted conduit through which control is said to circulate, to configure settings and levels of Web access based upon keyword and key pattern word searches that block entire Web sites, individual Web pages, and, perhaps, IP addresses. Like the V-chip, a technological solution is offered to regulate media content, and as the V-chip readministers a relation to the TV medium, we witness a reconfiguration of the networked computer. In this chapter, I examine how the computer screen is redesigned as a "front door" for home security in contrast to the television screen long conceptualized as a "window." The computer screen "armed" with filtering software becomes a control technology. The discourses through which Internet filtering software companies deploy their wares exceed content regulation as the ability to filter information is positioned as a practice for the securitization of habitat; the computer screen becomes a self-governed electronic threshold where control technology monitors who and what can pass. Filtering companies like Mayberry USA, CyberPatrol, CyberSentinel, NetMop, Screendoor, and Net Nanny seek to design a "family friendly Internet" in their own image, one that delimits a non-filtered Internet as dangerous, harmful, and hazardous. This chapter also looks behind the front door to understand the "invisible" workings of filtering software. The blocked site constitutes visible evidence of control, while the processes of rating the

Internet and the code that governs how filters perform their function are invisible since users are often unaware of what information is denied and thus banished from their screens.

Chapter 4, "Sanitizing," attends to the practice of reediting Hollywood copyrighted films to remove footage and dialogue deemed "obscene" by companies like CleanFlicks and ClearPlay. Through nonlinear digital editing software, CleanFlicks removed profanity, graphic violence, and scenes of sex and nudity from its clean-version DVDs until this action was ruled illegal in the form of *Clean Flicks v. Steven Soderbergh*. ClearPlay produces filtering software to work in conjunction with its DVD players that enable parents to select different versions of a DVD depending on the configuration of content selected. For example, we could watch with all profanity deleted, and the DVD player will mute the sound track when swear words appear. Sanitizing, it will be argued, is a practice of "versioning" that promises to safeguard domestic viewing experiences by literally eradicating filmic content. The designed-in quality and presence of control expand as it now fills our DVDs and DVD players. The reedited DVD and filtering DVD player instrumentalize control as a technology of choice in that both companies and film sanitizers in general regard their trade as empowering choice in the form of their versions. To acquaint us with the process of film sanitizing, I have elected to concentrate on CleanFlicks' version of David Cronenberg's *A History of Violence* as a case study of sanitizing effects. I consider *A History of Violence* in relation to the question that Jane M. Gaines sets for her own work on film censorship in the early twentieth century: "what does the censor's cut do to the film text." While this question will persist in the final chapter, it is raised within the context of film sanitizing to question how this process purports to "repair" what is presumed "damaged" and "damaging" for its audiences. This chapter also finds it necessary to provide a larger context for film sanitizing than CleanFlicks and ClearPlay. I turn to the notion of "viewer control" that became a popular marketing mantra in the 1980s for articulating social relations and understandings for domestic media like the VCR. In doing so, James Hay's work on governmentality and media technologies of the period elucidates how they instigated new social arrangements for self-regulation within the domestic sphere. However, rather than replicate Hay's engagement with the VCR, I look to the video store, namely Blockbuster Inc.'s radical redesign of the video store experience as a control technology that attempts to monitor and preempt what content is licensed to enter the home through its "family entertainment" policies.

Chapter 5, "Cleaning," continues to expound upon Jane M. Gaines's questioning of the "censor's cut" by redirecting it to the digital composite. Film production and postproduction increasingly rely on digital media for cinematic realism and narrative continuity. The "cut," too, is transformed by these same technologies as digital compositing "paints," "erases," "superimposes," "masks," and "fills" the shot with information rather than relying solely on the cut and splice technique long associated with cinema in its analog mode of production. Drawing from film and media scholarship on digital special effects, this chapter explores how these practices affect our understanding of film censoring as it becomes increasingly visible and pervasive in its digital manifestations. Stanley Kubrick's *Eyes Wide Shut* and its superimposition of digital images to mask "graphic" scenes to secure an R rating provides an intriguing case of such practices. Digital effects in the service of censorial practice display the censorial as an aesthetic effect that manages our viewing. I also consider modes of "cleaning" that do not directly invoke censorial measures required for a particular rating. Of interest are Steven Spielberg's decision to replace handguns with walkie-talkies in the rerelease of *E.T.: The Extra-Terrestrial* and the cleaning of images of the twin towers after September 11, 2001. The second section maintains an emphasis on cleaning via digital effects to question the production of clean-version CDs. John Corbett's work on the sonic techniques that hip-hop artists enlisted in the early 1990s to evade censorship proves invaluable for a critique of music in the way that Gaines's question shapes our understanding of sanitizing and cleaning filmic images. Engaging with practices like "masking," "deletion," and "replacement," we consider how the "cut" in music attempts to clean content for purposes of both distribution and consumption. Cleaning, it will be argued, is an active process that does not refer to any music free from "explicit" lyrics but one that has been corrected by the reediting process. This process renders other versions seemingly "dirty" in its censorial corrections.

"Patching" serves as the conclusion to *Edited Clean Version* and offers an overview of congressional outrage at the hidden sex scenes in Rockstar Games' *Grand Theft Auto: San Andreas*. Game "mods" and "cheats" allow players of the game to unlock explicit scenes that Rockstar Games originally denied existed in the game. Lawmakers have since called for increased scrutiny of the Entertainment Software Rating Board, and pending bills would increase fines for retailers who sell games to minors. Game console manufacturers have also responded by including parental controls in their systems that manage game content according to a game's rating, while policing online gaming in ways similar to Internet filtering software, particularly since Microsoft's Xbox 360 and Sony's PS3 are networked computers. The inclusion of parental controls in game consoles to monitor game content further evidences the *designed-in* premise of control technology while expanding the media technology through which the parental function of self-governance operates. In addition, I touch on the expansion of control technologies that concentrate on mobile devices while examining challenges that confront parental control's pledge of securitization since the iPod and user-generated Internet video content cannot be regulated through prevailing practices and processes.

1. Control

Control and Governmentality

The English translations of Michel Foucault's "Governmentality" and Gilles Deleuze's "Postscript on Control Societies" both appeared in the early 1990s.[1] While Deleuze's *Foucault* is often discussed within governmentality studies, control and governmentality are in the early days of cohabitation. Michael Hardt and Antonio Negri's *Empire* rests on the exchange between Foucauldian discipline and Deleuze's exegesis on control. Nikolas Rose's *Powers of Freedom* dedicates its final chapter to control in his analysis of neoliberal strategies of rule. The work by both sets of authors is valuable for identifying ways of configuring Deleuze's work on control as practice and process of governing. In "Control and Becoming," "Postscript on Control Societies," and "Having an Idea in Cinema," Deleuze attempts to illustrate an epochal shift in the rationalities and operations of power from discipline societies to what he posits as "control societies."[2] Deleuze suggests that "we're moving toward control societies that no longer operate by confining people but through continuous control and instant communication."[3] While Deleuze's discussion of information technology will be the subject of the next section, here I concentrate on how "continuous control" is manifest in new configurations of rule that beget control societies. More specifically, I attend to how control, and what it enables for the study of new forms of media regulation, can be situated within governmentality studies.

Control or control societies are the locutions Deleuze uses to elucidate the continuous displacement of disciplinary institutions and apparatuses by new technologies and social configurations emblematic of an emerging network of control throughout the twentieth century (accelerated after World War II) and well into our twenty-first-century present. This displacement by control is, for Deleuze, an unfinished process. "Entering a new type of society," as well as a "leaving behind of discipline," we witness a "taking over" from disciplinary institutions of the eighteenth and nineteenth centuries; modes of micro-power practiced through meticulous techniques of standardization, management, organization, individualization, examination, and observation enacted on and through enclosed bodies sought to produce normalized subjects for civil society. In the composite picture of the technology of discipline constructed by Deleuze, the new apparatuses and conditions of control differ from disciplinary procedures just as sovereign societies were distinct in terms of aims, operations, and objectives from discipline societies. These shifts ought not to be regarded as total linear replacements of one another. Foucault's lecture on "Governmentality" offers a triangular model of sovereignty-discipline-government with the management of population through security being the object of the ensemble of government. While not employing the concept of "control" in his definitions of governmentality, Foucault suggests that "we need to see things not in terms of the replacement of a society of sovereignty by a disciplinary society and the subsequent replacement of a disciplinary society by a society of government; in reality one has a triangle, sovereignty-discipline-government, which has as its primary target the population and as its essential mechanism the apparatuses of security."[4] Periodized differences and historical shifts nevertheless may overlap, coexisting as consonant logics in the formations of conduct.

When Rose directly addresses control, he reiterates the importance Deleuze attributes to the displacement of enclosure while also highlighting the pervasive qualities of the new configurations of control. He writes, "rather than being confined, like its subjects, to a succession of institutional sites, the control of conduct was now immanent to all places in which deviation could occur, inscribed into the dynamics of the practices into which human beings are connected."[5] Hardt and Negri reiterate this point well when they insist that "the passage to the society of control does not in any way mean the end of discipline. In fact, the immanent exercise of discipline—that is, the self-disciplining of subjects, the incessant whisperings of disciplinary logics within subjectivities themselves—is extended even more generally in the society of control."[6] Although Deleuze does not acknowledge governmentality in his writings on control, his conceptualization of control expresses a formation of power that is translucent enough to recognize what Foucault would call "governmental techniques" of governmental rationality. This is most evident in both writers' citing of the "incessant whisperings" of discipline not solely internal to the state and its institutional constrictions, but increasingly external, accentuated everywhere. When at the end of his lecture on governmentality Foucault advises his audience that his next lecture will continue this history through an investigation of the Christian pastoral, Deleuze is attempting to scout information technology. Furthermore, Deleuze insists that Foucault knew that disciplinary society, elucidated so well in *Discipline and Punish* and in numerous essays, lectures, and interviews, was coming to a close by the early twentieth century. In contrast to a sketch of contemporary society as one of discipline, Foucault's work on the subject functions as an epitaph for the historical periodization of disciplinary society while, concurrently, serving as a prelude to control.

The foremost characteristics of the shift from disciplinarity to control are multifarious. Diminished centrality of institutional enclosures for social administration, regulation, and management in the imposition of civil conduct and normalization exemplifies control societies. For Foucault, the institutions of disciplinary society, be they prisons, schools, hospitals, or factories, comprised the modern topography for the exercise of power. Foucault was also adamant that these enclosures be comprehended as institutional assemblages of the technologies of power, not as the basis of power relations in disciplinary societies: "Discipline," in an often cited passage, "may be identified neither with an institution nor with an apparatus; it is a type of power, a modality for its exercise, comprising a whole set of instruments, techniques, procedures, levels of application, targets; it is a 'physics' or an 'anatomy' of power, a technology."[7] The structural organization of institutions and enclosures constituted the means by which to confine, organize, distribute, and regulate bodies within a carefully demarcated spatial arrangement ("a space not too large") for the efficient employment and exercise of disciplinary procedures. These and other institutions of the modern period served as conduits for the meticulous enactment of the effects of power.

The shift from discipline to control signals a disintegration of the stalwart institutions once claimed by disciplinarity. "We're in the midst," Deleuze announces, "of a general breakdown of all sites of confinement—prisons, hospitals, factories, schools, the family. The family is an 'interior' that's breaking down like all other interiors—educational, professional, and so on."[8] Institutional assemblages assisted in the consolidation of techniques of discipline. In disciplinary society the body proceeded, calculatedly, from one structure of confinement to another: a scrupulous cycle—enclosed in systems of the family, schools, factories, prisons, churches, barracks, and hospitals—inscribed through an economy of power-knowledge relations where "each individual has a place and each place has its individual."[9]

Deleuze contrasts disciplinary society's dependence on perceptible "molds" of confinement to control's preference for "modulation." "Confinements are *molds,* different moldings, while controls are a *modulation,* like a self-transmuting molding continually changing from one moment to the next, or like a sieve whose mesh varies from one point to another."[10] In regimes of control, the erosion of molds does not signal the ineffectuality of strategies of power but rather a modulation complicit with the logic of control. Like Mark Poster's revisioning of panopticism (the panopticon remolded as the "superpanopticon," a control technology) whereby "the techniques of discipline no longer need rely on methods of regulating bodies in space,"[11] Deleuze's account of control does not rush to label disciplinary institutions as either liberated ruins or completely antiquated apparatuses. Instead, he foresees the materialization of a new system, one that exhibits both characteristics distinct from the recent past of disciplinarity and residual traces of the same. "To be sure," as Deleuze writes, "there are all kinds of things left over from disciplinary societies, and this for years on end, but we know already that we are in societies of another sort that should be called . . . societies of control."[12] This relation to the molds of discipline is articulated well by Michael Hardt's "The Withering of Civil Society," an essay that interrogates Deleuze's accentuation of control in a broader consideration of civil society and political theory. Hardt argues that "social space has not been emptied of the disciplinary institutions but [is] completely *filled* with the modulations of control."[13] The inundation of control technology, which this book studies, furthers Hardt's claim. Subsequently, Hardt and Negri would add to this postulation, suggesting that the passage from disciplinary society to control be viewed as an "intensification and generalization of the normalizing apparatuses of disciplinarity that internally animate our common and daily practices, but in contrast to discipline, this control extends well outside of the structured sites of social institutions through flexible and fluctuating networks."[14] Far from signaling the full extent of discipline, societies of control are constituted by discipline's ubiquitous accentuation.

Where Foucault described discipline as a technique surging through the various (molding) structures of confinement to perfect efficiency and control expenditure in the production of docile citizens, modulations of control circulate freely. Unconstricted by any given social institution, control operates a plurality of effects multiplied on, in, and across networks of contemporary society: "Wouldn't it be better to spread out the treatment?" prompts Deleuze wryly.[15] In being "completely filled" as Hardt illumes, control is exercised indiscriminately, ubiquitously. Its modulations are intensified, distributed, continuous, free-flowing. Freed of the need to "pass through the structures of confinement," control society is also consonant with tenets of advanced liberal governmentality.[16] Advanced liberal governmentality has been a major focus for a number of contemporary political theorists and sociologists who press for refined articulations of new social arrangements and technologies of governance as emerging forms of government lessen the explanatory capacity of traditional political philosophy and economic theory.[17]

Drawing on Foucault's 1978 lecture "Governmentality," Andrew Barry, Thomas Osborne, and Nikolas Rose position advanced liberalism as neither a new political philosophy nor a new type of society as they contemplate the politics of the present:

> It has proven difficult and painful for much political theory and political sociology to abandon the oppositions that have sufficed for so long: State and civil society, economy and family, public and private, coercion and freedom. Yet contemporary movements in politics show just how clumsy and inept such oppositions are: each, in different ways, demands a form of government that combines action by political and non-political authorities, communities and individuals. And the relations of force, of power, of subordination, of liberation and "responsibility," of collective allegiance and individual choice that are brought into being in these new configurations are difficult to visualize, let alone evaluate, in the language of orthodoxy.[18]

In the difficulty of visualization Barry and colleagues suggest that advanced liberalism be considered as a formula of rule, a "mentality of rule," or better still, an ethos of government. "Government" holds two senses for Foucault: one of practice and one of a mentality. The first sense demonstrates the "variety of ways of reflecting and acting which aimed to shape, guide, manage or regulate the conduct of persons . . . in the light of certain principles or goals."[19] Reflection upon conduct is realized through an emphasis on the practical to facilitate acts of governing and power relations between social dynamics and agents. The second sense analyzes the idea of government as a way to "think governmentally"; it represents a "how-to" of sorts: government as a mentality of rule systems for governing. Foucault's interest lies less with separating the two senses than in understanding their interconnections.

In "Government, Authority, and Expertise in Advanced Liberalism" Rose defines a new formula of rule for advanced liberal society that entails "the adoption of a range of devices that seek to recreate the distance between the decisions of formal political institutions and other social actors, and to act upon these actors in new ways, through shaping and utilizing their freedom."[20] The utilization and instrumentalization of political forces outside of those of "the State" leads Rose to articulate this process of governing as being "at a distance" and executed through an ensemble of governing techniques, as Foucault argues in relation to governmentality, that are "internal and external to the state."[21] Of key importance to the articulation of "neo" or "advanced" liberalism, and like discipline's multiplication and generalization under the auspices of control, is that direct state control in the form of governmental intervention is being dispersed and reasserted as a governmental rationality exercised through new techniques of self-regulation and free-market expertise in the constant management of freedom as a discipline practiced through the maximization of choice.

Freedom as a disciplinary mechanism is apparent when pairing Rose's governing "at a distance" with Deleuze's metaphor of the "highway" to account for the autonomy generated through numerous practices of licensure that enable subjects to regulate their own actions. "In making highways," Deleuze writes, "you don't enclose people but instead multiply the means of control. I am not saying that this is the highway's exclusive purpose, but that people can drive infinitely and "freely" without being at all confined yet while still being perfectly controlled."[22] The metaphor of the highway as the equipment of power seeks to express control's undulations of new freedoms—modalities of licensure regarded as beneficial, convenient, secure, enhancing, enabling, "freeing"—promised as well as implemented by instant and continuous self-regulation. Choice is enabled through the control of options. Freedom as a practice produced by control, to adopt Barry, Osborne, and Rose's position, exists as "a formula of rule" as opposed to a utopian condition free of determining restraints and governmental restrictions placed on autonomy, agency, and selfhood. Actions are not predetermined by the institutional processions of disciplinary society, yet the routes navigated— our choices for how we experience daily life—are always already carefully charted. Power is less obvious (power's masking of itself, as Foucault says), less constrictive in its dispersed thoroughfares and difficult to see distances. Rule is imposed through active choice. Its modulations are nonhierarchical with advanced liberal rule strategies set in place to safely facilitate the free flow of everyday movements and actions through, to continue with Deleuze's metaphor, the sprawl of control.

In contrast to subjects being "molded in" confinement, Rose alerts that "conduct is continually monitored and reshaped by logics immanent within all networks of practice. Surveillance is 'designed in' to the flows of everyday existence."[23] In being "designed in" or "completely filled," as Hardt states, the highway is less a governing structure, an advanced system of enclosures designed to "hold" the trafficking of bodies, than an ethos for the subject who, enabled by the instrumentalization of self-regulation, relies upon this specific system of rules to pass through freely. This ethos for a culture of control is best evidenced by the emphasis on choice, personal responsibility, self-reliance (after all Deleuze's highway does not seem to envision a mass public transit system but individual drivers), and self-governing capitulated in a free-market system where solutions to social and moral questions are offered as consumer choices purchased as devices for the management of domains—the family, the home, youths—deemed simultaneously at risk and in danger, yet protected and corrected by control technologies designed to secure them.

Expertise plays a crucial role in the policing of culture and administration of control technology. Tony Bennett describes censors and media regulators, among other examples of cultural workers, as having a type of "expertise subjected to particular forms of validation and translated into particular technical forms through their inscription within particular technical apparatuses."[24] Although these "particular technical apparatuses" are only mentioned and not discussed by Bennett, we can make a case for expertise within contemporary practices and processes of control enacted on culture and through culture. The expert of disciplinary society exercised authority over human conduct through power-knowledge relations passing through various sites of enclosure. As Rose writes, "the very powers which the technologies of welfare accorded to those who possessed knowledge and could speak the truth enabled expertise to establish enclosures within which its authority could not be challenged, effectively insulating itself from external political attempts to govern it."[25] Expertise assisted in the rationality of liberal rule by managing the limitations of political authority in governing people's lives. That is, the exercise of liberal rule was "rendered operable"; it deployed technologies of knowledge across a social spectrum by a range of experts who managed conduct via social apparatuses of authority.

Today, in contrast, people are called upon to become experts themselves, and *of* themselves in a variety of domains. For Rose, this speaks to a new relation between expertise and politics. "Individuals are to become 'experts of themselves,' to adopt an educated and knowledgeable relation of self-care in respect of their bodies, their minds, their forms of conduct and that of the members of their own families."[26] The category of "parent," like that of family, is an important indication of Rose's notion of expertise and a central principle and strategy for technologies of control in the digital age. Parent is a licensed category that fulfills the administrative duties of self-regulating culture for their domain and the domains of others. As a technique of control it "parents" culture not in the ethnological sense of biological birthing but according to other meanings of the word *parent*: guardianship, protection, as well as to cause to come into existence. Parenting is a function, a "parental function" by which to govern the domain of the family and insert itself across culture through practices that produce and ensure the "securitization of habitat."

In his discussion of the networks of security in control societies Rose offers the concept of "the securitization of habitat" as an instance where disciplinary techniques become generalizable to saturate the home with their meticulous rationalities of normalizing intent.[27] Securitization of habitat is the "simultaneous generation of anxiety and insecurity concerning property and personal safety in and around the home, and the marketing of a whole variety of devices and techniques, from insurance policies to burglar alarms, to securitize that habitat."[28] The prime example that Rose offers is the gated community with its maximum security facade designed to "keep threat out rather than keep it in":[29] an inverse of the prison whereby the entire "outside" is placed on permanent lockdown, "space is reconfigured in the name of security."[30] This reconfiguration is not a huge stretch from discipline's implementation of institutions as concentrated sites and apparatuses for power's designation of conduct and crystallizations of state power. One distinction is that Rose posits a different aim from discipline's goal of docility and the means through which it is practiced. In its place (or perhaps on account of discipline's intensity) security becomes an individual responsibility: the parental function's investment in and acquisition of measures to safeguard the family and culture in domestic space.

I would like to propose a more expansive position on the securitization of habitat that exceeds the processes that Rose has identified. The example of a gated community surrounding the domicile anchors control into already existing disciplinary institutions with their own sets of practices and strategies. It also locates habitat in a fixed place. Unfortunately, Rose's analysis of control strategies does not stray too far from the disciplinary institutions originally formulated by Foucault, and he seems reluctant to explore fully the new possibilities of security opened up by media technologies that regulate the flow of information that can take up residence in the securitized and securitizing home. For example, the increasingly securitizing microspace of the television and computer screen and their architectures for communication, visuality, and information within the space of the home as well as its abilities to extend beyond it would be one such instance where the "gated community" needs to be reconsidered as the prime signifier of securitization. The bolted lock on a door and human guard positioned at a gate are only a few means to regulate and manage who and what can intrude upon the spatial strategies of security. (Chapters 2 and 3 develop this line of thinking in more detail.)

In the securitization of habitat the family is a technology (in the Foucauldian sense of the word as a way of exercising power-knowledge relations encompassing a whole range of techniques, mechanisms, and practices) for the management of conduct and the regulation of domain: this takes the form of the family's domain, its home, its neighborhood and community as well as what can come into contact with this domain. While many gates are in place to generate freedoms for those within this domain, where, in fact, does the securitized domain terminate? Is it finite, dependent on the strict confinement of institutions like schools and prisons (if so, control is not any radical departure), limited to the citadels of the enforced gated community, or does "family" attempt to police, this action understood as developmental, not restrictive, a much wider parameter that is not so compliant with older markers of territory? This question is essentially a line of inquiry into the discourse of family as a technology of power that polices and administrates the sociopolitical conditions of culture: culture itself practiced as a locus of power-knowledge relations to shape conduct through the distribution of the parental function's inscription of securitization through the screens governing our well-being.

The family cannot be seen as an adjective for control devices; it must not be regarded as a mere description of some new technology or marketing strategy like "family entertainment." The family is attributed the status of a "kind of 'machine' for assembling citizenship" by Rose.[31] Its machinery transforms the home into a moralized and moralizing space. Yet, the family's mechanisms are not restricted by the doorway: "a 'private' ethic of good health and morality can thus be articulated on to a 'public' ethic of social order and public hygiene, yet without destroying the autonomy of the family—indeed by promising to enhance it."[32] Where in the nineteenth century Foucault assigns the family to the role of anchor to provide permanent support and assurance for production of power-knowledge effects in the deployment of sexuality and morality in general, the family as machinery for control is less fixed. It circulates and develops its practices through the heterogeneous ensemble of culture. Family does not necessarily aim to homogenize culture. Performed as a parental function, family is instead a strategy of rule that operates through culture to further an ethos of security that instrumentalizes cultural practices as they flow freely as solutions to the problematic of securitization. In its enhancement, the "family-machine,"[33] as Rose might say, or, as I prefer, the parental function,[34] becomes the normative basis for "goodness" and the administration of ways of being "good" through the surveillance, perfection, and maintenance of disciplined freedom.

As a technology of expertise, the parental function is neither restricted to its traditional residence of the home, nor are its protective measures only aimed at its family.[35] Securitization broadens the habitats that it can claim. In regards to control devices and technologies of control, the authority of parent and the consequent protection of family are scattered across culture to structure other cultural forms and practices to multiply the possibilities of securitization by claiming choice as the master key for the design of self-governance in the habitat of neoliberal politics. Its expertise leaves the domain of the home (after completely "filling up," to maintain Hardt's explanation of control, the home with its governing morality) to instrumentalize its knowledge in other spaces and upon other subjects not "biologically" linked to its rule but made expressive of governing. The parental function is outfitted with actions such as "warning labels," "ratings," "controls," "locks," "blocks," "filters," "clean" and "sanitized" versions that automatically enact "parenting" at a distance and across various distances. Family is central to strategies of control in its support and expression of the mechanisms of power throughout culture. For example, we see it enacted and enabled when Blockbuster Inc. and Wal-Mart, major retailers of media, designate their space, commodities, and services as "family friendly," places to find heavily policed "family values." "Family" is engineered as a proactive as well as prophylactic entertainment genre, a category that places the categories of "mature" and "adult" under surveillance as anomalies in need of "correcting" and "cleaning." Clean versions rehabilitate "recalcitrant" media by classifying them in opposition to the correct or approved (in terms of retail licensure) version. Once classified, techniques of family offer instruments to improve, repair, or render safe (filter their moral illegalities) that which was dangerous to the securitization of habitat while simultaneously safeguarding freedom of choice. Unlike the term *child* used to mobilize legislation, fear, and insecurity, parent is not a nebulous victim but an enabled solution to police the cultural spaces that most affect children and the family, namely media.

Rose's idea of how we become experts of ourselves indicates that the model of governing "through society" is fast being replaced by heterogeneous strategies of rule that specify governance through individual actions of choice and the recognition of people (normalized citizens) as active agents in self-regulatory practices. The parental function's positioning as a self-responsibilizing agent administers choice for the continued maintenance of regulatory freedom. This is a politics of the enabled in the daily pursuit of disciplined freedom through strategies of rule for the self and others in the self's domains (the family, for instance). It is a politics ruled by choice. The figure of the expert, the authority of expertise as a political force, is relocated from "the apparatuses of political rule" to the rule of the free market. This divested authority of the social institution positions "expertise" as a practice of decision making organized according to the enterprise of consumer choice rather than forms of obligation.[36] The most obvious instance for us is the consumption of clean version CDs and DVDs, the decision to install Internet filters, as well as the automatic inclusion of control devices in our many media choices (V-chips legally required in televisions manufactured for the U.S. market, "parental controls" provided by ISPs). Choice is imagined as an active, autonomous action: "making a choice" is a daily occurrence in modes of self-regulation unlike the oppressive resonance of "subjection to government." The complex of choice, a smaller triangulation in the exercises of governmentality where control, in the context within which we are studying it, is dependent on empowerment-parental function-freedom, becomes a preferred surrogate strategy in neoliberal societies for the presumed limitations and restrictions of regulation. The marketization of expertise aligns the accumulation of knowledge with the action of purchasing in the maintenance of the regulation of autonomy. Choice within this context functions as an enabling action for regulated and disciplined freedom: the paradoxical logic of choice in the era of control. This understanding of choice as a complex of strategies of control renders the function of choice autonomous, nonrestrictive, nongovernmental, deregulatory, and posited on a mentality of "self-reliance" and "self-help" that adopts regulatory practices of self-management as licensed freedom, not dominating. The practice of choice in the passage from disciplinary to control societies might thus be discerned as active compliance with a strategy of rule for the maximization of disciplined freedom.

In control societies, governance is exercised neither solely through the apparatus of rule located in the categories of "society" or "the State," nor is it located in the modern institutions that Foucault examined but through the exercise of rule illustrative of market-governed "regulated choices of individual citizens" in their maintenance of personal freedom and securitization of habit.[37] The V-chip, edited clean CDs, ISP parent control, Internet filters, content shifting DVD players, and video game consoles with parental settings suggest that family is far from a minority. Devices such as these allow the family to circulate its functionality beyond territorial restrictions to transform its social obligations of securitization into a control strategy that acknowledges choice as the ruling principle of regulation. These devices, as governance "at a distance" and channeled through Deleuze's metaphor of the "highway," are emblematic of freedom in service of the family and are not deemed detrimental to its cultural administration of security.

Control Technologies

In multiplying and generalizing the rules of disciplinarity to encompass emergent networks of control, Deleuze cites information technology and computers as expressive of the new paradigm of power relations. He writes:

> It's easy to set up a correspondence between any society and some kind of machine, which isn't to say that their machines determine different kinds of society but that they express the social forms capable of producing them and making use of them. The old sovereign societies worked with simple machines, levers, pulleys, clocks; but recent disciplinary societies were equipped with thermodynamic machines . . . ; control societies function with a third generation of machines, with information technology and computers.[38]

Deleuze does not in any substantial way expound upon the "third generation of machines" and leaves readers to contemplate for themselves the cultural value in the historical transformations wrought by the "digital," "computers," and "code" for an analysis of control. Current scholarly research raises questions of information technology and control, in effect, extrapolating from Deleuze's formulation.[39] Moreover, Deleuze neither demonstrates a critical awareness and understanding of information technology emergent at the time of his writings on control, nor does he enlist the work of media theorists or philosophers of technology in making his case for control's redesign of disciplinary *dispositifs*.[40]

Alexander R. Galloway's *Protocol: How Control Exists after Decentralization* has gone the furthest to flesh out how networked computers are coterminous with Deleuze's delineation of control societies. "Just as Marx," Galloway writes, "rooted his economic theory in a strict analysis of the factory's productive machinery, Deleuze heralds the coming productive power of computers to explain the sociopolitical logics of our own age."[41] The information technology that Galloway offers as exemplary of control is the distributed network of the Internet's technical protocols: "protocol is to control societies as the panopticon is to disciplinary societies."[42] In the imposition of conduct Foucault perceived the panopticon as a diagram of a mode of power ("a generalizable model of functioning") and technology of discipline. While the rationality of the panopticon serves as a model for disciplinary society—its formula of rule dispersed throughout other institutions to intensify control over bodies through docility—I shy away from such an analogy for control society. Control technologies permeate our daily lives; therefore any analysis of the machineries, environments, and programs of power ought to seek them out not only under every stone but *in* every stone, so to speak: in the constant convergences, remediations, and intermedial processes of our present sociopolitical and technocultural networks where power is exercised. This is neither to dispute the importance of the Internet protocol, nor to ignore its relevance for the study of control. Control's "third generation machines" are multifarious and diffuse, not restricted to a single medium or "network of networks," but disseminated incessantly across the converged and increasingly mixed media of television, film, video games, CDs, and DVDs, to which networked computers and the Web are undeniably crucial. Some characteristics of control reside in networked computing; others do not. Though Galloway's analogy is striking as well as both historically and theoretically rich, the logic of control would suggest that no single network (even one that is distributed) ought to subsume the multiple possibilities and permeations of control strategies that currently coalesce to provide safe and continuous passage on our regulated and regulating Deleuzian highways. If control's proliferation, per Deleuze's warning, leads us to "see the harshest confinement as part of a wonderful happy past,"[43] then we need as many vantage points as possible from which to envisage and materialize this shift. My central concern here is that in positioning Internet protocol and computer code as the definitive characteristics of control society, we may divert attention from other nodes in the diagrams that define and produce new relationships between neoliberal subjects and communication-information technologies.[44] These other nodes represent a range of devices, techniques, and practices that function as technologies of control and warrant comparable attention if control is to be studied as it is practiced across and through media.

The passage from Deleuze's "Postscript on Control Societies" that appears above is generative not only because it illustrates the movement from disciplinary to control societies in terms of the different periodizations of media technologies that Galloway references, but also because its formulation bars technological determinism. By not prescribing a definitive political direction for information technology, Deleuze leaves the problematic question of how media technology may transform culture open and unresolved. Technological determinism is less of a problem for Deleuze. The "correspondence between any society and some kind of machine" draws the conclusion that "machines determine different kinds of society but that they express the social forms capable of producing them and making use of them."[45] My articulation of control technologies is less about inventorying specific media than about trying to identify where and how the ethos of neoliberal power relations are multiplied and exercised through a complex configuration of devices, techniques, and practices that ensure the productive management of choice as active governance in the administration and instrumentalization of licensed freedom.

In what follows I describe the key characteristics of control technologies.

1. Instrumentalized protocols delimit a social relation to emerging devices of control.

Neoliberal control strategies are enacted and mediated through a range of devices, techniques, and practices that seek to regulate media and the subject of rule through "empowered" practices with media technologies. In doing so, a liberal humanist understanding of technology is upheld that relies on an instrumentalist view of technology that renders all technology as neutral means, or "tools," for the realization of some human ends.

Solutions to the surmised dangers and risks of media that often fuel moral panic and censorial policy are practices with technology: how devices can be enabled and activated to achieve the goal-oriented task of multiplying the possibility of security by manageable measures. Social, economic, political, and cultural value depends on the uses of a particular tool, artifact, mechanism, or instrument. Objections arise when a specific technology is employed in a way deemed socially inappropriate, dysfunctional, or possibly harmful.

The instrumental view of technology allows for only a one-dimensional examination of tools, what users do with them and how they use them. It is reductive and cannot account for the profound ways that technology has helped to transform culture, and my description of technology-as-tools implies *not* a compliance with the instrumentalist view of technology but the establishment of a problem that will be addressed throughout this book, namely, how control and neoliberal governance perpetuate this model to maintain self-governing rule at a distance. Rather than "big" government breathing down one's neck with its large bureaucratic institutions and legal processes for an imagined national citizenry and body politic, little practices located directly in our governing hands emanating at the point of purchase (whether "one click" or scanned across a register) can achieve similar goals in managing and securitizing our everyday lives. In examining control devices, techniques, and practices, I posit technology as an ensemble of relations among various devices, tools, machines, environments, and human beings rather than an inventory of independent and objective tools activated by an autonomous human user. To make sense of the relations between users and the promises of control technologies themselves, the instrumentalist view is positioned as part of the rationalities and discourses of subjectification that bespeak mentalities of rule and active self-governing as practices of "empowerment," "freedom," and "choice" precipitated by the licensure of disciplinary strategies being intensified and accentuated as "free floating control." New strategies of control produce technology as a network of power relations that perform alternatives to the hierarchy of the governing-governed relationship.

In instrumentalizing the protocols of control the "user" is regarded as autonomous (rather than passive) and "made" responsible as a governing agent for interactions and interfaces with these technologies. Our governance is regarded as not external, institutional, and authoritative but internal, parental, and beneficent: literally located in our own hands and sound judgment. Our relation to technology as control is surmised as "empowerment" in that a specific technological artifact's "neutrality" *serves* the user who can achieve a certain aim: to control, to liberate, and to manipulate our surroundings.

In being a "user," for example, we are afforded and aided with a new ability: to multiply our judgment on and across, more often than not, screen space. This judgment is not figurative but a literal action: the ability to go beyond the "power button" (to turn the television on or off) as a solution to managing cultural information. The market provides blocking technology like the V-chip that enables parents to monitor (literally through, excuse the pun, monitors) and safeguard, as an exercise of the parental function, their family's television viewing without having to depend solely on the standards of large profit-driven media corporations that require a broad audience to secure advertising revenue. The censorial is becoming a niche-driven operation, or better yet, a customized operation whereby users can "personally" select, set, download, program, purchase, or choose particular versions that correspond with their own regulatory requirements; this is perceived not as a censorial action but, in accordance with legislation and market rhetoric, as a matter of choice and an index of freedom cast as consumer choices. The surmised neutrality of technology allows for activity rather than constraint: through the use of these devices one possesses the ability to control what information enters the home and what information can be displayed on a screen. Governance comes from within and is orchestrated within the familiar space of the home and in cultural technologies like television. Its practices are not described as dominant or oppressive but simply a new ability within an already depended-upon medium. Presented as neutral tools, control technologies disassociate themselves from restrictive measures that clearly succumb to accusations of censorship. Instead we come to regard our media technologies empowering choice through the discipline of freedom. Any limitations placed on, in the case above, television, cease to be construed as censorial and come to be practiced in the governing circumstances of *using television to watch television*. Our media are our regulators: not an oppressive Orwellian caveat but an actualization of control's multiplication and generalization for new freedoms.

2. Control is "designed in" our media technology.

Rose offers a broad survey of control strategies that engage with health care and families, risk management, practices of security (securitization of identity, the home, and cities), lifestyle management, consumerism, and electronic identification and surveillance. The study of surveillance in media studies and cultural studies has received a great deal of attention on account of Foucault's work on panopticism and the use of new media in multiplying modes of identification in virtual form.[46] I am less interested in the "observed" subject of surveillance and more interested in control devices that license us as governing users and viewers. In a sense, I am asking what does control look and sound like in the early twenty-first century?

Likewise, I am inquiring into the technological means through which control manifests and displays itself. The condition of disciplinary technology being "designed in to the flows of everyday existence" that Rose spoke of previously multiplies the effects of control, embedding these effects in protocols of rule contained within familiar devices. Control becomes normalized, if not willfully accepted and embodied, as a preference, action, and product for free choice. Yet the immanence, accentuation, and continuity of control do not even require utility on the part of the subject. In the condition of "not being used," control devices *still* resonate with the workings of disciplinary logics. Our lives and relations to technology are still affected as nonusers of control devices by the very presence of software, chips, clean versions, and digital correction in our everyday media as well as the generalized mentality of rule that offers control technology as a viable solution to social problems as a new modality of authority and expertise through self-governance. The "success" of clean-version CDs and DVDs, Internet filters, and V-chip–embedded televisions lies in control's continuous presence as "designed in" measures of opaque governance. In this sense, "tools" may be actively used, or passively used, or never used, but their ubiquitous presence cannot be construed as ineffective.[47] The effect is already being there. The defense that one does not have to "use" control technologies yields little critical insight when their presence redesigns and redefines media technology and our social relations to it. The fact that devices of control are *already* present intensifies our understandings of media as communication and information machines to infuse disciplinary logic in this flow, transmission, feed, encoding, display, or download.

It is necessary to introduce a few aspects of Jay David Bolter and Robert Grusin's concept of "remediation" to clarify control's process of redesign.[48] One definition of remediation is that newer media are offered as improvements to existing or older media. Here we could argue that the improvements offered by control devices enable their users to "customize" their own personal relation to media regulation. For example, some Internet filters allow for levels to be set by the possessors of passwords (i.e., parents). Parents might raise or lower levels based upon their own discretion. The improvement here is the greater autonomization of control in that one enters into a process of cultivation that reconfigures how censorial processes are administered as self-regulation. Another definition of remediation offered by Bolter and Grusin is that newer media may refashion existing media. The process of refashioning, understood as an ensemble of social forces and technical forms, requires that we insert remediation into a context of regulation (something the authors overlook in their discussion of media technologies as a network of physical, social, aesthetic, and economic hybridizations). In this context, control reveals that its stakes are also ontological: our very understandings of media are redesigned when placed into the context of control. The playback medium of the DVD player now extends the terrain of the V-chip/television synthesis when it, too, is equipped, like ClearPlay's content-filtering DVD player, with "parental control technology" that enables users to "customize the ClearPlay settings each time you watch a movie" in order to skip and mute specific segments of a film that contains strong language, nudity, or graphic violence. The DVD player, once touted to offer remastered digital quality films and greater storage capacity on account of DVD's compressed technology (to house all of those indispensable "extras"), is now redesigned as a "content shifting" device, not for temporal management as was the case with the VCR's "time-shifting" capabilities, but for morality management. Technologies of control refashion existing media in order to multiply the possibilities of choice in the name of security, protection, and parental agency. Thus, control devices follow the path of remediation to further ascribe control through improvements to how we use and rely on various media technologies to advance our goal of self-regulatory freedom.

In being "designed in," control protocols come to redefine and redesign our media. For example, media are produced in "versions"; these can be based on different MPAA-approved ratings like R or NC-17. "Clean" version CDs are offered to expand the market where a denounced "dirty" version cannot penetrate. Sanitized versions of Hollywood films become the only accepted print for subscribers of CleanFlicks, ClearPlay, and Family Flix. Digital editing allows professionals and amateurs to excise or correct "harmful" images, "suggestive" dialogue, or "explicit" scenes from films. And, to return to my opening predicament, Sony PS2 and PS3 will not play an MPAA-rated Hollywood DVD without the proper password. Furthermore, filtering software and parental controls (a service provided by most operating systems and ISPs) may coalesce to "centralize" the Web morally according to an instrumentalist paradigm that refuses to understand the Internet as anything but a tool and potential danger in need of continuous supervision through empowered end users. To speak of control devices is to address the media that fill our everyday spaces and mediate our everyday life. (Therefore, this book is as much a study of censorial practices recapitulated as control technologies as it is a study of new digital media. For me, the two cannot be separated.) The protocols of control are familiar: here control becomes as mundane as stupefied channel surfing, downloading an "EXPLICIT" track from iTunes, interfacing with a DVD menu screen, or googling. Its protocols are only another option on a pull-down screen or a button on an RCD or game console controller.

Lastly, the process and condition of being "designed in" demonstrate that a separation between "media" and "content regulation" becomes untenable. We can say that censorship has been remediated to the extent that newer media and their networks refashion previous technological means of extending censorial actions. Censorship has been regarded as an imposition of rules carried out on media. This harkens back to Kuhn's discussion of the prohibition/institutions model whereby media are passive entities subjected to the governance of institutions of censorship. To interact with media today is also to interact with control: to be *in* control as a user who self-regulates and a user produced by disciplinary logic out of bounds. Our televisions, computers, DVDs, CDs, and video game consoles now provide us with the means to regulate not just their content (be it prerecorded, encoded, downloaded, or broadcast) but "the medium" itself and the environments it helps to construct. Marshall McLuhan's post-Gutenberg galaxy still operated within the constrictions of institutions: "Once these censors became aware that in all cases 'the medium is the message' or the basic source of effects, they would turn to suppression of media as such, instead of seeking 'content' control."[49] Perhaps "the censors" became aware, but rather than suppressing media, as McLuhan alerts, our media technology became rationalized as censorial instruments, and users became self-censors in effecting their own mediated environs.

That which is regulated also regulates. Media still come to us through the old institutional practices of censorship (ratings, classification, restricted access, the policing of obscenities, fines, standards), yet we can further impose personalized preferences when using our media as regulatory machines to preempt exposure and access. Hence, to *use* media is to enable and engage in the "designed in" practices of control.

3. Control technology is devices, applications, techniques, and practices that enable choice for disciplined freedoms.

Just as the highway "multiplies the means of control," protocols of governance are inscribed, embedded, and encoded into the dynamics of our practices. Control technologies multiply the possibilities of administering and managing our regulated freedom of choice. Deleuze's highway metaphor demonstrates control's extension beyond disciplinary apparatuses, a smoothing over of institutional restrictions. Control enables circulation. It neither impinges upon movement nor forbids action. I find the verb *enable* highly illustrative of power's productive effects. *Enable is to control what docility is to discipline.* Enable implies a relation: 1. To supply with the means, knowledge, or opportunity; make able. 2. To give legal power, capacity, or sanction to. 3. To make operational; activate. If we maintain the instrumental understanding of technology prescribed by control, we can see how parents are equipped with technical means and knowledge-producing tools to protect their family and secure their household. Practices like "blocking," "filtering," "sanitizing," and "cleaning" are functions and results of control technologies.

Strategies of control license and sanction the subject as autonomous only in that their choices are regulated through their relation to the devices that enable them to exert control. Strategies of control do not focus on a subject's ability to use various devices (recall they do not have to be used) or seek to impose restrictions on the subject's possibilities (the means of control multiplied). They govern, rather, through the regulation of choice. Choice becomes objectified through the modulations of control: like the body in disciplinary societies, choice is "subjected, used, transformed and improved."[50] In this sense choice is a normalizing "object"; its strategy is to become the only acceptable condition for the discipline of freedom. The multiplication of devices for control—the multiplication of the means of governance—enables objects for choice; it provides highways upon which "to drive infinitely and 'freely' without being at all confined yet while still being perfectly controlled."[51] In return, control devices make operational a series of practices that provide assurance that some action is being taken to further maximize choice while extending it as a self-regulation across media. As practiced in the porous constrictions of technologies of control, choice is enabled continuously and freely.

To continue with the "freeing" effect of control, McLuhan's afore-mentioned discussion of content censorship requires further engagement. In *Understanding Media* he plotted transformations of space and the importance of space in relation to politics, aesthetics, communication, and consciousness within his larger study of the shift from the order of the fifteenth-century technological revolution of print and movable type to the late-nineteenth-century "electronic age" founded on the invention and application of electricity. Each order, the order of "typographic man" and the order of "graphic man," as McLuhan put forth, instigated perceptions of the world ("the very large structural changes in human outlook") shaped through the inverse relation that we hold to tools in their impact on "the whole psychic and social complex."[52] McLuhan's famous (to some, infamous) aphorism "the medium is the message" can be considered, among other things, a problematic of space: in the mechanical age it was the body (Foucault's disciplinary technologies) sprawled across terrains encased in steel and steam; in the electronic age the central nervous system is inordinately technologically extended, the senses propelled beyond their corporality. The result of such "extensions" is a "new scale" produced by media. Media both shapes and transforms our environments; it "controls the scale and form of human association and action" within the new scale of electronic mediation.[53]

What is of importance for control technology and the parental function with its machinery of family is that the environments enabled by media are regarded as active processes and "not passive wrappings."[54] McLuhan's extension thesis weds loosely to Deleuze's conceptualization of the highway and begets a process that can be described as enabling. Lewis H. Lapham in "The Eternal Now," his introduction to the MIT edition of *Understanding Media*, clarifies McLuhan's usage of "central nervous system" not as one of any neurological truth-description but rather as, what I would dub, an enabling system: "He was talking about the media as 'make-happen agents,' not as 'make-aware agents,' as systems similar to roads and canals, not as precious art objects or uplifting models of behavior. . . ."[55] Where I have suggested that control devices are "designed in" to enable regulatory practices *as common practices with media,* it is also conceivable to understand these practices as exerted to gain control of media and mediation rather than to limit content. In other words, control devices extend strategies of rule across new scales, new environments through the very media that enable such extensions. The instrumentalist view attempts to account for a relation with discrete machines held hostage to utilitarian principles, and as such it fails to consider how use enables new technological environments. While the parental function exercises power through a technological ensemble, its ultimate goal is to build environments as secure spaces. The scales and environments are not fixed but rather multiply to fix every space as parented and "family friendly." The parental function is a measure occupied by anyone who looks to control technology as a means to perfect the ongoing securitization of habit. Therefore, control devices, while specifying access to media and attempting to regulate and produce what can come into contact with us, are in the business of perfecting practices to ensure the multiplication of control in the service of disciplined freedom, filtering where our eyes and ears can travel in order to *involve* them securely in the network of control. Where discipline concentrated on the body, control seeks to regulate its mediated trajectories.

2. Blocking

Each new means of extending the viewer's control
seemed to entail unwanted side effects or else whet
the appetite for new types of control.

William Uricchio, "Television's Next Generation"

. . . it's probably at your fingertips right now. The
v-chip.

www.rca.com

A Rogue Breast

"Let's do something, let's make a bet, 'cause I gotta have you naked
by the end of this song." On the evening of February 1, 2004, Justin
Timberlake's lyrics were just too compelling for their portentous
singer. Near the end of the Disney protégé's now infamous performance with Janet Jackson at Super Bowl XXXVIII, Timberlake
reached across her chest and removed a cup from her black leather
bustier, exposing her right breast to prime-time broadcast television
audiences. This incident, hailed as one of television's most TiVo'd moments, was ultimately proclaimed a "malfunction of the wardrobe"
according to Ms. Jackson's spokesperson Stephen Huvane. In defense
of the mishap Huvane attempted to clarify that Timberlake "was
supposed to pull away the bustier and leave the red-lace bra."[1] MTV,
which produced the choreographed half-time show witnessed by an
estimated 140 million viewers, maintained that the uncovered right

breast was an unfortunate accident and not intentional, as many suspected.[2] Michael Powell, then chair of the Federal Communications Commission (and son of former Secretary of State Colin Powell), felt otherwise. On September 22, 2004, the FCC unanimously agreed to fine twenty CBS-owned television stations the maximum penalty for indecency, $27,500 (total: $550,000).[3] CBS (owned by Viacom Inc.) appealed the FCC's fine for indecency. Oral arguments for the case began in September 2007 in the Third Circuit Court of Appeals in Philadelphia. In July 2008 the court dismissed the case, ruling that the 9/16ths of a second flash of nudity did not justify the $550,000 fine imposed by the FCC.

While the prime-time visibility of Jackson's lone breast (in *Everything You Always Wanted to Know about Sex but Were Afraid to Ask,* Woody Allen reminds us that breasts usually roam in pairs) prompted CBS's cameras to cut away quickly, they were not fast enough for the FCC or the alleged flood of complaints from concerned citizens produced in its wake. What exactly was the concern? Seeing unscripted nudity on terrestrially broadcast television?[4] Seeing a black breast rather than a white one owned by hotel heiress Paris Hilton? Seeing the breast of a woman in her forties? Perhaps it is the lucidity of a cheap stunt (as seen on MTV's *Punk'd*) or the shock of the unexpected in the routine comfort of television viewing? Powell provides an answer: "Like millions of Americans, my family and I gathered around the television for a celebration. Instead, that celebration was tainted by a classless, crass and deplorable stunt."[5] In his official statement Powell reports that the FCC received 540,000 letters of complaint and proceeds to de-personalize his experience to speak for a national imaginary: "As countless families gathered around the television to watch one of our Nation's most celebrated events, they were rudely greeted with a halftime show stunt more fitting of a burlesque show."[6]

Jackson's performance at Super Bowl XXXVIII has caused a ripple effect across television and its presumed lack of "decency" as well as regulation. Conservative media watchdog groups like the Parents Television Council, the Kaiser Family Foundation, and the Media Research Council as well as Capitol Hill lawmakers like Senator Sam Brownback (R-Kan.), Senator Hillary Rodham Clinton (D-N.Y.), Senator Joe Lieberman (I-Conn.), and Representative Fred Upton (R-Mich.) have since been advocating tougher FCC content regulation. In summer 2004 Congress voted to allow the FCC to raise the maximum fine from $27,500 to $275,000 for broadcast-radio and television violations of decency (the measure was slotted into the 2005 defense authorization bill as the televisual became a matter of national security).[7] More recently the Broadcast Decency Enforcement Act of 2005 (signed into law by President George W. Bush in June 2006) increased the fine to $325,000 *per violation* with a cap of $3 million. These calls generally take the form of demands for higher fines as in the Broadcast Decency Enforcement Act, revamped ratings, prosecution under federal laws of obscenity and indecency, and the imposing threat of new congressional legislation. One immediate response was the much publicized use of time delay to manage impromptu televisual actions and to preempt the possibility of Jackson copycats or, worse yet, someone going one up on her and exposing a pair. The control of "live-broadcast" also appears to have redefined the realm of the "indecent" to include celebrity political activism. During another prime-time gala event, the 2004 Oscars, it was criticism of the U.S. invasion of Iraq and the Bush-Cheney regime that was deemed inappropriate for broadcast and, therefore, subject to time-delay monitoring. It seems that in the early twenty-first century, a desperate attempt to revitalize a diva's career and a few outspoken Hollywood actors verbally protesting an illegal act of war are equal threats.

Time delay, not by any means new to television, is a measure designed to manage what enters the home from the point of transmission. The V-chip, on the other hand, is an electronic circuit *already embedded* in your television to manage at the location of the end user. It is a technological measure designed to promote viewer-centered control for parental self-regulation of television content and the conduct of viewing. The television "receiver," the machine as well as viewer, not the sender, is given the final word on what is displayed on-screen. Ms. Jackson's half-time performance not only revealed an exposed body part outlawed from broadcast, it also exposed a televisual moment of failure at the layer of content-based regulation of broadcast media and at the layer of self-regulation enabled by the "parental control" of television ratings and the V-chip. Media simply "got out of hand." Not just televisual content but media itself: the institution of mass media, the medium and cultural form of television, and the social act of television viewing. The significance of the Jackson-Timberlake performance within the context of this book has less to do with the presumed shock of seeing partial nudity on television than it does with revealing how technologies of control are multiplied and exercised through a complex configuration of devices, techniques, and practices that attempt to ensure the productive decentralized management of media as an active process of self-regulation in the hands of viewers. What happens to security if the promises of "empowerment" and "control" are easily ruptured by a rogue breast?

The four major networks, ABC, NBC, CBS, and FOX, responded to the Super Bowl debacle by launching campaigns to further educate parents about the V-chip's filtering function, that is, its ability to block information from entering the home.[8] The V-chip is a medium-specific filtering technology that relies on the blocking of television signals in conjunction with television ratings. According to law professor J. M. Balkin, who wrote one of the earliest articles on V-chip filtration, filtering mechanisms organize, select, and block information. In the case of the V-chip, the block restricts access to television programming. As Balkin explains, "the v-chip is a blocking filter for children, but it also is a selecting filter for their parents . . . [It] is an organizing filter, because it creates two types of programming—programming that is blocked by the v-chip and programming that is not."[9] Network parental education schemes seem utterly futile considering that sports and news programming are exempt from the new television ratings code, also known as The TV Parental Guidelines; the V-chip is quite ineffective in such instances as a blocking filter. Nonetheless, the National Cable & Telecommunication Association developed a Web site, www.controlyourtv.org, to promote its "Cable Puts You in Control" campaign for parental education on the V-chip. In August 2004, Cox Communications began running public service announcements that included a Web site with the campaign mantra "Take Charge!" Its spokesperson is John Walsh, the tough-talking, no-nonsense presenter of *America's Most Wanted*. "We all respect the First Amendment," Walsh reminds, "and no one wants to burn books or regulate what's on TV. . . . But Cox will help block out *The Texas Chainsaw Massacre*."[10] Contrary to Walsh's defense, the V-chip does regulate "what's on TV." This is its raison d'être. Television, in Cox's "Take Charge!" campaign, is a suspicious character: Walsh lends his law-enforcer persona to apprehend and protect us against an ethereal criminal. It is not the streets that he is keeping clean, it is the television screen.[11] (In this mode of policing it is imperative to consider how the V-chip affects a new way of seeing: television as a control technology and the mediation of vision through the technology of the V-chip's protocols of visuality. At stake here is an abnegation of vision where the discerning parental eye is assisted by technology that relocates the act of watching away from an ocular activity to an informational mode of monitoring. To investigate the visuality of the V-chip, I will consider it in relation to Paul Virilio's concept of "sightless vision" later in this chapter.)

A prime-time breast in the American living room makes Powell's recollection of how families watch the Super Bowl seem too tranquil, perchance intentionally idyllic. Super Bowl "gatherings" are far removed from a rosy-cheek Norman Rockwell picnic. Janet's breast would be right at home with party kegs, pizzas, pretzels, chips, hamburgers, and hangovers. I am not trying to delimit *the* audience for, much to my chagrin, one of our "nation's most celebrated events," though I am suggesting that Powell's scenario of how television and televisual images are experienced in the home is only one possibility among many. Counter instances of televisual reception and empirical work on viewer practices reveal little when the imagined scenario verbally depicted by Powell is more prescriptive than descriptive. The problem as presented within this book is that the new freedoms of control operate through the constant management of ideological positions that attempt to engineer concepts like family, domesticity, and security through definitive proclamations on media. Each new instance of a control technology enabling choice and freedom is also an instance of the cultural importance of media being redefined and reconfigured as practices and processes of control. This change affects both the media in question and, perhaps more importantly, our understandings, experiences, and relations to them. This is most apparent in the enabling of choice through control devices, the ease and magnitude of self-regulation, and in the promises of security and expanded control that new technologies bolster.

Although not writing on censorial practices and media regulation, William Boddy offers an assertion that can easily pertain to control technology. He writes, "Every electronic media product launch or network debut carries with it an implicit fantasy scenario of its domestic consumption, a polemical ontology of its medium, and an ideological rationale for its social function."[12] Filtering technologies for television like the V-chip, of which blocking is the pervading technique, and computers (which I will discuss in the next chapter) ought to be included in Boddy's exegesis, just as new modes of regulation ought to factor into the study of media in general. Blocking expands the cultural practices associated with television while also augmenting a new interface between the television viewer/listener/ user, television programs, and the medium itself.[13]

As this chapter argues, the V-chip expands "the ontology of its medium" to further stretch the logics of television to investigate viewer-centered control in a schema of neoliberal governance. The next section of this chapter addresses this expansion through William Uricchio's reconsideration of televisual "flow" and viewer-centered practices that purport to interrupt this experience. Polemics and promises of blocking-filter devices like the V-chip redesign television as a control technology for self-regulatory practices where the notion of control surpasses the forms of programming management and content selection discussed by Uricchio. The cultural practice of watching television in the era of the V-chip endorses the reformulation of the "governor-governed relationship" discussed previously. Governing content through the V-chip's blocking capabilities is also a governing of conduct located in the expertise of the parental function. The V-chip targets conduct—the act of watching television—by eliminating what televisual information can come into contact with potential viewers.

To understand how the V-chip redesigns our relation to television, we will examine the "original" meaning of the V-chip as a device for controlling the visual ("Vyou Control" as in what and how you "view") to situate this meaning within the context of Paul Virilio's concept of "sightless vision," introduced in *The Vision Machine*, whereby perception becomes an automated practice. Virilio's concept of "sightless vision" allows us to posit other questions for the V-chip that cannot be answered well by another reexamination of its constitutionality or legality, or for that matter, the study of censorship. In considering the V-chip within Virilio's scheme, we can direct questions concerned with governing and regulation, *alongside existing ones*, that have overlooked the V-chip as a visual technology, mediation, a new social relation to information, an interface, a human-machine system, and a peculiar mode of visibility. In other words, we can begin to consider what blocking actually does for viewer control and the "view" that television presumes.

V . . . Viewer-Centered Control

The Telecommunications Act of 1996 required half of all new televisions manufactured for the U.S. market by July 1, 1999, "that have a picture screen 13 inches or greater in size" and *all* televisions by

January 1, 2000, to "be equipped with a feature designed to enable viewers to block display of all programs with a common rating."[14] Though the V-chip was not the only filtering technology circulating in the mid- to late 1990s, it is the only filtering technology required by law to be *built into* televisions in the United States. I stress *built into* as the V-chip is not a stand-alone device, like Scientific Atlanta's digital set-top box or Motorola's digital set-top box for cable, but an actual part of television, a part of how we conceptualize and watch television. This requirement embeds the practice and process of control in our most prevalent cultural technology regardless of whether or not we comply with its promises to safeguard television, utilize its functions, or happen to be parents.

The V-chip falls into the larger category of "consumer discretion technologies."[15] Bearing names like Channel Block (Sony), Parental Control (Zenith), Tele-Commander (Protelcon Inc.), TV Lockout (Recoton Corp.), and Channel Guard (JVC), in the mid- to late 1990s over thirty televisual filtering devices were available in the United States. Most have vanished from the consumer market, having been replaced by newer cable box parental-control models. Consumer discretion technologies are split into three groups: time period–based blocking, filtering, and transmitted ratings-based blocking.[16] Time period–based blocking allows viewers to determine how much time is spent watching television. When a viewer's predetermined time amount has expired, the television turns off. One example is the TV Timer BOB, which also controls video game consoles and computers. Screen time is selected by parents. The child-user then has to enter a PIN in order to use an electronic device time-managed by BOB. Once the allotted time expires, the system shuts down. In contrast to time-managing devices, filtering allows viewers to block specific channels, and this feature is now default in U.S. televisions.[17] On account of its legal requirement, the V-chip is the most publicized example of transmitted ratings-based blocking. Still, many feel that the V-chip does not adequately monitor television and rely upon additional layers of regulation to go beyond the V-chip's capabilities. The TV Guardian Model 201 and Model 301 from Family Safe Media were designed in this way. These devices police language within television programming. They automatically scan the closed-captioning signal that provides metadata for television ratings to identify words judged "offensive" according to their database. These include profanity and sexual and religious references. Once identified, these words or phrases are automatically muted out. Lastly, independent devices like Intelevision (Spruce Run Technologies) are designed to work in conjunction with additional ratings systems.[18]

The operation of the V-chip is based on several factors. TV Parental Guidelines, in the form of an electronic watermark (an image embedded with metadata about the particular media object within which it appears), appear for fifteen seconds at the beginning of a rated broadcast and at the beginning of each program segment (after commercials, for example).[19] Since 1997 the following ratings, much like age-based ratings for film, video, DVD, and video games, have been introduced in the United States: TVY, TVY7, TVG, TVPG, TV14, and TVMA. After October 1, 1997, content ratings providing additional information to parents began to accompany the age-based descriptions: for example, V (violence), L (strong language), D (suggestive dialogue), and FV (fantasy violence). Provisions for informative televisual descriptions are innocently hailed as advisory, protective, and parent-friendly measures rather than categorical actions administered on and through television. Electronic descriptors, enlarged since the 2004 Super Bowl, imbue our television screens with metadata for program approval or blocking. With the screen rating meshed to our screen, it becomes a framing mechanism for regulation as the V-chip receives its signal. Ratings descriptors fill up the screen in ways similar to channel identity descriptors, for example, pop-up icons that announce what is "coming up next," on-screen data called up by a remote control device, sped-up end credits "windowed" to one side while previews for another program are shown, as well as voice-over announcements for the news and other programming. Control shares these processes since regulatory practices are deemed informational. Like still and animated on-screen graphics, rating codes are another example of television's hypermediated fragmented flow and the televisual metadata crowding our screen. On-screen ratings that are demarcated as *suggestive* and *assistive* rather than overtly restrictive may dodge the association with any type of censorial action. They easily dissolve into the nebulous category of on-screen "information" or "visual noise" we have long become accustomed to when watching TV on a nightly basis. If the V-chip is programmed to block according to a particular rating, then these televisual descriptors become translucent; their visible presence matters little to our direct vision. An electronic circuit automatically and instantaneously blocks as a parental function in lieu of a parent's actual awareness and physical presence when the V-chip is enabled. In this case, the V-chip "sees" for us: it monitors regardless of our attention. It does not blink.

The V-chip's promissory note of choice and control is directed at the instrumentality of the parental function that is enabled with improved (super)vision and the technological means to regulate television (content and the medium itself) in and from the home. The television itself becomes a governing agent for control as parents become "empowered" through such a technological solution. An electronic cordon sanitaire protects against on-screen contagions, or at least this is the promise: to keep "sex," "language," and "violence" away from children. To cite an example of this instrumentality, during the design of the new television ratings system Jack Valenti, former president of the MPAA, issued a statement in line with the paternalism constantly invoked to discuss the protection of children from violent cinematic and televisual images: "I see nothing wrong with giving more information to parents. I don't know how anyone could be against that."[20] According to the logic of the MPAA, ratings are understood as neutral and transparent, never biased or explicit: the MPAA is in the business of information dissemination, not censorship, or so the story goes. Yet, we could also regard ratings as active in shaping content, organizing viewing in terms of either "allowed" or "disallowed" (in the way that filters organize information, according to Balkin), and an additional layer of censorial protocols and prescriptive precautions.

The expertise of the parental function is implicit throughout debates concerning the V-chip, and it is always already present in the MPAA's rating system. The mechanics of the parental function dislodges the category of adult as a signifier of maturity and responsibility. According to its official home page, the MPAA sees its ratings "designed to serve—parents of America," and when still in office, Valenti was cited as saying that the ratings system is not for adults, instead it "is for parents only."[21] And following on from that, he maintains, "all we're doing is giving more information to parents so they can make the final decisive judgment about the conduct of their children."[22] Conduct and content are conflated here in that managing the "conduct of conduct" as governmentality prescribes is, in the context of the V-chip, a matter of *governing conduct by governing content*. Insofar as MPAA ratings are not "for adults," the legal requirement of the V-chip and a new ratings system position the medium of television as a cultural technology predicated upon parental presence regardless of whether or not a parent resides in the television household. Regardless of who owns, views, or uses a television, the mechanics of, one might say, "parenting at a distance" (to maintain

Nikolas Rose's notion of "governing at a distance") is a designed-in component of each television. The rationalization of parenting as an action stripped of parents is infused across culture and technology. And this parental function becomes omnipresent with each new TV sold on the U.S. market, as control becomes a closer and more immediate practice.

Here the category of "parent" is a protective measure used to transfer and extend control into a voluntary process rather than a demographic appellation. The ratings system assumes, if not invents, the category of "parent" as homogenous, rallied around securitization. Who are these parents? Are they heads of the family for whom Powell spoke when he blasted the Super Bowl performance? Are they the father who has one drink too many to celebrate his team's victory or to nurse an agonizing defeat? Or, maybe, the American parent who does not watch this spectacle? The ability to filter televisual images through V-chip blocking is a display of a technique and mechanism for governance, censorial self-regulatory practices and control through and simultaneously over a cultural technology. Parents are outfitted not with the ability to discern televisual content, but to reactively enforce and display standards for acceptance and disable visual access. In doing so, parents can accept, through practices with the V-chip, that broadcast is too indecent, violent, or obscene for younger viewers, and that television ratings are in place to protect, enable, and inform rather than to restrict. A corollary to the V-chip's effect is that public debate on issues of "indecency" becomes muted as the V-chip's neoliberal emphasis on self-regulation makes the censorial a private matter where each television screen monitors according to individual user preferences. The debate shifts from identifying and addressing a "problem" to embedding a proposed "solution"; further opining becomes redundant.

Leading up to its partial debut in 1999, the V-chip's "at a distance" functionality was championed as the latest example of neoliberal policies of deregulation and decentralized governance. Vice President Al Gore celebrated the approval of the new television ratings to coincide with the V-chip by proclaiming: "Today, America's parents have won back their living room."[23] Accompanied by Gore and Senator John McCain (R-Ariz.), Representative Edward Markey (D-Mass.) proudly, if somewhat inanely, announced: "Today we have a V for victory—and also a V for violence—but a V for victory for parents in our country."[24] Bipartisan congressional support praised the V-chip as an enabling rather than restrictive consumer technology premised upon viewer choice, agency, and the self-governing of televisual content as opposed to federal interventions. It functions, according to such arguments, as a beneficent solution and preferred alternative to state intervention into the domain of television programming and the restrictive imposition of additional governmental layers of regulation. The key to the "success" of the V-chip was to be the availability of information, empowerment, and enactment of so-called parental involvement. Writing prior to the V-chip's introduction into the U.S. market, Matthew Murray argued that "by ostensibly locating content determination with the receiver, rather than the sender, the V-chip legislation professes to permit interactivity and viewer choice."[25] Its appeal—and the basis for its alleged ability to thwart accusations of state censorship and elude accusations of unconstitutionality—is that the V-chip is said to allow parents to determine, through the filtering of cultural information, the suitability of broadcast content for their children. This is do-it-yourself regulation without the mess and fuss of bureaucratic institutions: the decision to block or not to block is not handed down to parents but emanates from parents, thus positioning the control of media within the home, within the family, in the hands of the parent and not the state. Rather than impose regulation, the state appears merely to legislate the implementation of resourceful tools for our utilization and security.

If the V-chip is meant to empower parents and relocate the source of censorial power away from divisions of network standards, then ought we to experience a radical openness in television programming? Could V-chip technology be read as a license for the production of more "explicit" broadcast content to recognize and program to an adult audience? Locating the decision to regulate in the sphere of the end user would seem to suggest so. We could consider how network broadcast is stunted by such regulations while cable is able to develop provocative programming (*The Sopranos* being only one example) to attract growing audiences. Although an argument for license could be made, it would not be that convincing when one considers that the FCC increase in fines for "indecency" occurred almost a decade after the V-chip became a legal mandate in U.S. televisions. With higher fines for broadcast, the major networks are not in any position to offer content that would challenge existing television ratings systems even with V-chip–embedded televisions firmly in place. Despite the emphasis on user-centered control for negotiating televisual viewing, content is still policed by oligarchic consolidation of ownership that seeks to appeal to a broad demographic of audience taste and moral propensity. The V-chip is a license for yet another layer of censorial practices and processes that transform the television into a self-governing device and further a neoliberal investment in the self as a deregulatory political agent.

After half a decade of V-chip availability and politicians continuing to sing its praises—as did President George W. Bush when signing the Broadcast Decency Enforcement Act into law—it is worth asking: What has the V-chip actually accomplished?[26] Having survived the hollow threats of Y2K, did Americans awaken to a radical new dawn in television viewing and content management? Were domestic television screens somehow "safer," less prone to display the likes of *Buffy the Vampire Slayer, Mighty Morphin Power Rangers,* or *South Park,* television programs often pointed to as violent or indecent?[27] Did Edward Markey's victorious parents form an info-matic dragnet to catch every single stray televisual perpetrator? Even in 1997 Paul Levinson was quick to point out the fragility of this promissory trawl on account of television's diffuse qualities: "parental attempts to control the TV viewing of their children via V-chips can be defeated by just one parent who elects not to use the chip, and whose children are friends or in school together with the other children."[28] High on choice (but not from inhaling), were parents somehow more in control of their children's everyday environments? After all, as Marjorie Heins correctly acknowledges, "parents concerned about racism, drugs, drunk driving, religious cults, or homophobia would receive no help from the v-chip law."[29] This concern remains unaddressed.

When the V-chip actually began to appear on the U.S. market in summer 1999, its debut did not mirror the fervor of congressional self-congratulatory applause. Despite early efforts by the Kaiser Family Foundation, the National Cable Television Association, and the Center for Media Education to educate users about the new filtering device, it seems that Dick Wolf, executive producer of *Law & Order,* proffered a more accurate appraisal of the V-chip's debut: "Nobody cares. Take a poll, and see if anyone even knows how to activate their v-chip."[30] Polls were of course taken. Kaiser Family Foundation reported that only 17 percent of people who owned a new television with blocking capabilities actually put it to work. The Annenberg Public Policy Center found that only 50 percent of parents surveyed were actually aware of the new parental guidelines rating system that works in conjunction with the V-chip.[31] These statistics may suggest that television content is less a problem for parents than their presumed technological incompetence. Where the latest example of a "quick-fix political remedy,"[32] as Jack Valenti once described the V-chip, did receive notable recognition around the time of its debut was not on the small screen, as intended, but on the big screen. In *South Park: Bigger, Longer, and Uncut* (Trey Parker, 1999) the ill-tempered Eric Cartman has a V-chip implanted in his brain to regulate his fondness for profanity (an update on the Ludovico Treatment Technique from Stanley Kubrick's *A Clockwork Orange*, 1971). Cartman's inability consciously to repress his vocal urges coupled with a malfunctioning V-chip gives him the power to convert energy into some kind of destructive energy ray. This, of course, helps the good citizens of South Park, Colorado, defeat Saddam Hussein and Satan! At the turn of the millennium the V-chip was an overripe technological lemon for cultural satire. Yet, being an object for satire in such a popular cultural phenomenon as *South Park* suggests that the V-chip possesses cultural significance and speaks to social anxiety as the show is fond of providing commentary through its characters, Stan, Kyle, Eric, and Kenny.

The question of the V-chip's accomplishment is best responded to by examining how it extends our understandings of television within the context of the viewer centeredness of the televisual interface and in return how this envisages the practices and processes of technologies of control. Like the persistent expansion of how we watch and use television (and its content) through remote control devices (RCDs), cable, satellite, video game consoles, VCRs, pay-per-view, DVD players, video streaming, HDTV, WebTV, TiVo, DVR, EPCs (entertainment PC), TV content on the iPod, Apple TV, user-generated YouTube, Microsoft's Windows XP Media Center (Edition 2005), and Microsoft Vista, the V-chip, as well as other content-filtering devices discussed previously, ought to be considered an element in the expansion of the televisual apparatus as it facilitates how we "safely" watch, use, and understand television, be it LCD, plasma, or CRT. This is not to suggest that the variable conditions of televisuality and television take the place of the V-chip's censorial intentions and effects, but rather, that both must be attended to together. While medium-specific differences are increasingly difficult to ascertain and media scholars increasingly lean toward the process of convergence "as a way to bridge or join old and new technologies, formats, and audiences,"[33] filtering technologies (and this can be extended to the other technologies and practices discussed throughout this book) are becoming part of our everyday experiences of and subjective positions within the cultural formations of media. Its legislative pledge is to extend the viewer's control over televisual content (to assist you in "taking charge" as COX Communications promises) and other viewers, as well as the medium itself. This pledge redesigns the V-chip–enabled television as a control technology for governance. In the case of television, the V-chip is now part of television's flow, part of its televisual style, part of televisual space, part of television's domestic milieu, part of television's polysemy, and a legally required *part* of television.

William Uricchio addresses historical specificity and the "constellation of technologies and practices" that affect the identity of television well when he repositions Raymond Williams's well-known formulation of "flow" to account for the historicity of the moment within which Williams encountered U.S. television programming and, more importantly for our immediate concerns, the continued technological changes to the medium and the shifting modes of how we experience it.[34] Uricchio looks toward various viewer-centered means that disrupt flow as a programming-based enterprise and emanation to the notion of a user-based flow located in the hands of the viewer. VCRs, the RCD, and DVD players mentioned above attest to a viewer-dominated flow. Let's consider Uricchio's comments on the RCD as a way to argue for the V-chip as part of this constellation of viewer-centered control over the TV medium. "The ability of the RCD," Uricchio writes, "to silence advertising by muting the sound, and ultimately its ability to switch away from it altogether by changing channels or turning off the set, was a site of enormous anxiety for the industry because of the implications for the logics of commercial television. But from the public's perspective, such uses were precisely the point of the new control promised by the RCD."[35] James R. Walker and Robert V. Bellamy Jr., in their introduction to their edited collection dedicated to the RCD, address the idea of "new control" as a matter of reinvention, in that "although remote control devices were designed to make existing television operations more convenient, the technology has been used by the consumer to facilitate grazing and multiple program viewing and to change the relationship of viewer to the television medium."[36] Designed into U.S.

televisions on the market after 2000, the V-chip changes our relation-ship to the medium of television once again as it is yet another way to exert control over programming as a filtering practice similar to that of grazing while enabling the exertion of control over television and the conduct of viewing through the medium itself. The importance of the V-chip in relation to Uricchio's discussion of the RCD is that it too extends control over the viewing experience, providing options to parents beyond changing channels when a forbidden program airs or the cultural deprivation of totally switching off the television. "Switching away," "channel changing," and "muting"—practices we have come to regard as "grazing," "zapping," and "zipping"— made possible by the RCD (or, at the very least, made easier by it) demarcate a televisual interface enacted as viewer control. It makes the medium "do things" easily, like, as Balkin discussed, filtering the volume of programming, as in channel surfing, where we visually feast upon sporadic program segments, or, in the case of the V-chip, blocking incoming information.

Where television programming can be changed at the touch of a button, the same button pad now allows parents to "program" their television to monitor its content according to a new ratings system. *Program*—a term constantly invoked in V-chip marketing and in-structional information—is misleading and serves only to main-tain the emphasis on viewer-centered control and interactivity. It is another market incentive dressed up as empowerment. Code is not being written, programming language is not instructing; instead, one is "selecting" options and assigning a PIN (would we refer to an ATM transaction as programming?). Parents remain users as opposed to coproducers, and this status continues to reaffirm the instrumentalist view that characterizes the V-chip as yet another legally sanctioned tool at their disposal. The "muting" that occurs here is not akin to "turning down the set" but a resounding of how we use television. The block is visible evidence that the V-chip is doing its job and that television is "working" to protect and secure habitat. It now possesses the capabilities to display/project cultural information as well as filter and block cultural information. While this resounding has been a muted affair, in its short history the physical presence of the V-chip and other televisual filtering devices do expand as well as expound upon television as a cultural technology and practice within the pro-cesses of control. Filtering capabilities usher in a new phase in the logics of television that relocates the determination of content from programming and content standards to a supplementary layer of self-regulatory filtering as a viewer-centered practice in home securitization via the management of conduct from the home. The pushing of a button on the same RCD that "controls" the television—and possibly one's VCR (if still in use), DVD player, and game console—is also a push on our very expectations for and experiences with television, that is, how information can be disseminated within the home and experienced, and how regulation is administered within contemporary culture—through the interconnected hands of governing and governed.

To return briefly to Murray's skepticism about the V-chip as an interactive device, we can liken claims of interactivity to the capabilities of an RCD. In the same way that "programming" is a misnomer for selecting available options within the apparatus of our televisions, so is interactivity. Viewers have no interaction with the ratings system design or the close-captioning signal that transmits them. This process is out of our hands. It resides behind the secrecy and authority of the MPAA and the FCC. Even though, as Uricchio instructs, we ought to be careful to attend to both historical specificity and the changes to the technology and our practices with it, the historical period within which Williams wrote about U.S. television still offers us an insight into the V-chip. In the mid-1970s, Williams discussed how "applied technologies" within the home could institute a "new kind of 'communication' news from the outside."[37] In this passage Williams is referring to radio broadcast in the 1920s and 1930s. He draws from its history to discuss the culturally constructed process of television's development in relation to "home-centered" technologies. I have already mentioned a score of pre-digital and digital television consumer technologies that promise to foster a more interactive engagement with television. Williams speaks of interactive television, by way of cable systems, that were attempting to use the idea of "instantaneous audience reaction" to measure audience viewing habits as well as devising a system whereby audiences could vote on endings to programs (which has been realized in *American Idol*). Williams is also quick to point out that these instances of audiences interacting with television broadcast are, in fact, examples of "reactive" rather than "interactive" practices. He writes, "nearly all the equipment that is being currently developed is reactive; the range of choices, both in detail and in scope, is pre-set."[38] Likewise, the V-chip is modeled on a reactive relation to content ratings and on-screen electronic watermarks, one premised on the parental use of "button-pressing reactive equipment" (Williams's phrase for the stage of development in interactive television of his era). The V-chip has not really moved beyond this stage despite advances in television design and technology. Ratings, in conjunction with the V-chip, provide categories predefined to signal the reactive practice of acceptance or rejection. Marjorie Heins, in her excellent article "Three Questions about Television Ratings," draws attention to the fact that

> Those parents who choose to activate the chip will not be evaluating programs themselves to determine if they are consonant with their own values or appropriate for the age and maturity levels of their children. Instead, parents will be blocking programs based on simple, conclusory labels. . . .[39]

Parents can now simply "vote"—in the sense that Williams discussed decades ago—for a rating while administering the ability to screen the domestic from the insecurity of the outside.

The presence of the V-chip reconfigures television—a medium often surmised by the Left and Right as a source of moral danger, disruption, threat, and harm throughout its short history—as an employable and productive component for regulating its content. The V-chip is embedded as yet another "option" on our ever-crowded RCD, and ratings are another descriptor competing for our impatient attention on-screen. A repositioned commodity allowing the receiver-user to exert an action over the sender, rather than a social program or agency, it offers a solution to the control of televisual information entering the home and furthers the securitization of habitat through the expertise of the parental function as self-regulatory practice and beneficent mode of governing.

While in 2004 the V-chip was still regarded as a "multi-system failure,"[40] since Janet Jackson's Super Bowl performance the V-chip has garnered a renewed interest. As mentioned previously, this interest is in spite of the fact that the V-chip is ineffective against sports and news as they are exempt from the television ratings system. As Lynn Smith reports in her *Los Angeles Times* piece on the reassessment of the V-chip:

> networks, cable companies and manufacturers are rushing to jump on board. Fox and Thompson/RCA are already running spots and print

ads in a high-profile, national ad campaign, and FOX has promised a one-hour special on the V-chip and indecency. ABC and Pax have agreed to show the ratings icon more often and with a voice-over to alert parents to the content of a show.[41]

In regard to RCA and other manufacturers this renewed interest means an increased sale in televisions if viewers do not currently own a television with V-chip capabilities. RCA's home page is a good example of the recent high-profile campaign that Smith underscores, and promotes the viewer centeredness of control that I have been discussing. "The V-chip puts YOU in control even when THEY have the remote" is the slogan that greets visitors to RCA's home page. With links like "How V-chip Works," "V-Chip Content Themes," "Setting Up V-Chip," and "V-Chip Rating System," RCA assures customers that its products will meet the needs of parental control, that they will enable the parent, as an expert, to administer culture. "As a parent," RCA's precautionary marketing rhetoric promises, "you want some control over what your children see on TV. But you can't always be there to make sure that what they are watching is appropriate. The good news is you have a tool already built-in to your TV to help you control what your children are viewing even when you're not around. And it's probably at your fingertips right now. The v-chip."[42]

Right-under-our-noses typifies the commonplace approach that V-chip education bolsters and reaffirms the designed-in processes of control. After all, it is located in the most dominant object within the majority of U.S. households. Now self-regulation through control technology too is a commonality, as ordinary as using an RCD, as everyday as watching television. The V-chip's millennial premier does not carry the same shock of the new that television and computers carried during their initial introduction and historical placement within domestic space (the newness of the computer was tamed as an appliance to catalog recipes, plan meals, assist with homework, balance the family budget, play games, and print dot-matrix "Happy Birthday" banners). The V-chip is simply already there, lodged in the guts of our televisions, managing invisible signals in silence. RCA's emphasis on "your fingertips" harkens back to Uricchio's discussion of the RCD as a viewer-centered technology; it stresses the ease, convenience, familiarity, and choice of the V-chip interface as well as its position *already* within the disciplining hand of parental control. The RCD, an instrument firmly grasped for zapping, zipping, muting, and grazing on, past, and across television programs, now adds blocking to its handheld, eye-line lexicon and technocratic command capabilities.

The V-chip's propagation of choice in accompanying viewer-centered control is a slippery enterprise. In fact, we should ask how the question of choice figures in relation to the V-chip. For Murray, notions of "choice" and viewer "selection" come to mean "limited selectivity based upon predetermined categories and previously formulated decisions over what constitutes violence and indecency."[43] In terms of the ratings system, the viewer may comply with existing categories rather than engage with the content directly. Heins makes a similar argument. "Parents who use the chip," she writes, "will do so on the basis of Congress's determination that it is sex, 'indecency,' and violence that must be restrained, and the industry's interpretation of 'indecent' to mean 'coarse' language (L) or 'suggestive dialogue' (D)."[44] In both instances parental choice is consigned to determining a PIN necessary for setting (not programming) the V-chip. This is not an example of viewer discretion; any claim to viewer agency is deferred to a pre-programmed response: even the burden of turning off the television is removed.

Balkin shares the skepticism of both Murray and Heins. The promise of enhanced parental control through choice balances between technological enabling and the obviation of choice. As Balkin writes, "filtering, especially in the Information Age, increasingly involves delegation of choice to another party. Thus, it is very important not to collapse filtering into choice, thereby absorbing the latter's positive moral connotations."[45] In control societies, as imagined by Deleuze, this collapse would occur continuously, and it is increasingly challenging to mount a convincing case for where "actual" choice resides in the process. For example, we could argue that in control society choice is replaced by actions of choice that are technologically enabled by consumer media. Choice increasingly becomes instrumentalized across a range of devices and efficient techniques for managing information rather than being external to mediated processes. While Balkin is quite right to debate the effectiveness and moral responsibility of such matters, we still need to consider control technologies as the licensing of autonomy in the service of self-management and self-selected regulation in order to gain any understanding of cultural formations as means of governing. The V-chip garners a positive moral experience insofar as its capabilities are construed as a matter of personal choice and assurance of control. Instead of a negation of choice, filtering technology reassigns the responsibility to an instant result: in the case of the V-chip, blocked access to selected programming. The choice exerted by a parent complies with the V-chip's *response abilities*. Whether an informed choice or not, this action is a choice that leads to a blocking practice in the name of security. This compliance exceeds the viewer-centered televisual interface as it also indicates a compliance with a strategy of rule for the maximization of personal freedom as security maintenance. The delegation of choice is already a facet of democratic society. Why would the self-regulation of media within the fabrication of the private sphere be exempt? What becomes increasingly apparent is that instead of delegation, filtering technology functions more as a replacement for augmenting our own presence in decision making and moral practices through technology. Our sense of choice is located in the practice of button pushing within the digital logic of "block" or "enable": *enter* choice.

To best articulate my position on choice, a summation is in order. The V-chip embodies many tenets of neoliberalism. It enables parents to control and discipline their own children and televisual information without direct state intervention at the level of programming (or so the story goes). In return parents are implicated in a regime of discipline as they function as experts in delimiting access. They "program" to comply. In line with the instrumentalist view of technology, the state and the market take a "hands-off" approach that refines their role as supplier of tools legislating to enable through self-regulation. In our hands is placed a beneficent technology that will enable parents to exert more control over culture with ease and automatic results (the blocking of televisual content). Security resides in the home and in the hand of parental control. Proponents of the V-chip (these can range from television executives to watchdog groups, members of Congress, parents, and television manufacturers) codify its abilities as an exercise in choice. The Clinton-Gore administration, and this approach is echoed in the wake of Janet's breast, hailed the V-chip as empowering parents and affording control over television content. President Clinton went as far as to claim that the V-chip is a matter of "handing the TV remote control back to America's parents."[46] Of course, in "handing the TV remote control back" it contains an additional feature, one reminiscent of Williams's television period but one also unique to television's current logic and control capabilities. Critics like Murray, Heins, Balkin, and others regard V-chip–enabled choice with warranted skepticism. The delegation of choice, as Balkin writes, is a delegation to the invisible process of filtering and blocking. The exercise of choice here is a matter of compliance rather than earnest deliberation and personal autonomy. I am inclined to argue that both parties are correct. As a control device, the V-chip exemplifies disciplined freedom, choice that is regulated through mediated acts of choice. A technological means secures the *ends* of choice and not the end of choice. The V-chip helps shape the field of choice as a practice and process of parental control and empowerment through expertise. It is at this location that criticism must be directed, criticism that regards the V-chip as a practice and process of control within the larger study of technologies of governing. Choice is licensed through the intentional and compliant restriction of choices (the allowance of freedom provided by Deleuze's technology of the highway). Here choice is concerned less with the concept of personal autonomy and more with a rationalized practice of securitization whereby technology functions in the service of the user; choice is regarded not as an act of delegation but, in a reductive sense, as the use of tools to assist in self-regulation. The question becomes not "what do you want?" but "do you want A or B?" Blocked or unblocked.

Perhaps of equal importance, the question of "choice" may not even be the most productive way to assess the V-chip's functionality when it comes to the question of viewer-centered control and the televisual interface. As I continue to stress, the actual utilization of control devices like the V-chip is less vital for understanding technologies of control than their embedded status: the transference of censorship into censorial practices throughout intermedial experiences. With control designed in, our media are reconfigured to position us within the discourse of control technology. We are subjected to the position of the parental function of authority and expertise. When enabled, to watch television is to watch through the V-chip. When disabled, or simply never used, all viewers are positioned in the field of the V-chip as it is already present. It is usually at the level of practice that questions of choice arise: the decision of whether or not to "use" the V-chip. We could argue, and this point is argued to death in neoliberal circles, that the V-chip commands no new level of censorship when the "user" decides whether or not to use it. The question of whether or not to block is left entirely up to the parent.

At the risk of sounding crass, if choice were a major point for debate and not simply a marketing device to recapitulate viewer-centered practices with control devices, then one could argue for having a choice in purchasing a television with or without a V-chip in lieu of having all televisions sold within the United States bound by the legal requirements of the V-chip.

V . . . V(you) Control and Vision Machine

If the V-chip expands the logics of television and furthers a case for viewer-centered control, then it is worth seriously considering what the recondite V in V-chip actually means or has meant in an earlier phase of its development and implementation. I believe that the "V"-chip's initial meaning, before the U.S. congressional hullabaloo seized upon it, demonstrates the importance of vision and visuality within viewer-centered control at the televisual interface. In the mid-1990s, as demonstrated by Representative Edward Markey's fervor, substantial interest was dedicated to the elusive v. The heated debates over industry interpretations of ratings like "D" (suggestive dialogue) would suggest that V stands for "vague." Proponents of Sec. 551, "Parental Choice in Television Programs," of the Telecommunications Act of 1996 subscribe to an interpretation of "voluntary" as in "voluntary rules for rating video programming." However, if one looks at the MPAA ratings for film classification, the concept of "voluntary" dissolves when major cinema chains refuse to run unrated or NC-17 films (and when Blockbuster Inc. and Wal-Mart refuse to carry NC-17–rated videocassettes or DVDs). Aspirations to a "voluntary" quality severely collapse at the point of distribution (or in the case of television the necessity of advertising revenue). Claims of graphic violence on television would presume that V is for "violence" (this meaning prevails), while media watchdog groups may define V as "values" (as in family values). Perhaps it stands for vertical interval line, the part of the bandwidth that carries the ratings signal? For its creator, Tim Collings, V stands for "Vyou Control," as in "view." "You" control the "view." The agency of a universal seeing subject converges with technologically enabled control.

While managing violent content was clearly on the agenda of development, the V-chip was conceptualized to manage the televisual. More precisely, its development was meant to impact not just how we watch television (in terms of what programming is blocked), but how we come to *view the television*. Consequently, it is significant that Collings opted for *view* instead of *watch* in his conceptualization of the V-chip's capabilities. *View* accounts for the act of looking, a particular position from which to look at something (as well as the expression of one's opinion as in having a "point of view"). Views are framed; they are constructed for us (think of postcards, staged photographic opportunities, art in museums, holiday brochures, the cinema) as well as by us where a perspective is facilitated or imposed. The *OED* defines *view* in the following manner: 4. The exercise of the faculty of sight; the faculty or power of vision; the possibility or opportunity of seeing something. 4.e. Range of sight of vision; 6. The sight or vision of something.[47] *Watch* is a verb for the act of looking and does not, like *view,* command the broader meanings of power, range, activity, and position. "Vyou Control" suggests that the V-chip is concerned with both *an object* and *an action* in the way that Tony Bennett configures culture as both an object and instrument of government for the facilitation of conduct. The "view" and the conduct of "viewing" become both through the presence and practice of the V-chip. The object is the visibility of television's information, and the action is the practice of controlling how the view is accessed and how viewing is conducted. Television is both a target (disallowing access to television programming) and means (television as instrument for regulation) of control in this dynamic.

Furthermore, it ought to be noted that the V-chip was designed for the wrong medium, or at least Collings's protective intentions stemmed from an event associated with a different medium. Brian Lowry, writing for the *Los Angeles Times,* recounts Collings's motivation for designing the chip; he "decided to explore that area in the wake of an event that occurred a decade ago: the massacre of 14 engineering students in Montreal by a man whose apartment contained numerous violent *videos.*"[48] How would a technology designed to block audiovisual access to broadcast programs affect the viewing of a videocassette? The V-chip is powerless over this medium. Any blocking would take the form of retail outlets like Blockbuster refusing to stock certain titles, blocking devices that lock out channels 3 and 4 for VCR/DVD use, reedited DVDs like those sold by CleanFlicks, the use of filtering DVD players by ClearPlay, or simply fast-forwarding or scanning past "indecent" scenes. In addition, Collings expressed concern over violent content, but the V-chip far exceeds this category. Heins offers the example of how documentaries, docudramas, and films based on historical events could get easily lumped under content ratings of V. She writes, "works of film or TV art, from *Bonnie and Clyde* or *Psycho* to documentaries on the civil rights movement, would receive violence ratings."[49] And, of course TV-M, and V, or S may discourage lucrative sponsorship, and the television ratings, much like film ratings, would result in ratings determining content for audience figures. The action of blocking is far from accurate management of content. But then accuracy is not the point. While a program may carry the content rating D (suggestive dialogue), if programmed, the V-chip will automatically block the entire program; it cannot consider dialogue that is not suggestive (whatever that would entail). The same applies to other content warnings. The presence of a single element warranting the rating of TVMA initiates the V-chip's blocking ability. The V-chip, and we could say the same for the parental function's indebtedness to the V-chip, cannot be selective. Nor can a parent's own decision making under its training and constraining regime exceed the RCD.

Although the V-chip may be a relatively new way of regulating televisual images (we have recently passed the tenth anniversary of the Telecommunications Act of 1996) and the conduct of viewers, as opposed to previous efforts by institutions and divisions for broadcast standards, it is housed within a familiar object and longstanding source for "news from outside," the television.[50] The embedding of the V-chip within television manifests a new visual protocol; it makes visible the positive effects of television that it enables: choice, self-regulation, interaction, safe images, and security. Here choice becomes a matter of display, not contemplation. The "object" of the V-chip is less the blocking of individual programs in compliance with a ratings system than a redesign of viewer control and further "empowerment" of parental expertise as the self-regulation of culture. When Valenti exclaimed that the V-chip is for parents, he was 100 percent correct. Yet where Valenti applauds an informational service, we can see far more at work. As discussed previously, the tangible ability to exercise control over televisual images in the form of embedded filtering technology comes not from a remote sender exclusively assigned to an elusive corporate policy or government agency. It is instead effortlessly (at least in theory) practiced by the parent through the television, the technocultural object of domestic commonality and social experience. Again, control is literally "at your fingertips." And in being so, control shapes conduct in a manner that enables the self as an active agent in the administration of its own governance through choice and consumer practices. The ends are instantaneous and automatic. Parents do not have to deliberate, research, or even understand the various ratings or the workings of V-chip technology much less the content of broadcast programs. Parents simply continue to use the available features of their television, viewer control at their fingertips.

To sustain an engagement with viewer-centered control through the V-chip as "view" control, I would like to expound upon an alternative meaning of the *V* abbreviation in V-chip. In this case *V* would stand for "vision" as in "vision machine" and point to the question of visibility that ensues. Paul Virilio's *The Vision Machine* explores the ways that perception and representation are modified by technology. *The Vision Machine* is a second volume that greatly expands his project on the militarization and industrialization of vision initiated four years earlier in *War and Cinema: The Logistics of Perception*. As John Johnson explains in "Machinic Vision," the logistics of perception account "for the operational agenda according to which perception is appropriated, delimited, and further produced by means of various technologies mostly controlled by the military and police."[51] While *War and Cinema* remains true to its title and confronts the relational developments between warfare and cinema during the world wars, the expanse of *The Vision Machine* accounts for a concatenation of art history and avant-garde aesthetics, communications media, digital photography, urban planning, television, surveillance, and computer technology as well as the military industrial complex (and one could easily imagine this series being broadened to include the military entertainment complex of video games), cinematography, and histories of cinema in its attempt to delineate the "paradoxical logic" of the changing conditions to vision and images wrought by the automation of perception.[52]

While Virilio's logistics of perception do not consider the V-chip, as *The Vision Machine* was written over a decade before the V-chip began to appear in U.S. televisions,[53] it does provide a conceptual scheme within which blocking can be assessed as it pertains to viewer-centered control. Virilio's concern with computer-controlled perception, where the eye of the human observer is displaced by technical devices, can function as a catalyst for asking how the V-chip exerts control over the presence of televisual images in the domestic field of television and televisuality. To reiterate, the V-chip allows for parenting at a distance in that the physical presence of an authoritarian gaze does not have to be present in front of the screen, or in the same space, for that matter. Virilio would address this distance as an example of sightless vision. "Aren't they also talking," Virilio queries, "about the new technology of 'visionics': the possibility of achieving *sightless vision* whereby the video camera would be controlled by a computer?"[54] Famous for reliance on neologisms and epigrammatic allure, Virilio offers "sightless vision" as a way to account for the surrogacy of human vision by machines of vision.[55] This is best exemplified in technologies for sightless vision that enable machines to replace human perceivers. Rather than a pair of human eyes behind a lens or screen, a surrogate information system—what Virilio often refers to as automation of perception—occupies the position of active observer.

Technology is charged with "looking for itself."[56] To provide a contrast to sightless vision machines, Virilio offers the model of the surveillance camera. The vision machine, according to Virilio in an interview with John Armitage, "means that an inanimate object now can see *for itself.* A remote camera, for example, is for the use of a policeman or a security guard. There is someone behind it who does the viewing. . . . But behind the vision machine there is nobody. There is only a micro-receiver, and a computer."[57] Virilio's assertion that a seeing subject presides behind the camera speeds past Foucault qua Bentham's well-weathered insistence that the actual presence of the guard is less pertinent than the disindividualized modality of power being simultaneously "visible and unverifiable."

Prior to the interview and in the chapter from *The Vision Machine* where he elaborates on the concept of sightless vision, Virilio discusses the television (in his beloved italics as a *domestic display terminal*) as occupying a panoptic position far removed from Bentham's reliance on human centrality. Discussing the installation of television in individual prison cells (we are not privy to exactly where this occurs), Virilio regards the presence of television as complying with a mode of surveillance: "as soon as viewers switch on their sets, it is they, prisoners or otherwise, who are in the field of television, a field in which they are obviously powerless to intervene. . . ."[58] The punishment, according to Virilio, is envy: seeing but unable to have. The imprisonment is being in the field of the cathode-ray tube or plasma screen.

Just as Uricchio placed Williams's experiences of televisual flow within a historically specific moment of television's practices and technologies, sightless vision and Virilio's address of television require similar consideration. Firstly, Virilio's ellipsis can be filled with a corrective. We are not powerless in the field of television as Virilio asserts. While the notion of the "powerless" can be ambiguous and Virilio does us no favors by providing a clear explanation, we have seen that various devices and technologies expand the conditionality of television to allow for greater management of programming by the viewer. Uricchio's argument of viewer-centered flow makes this case very clear. In the current historical moment, the V-chip, many proponents would argue, attempts to prevail over the inability to intervene in controlling television and the cultural information emanating from its screen. I will allow that Virilio's audience is literally "captive," but he does impose a similar form of imprisonment on all viewers of television by virtue simply of proximity to its screen. Within the processes of control, being in the field of television is less expressive of regulation than of the technology, television, being transformed by being embedded with a device for control. For it too is on lockdown.

Secondly, is the V-chip a type of surveillance technology, an electronic security guard? The V-chip, and this criticism will be continued with respect to Internet filters, does not function as surveillance technology as illustrated by the camera-guard scenario. The V-chip displays a view and manages a way to view. Its "surveillance" is of incoming information, not bodies in space. It does not observe but shows what can and will not be seen. Virilio attempts to rethink the camera-guard scenario in his turn to the notion of the vision machine. From the rapid deployment of the logistics of perception, a blinding of "natural perception" perpetuated by the accelerant vision machine occurs. Many media scholars have taken issue with Virilio's insistence on a crisis of perception and his catholic maintenance of a stark separation between the categories of human and machine.[59] Virilio's dependence on categories like "natural perception" and the procession of mourning that lambastes its erosion by emerging information and visual technologies would lead to the conclusion that the V-chip is yet another instance of replacement (and this charge is often leveled against parenting) or would invoke the careless application of prosthetics to account for its practices. While a more dedicated critique of the limitations of Virilio's work on account of his unapologetic humanism exceeds the confines of this immediate project, it is necessary to reconsider the role vision plays in the practice of manifesting a vyou/view.

The question of "who" watches and "who" is watched is compounded when filtering technology like the V-chip becomes a part of our practices with television. Children are watched in that their access to programming bearing ratings deemed inappropriate is denied automatically, even in the absence of "direct" parental supervision. Television is watched by viewers while it "watches" information and displays its ability to regulate information, the display of our "view" we could say. The evidence for this takes the form of the actual block displayed on-screen to restrict access to select programming. The block itself, regarded as denying access to information, is actually high in informational content. Its "message" is security and the practice of control. Where the message of television for McLuhan was not its content but its ability to design (and discipline) a new environment and mode of perception, the V-chip's "message" (or its retinal "massage"), to follow McLuhan, is the enabled environment and encouraged perspective of the audiovisual block: a "programmable," self-afflicted, and allegedly beneficent blindness displayed on screen. The question for the V-chip is not what it "sees"—it in fact sees nothing—but what kind of censorial perception it enables as a vision machine designed intentionally to impair vision. Viewing the block is a form of visible assurance. This is not imposed from above—a negative dominating expression of power and restriction of choice—but from within: within the family, within the home, and within the television set. Television ratings, coupled with the V-chip, determine what is acceptable and what is accessible. Outfitted in all televisions, the V-chip introduces a discrete member to the family (another member under the parental function): the permanence of control and the sign of security. Not just the observation of bodies in space but the compound relation of bodies around the television, televisual images, technology, and visibility all come under the jurisdiction of the V-chip. We "view" television as a technology that enables choice. An audiovisual cultural technology enables viewer-centered control through the familiar and familial circuits of television.

What type of "viewing" is practiced through the V-chip? While vision and visibility mutually impact one another, the watching of the V-chip is a sightless vision of informational seeing rather than ocular seeing. Virilio moves into this type of distinction in 1990 with *L'Inertie polaire* (published in English as *Polar Inertia* in 2000), where he returns to the vision machine to account for the "transformation of ocular optics into a truly everyday electro-optics."[60] The "viewing" (our present vocabulary lets us down here) is information processing invisible to the human eye. We cannot observe this process; all we can see are its results. No optical "watching" occurs. No vision is present unless we maintain the notion of sightless vision as informational seeing. Transmitted numerical code embedded in the signal of rated programs is decoded by the V-chip and measured against parental options (preset levels of access) and proceeds to block the signal or allow access until instructed otherwise. Virilio would agree that models of surveillance premised upon vision and perspective—that is, ocular seeing—are cumbersome here. However, a system of visibility is present. The visibility made possible by the V-chip is seen in its effects, its "view" displayed for all to see.

If the V-chip's function within the television can be understood as a sightless vision machine in the way that Virilio insists, then its aim would be to degrade vision and displace the human viewer. However, the V-chip can hardly be regarded as an animistic technology. And displacement is not the practice of the V-chip. It requires a complex of human-technology interaction in order to regulate television. Rather than purport to "see for itself" in order to assist in the policing, management, selection, and regulation of televisual content, blocking technology relies on encoded signals, not the discerning eye of a remote human spectator. The image seen on a cathode-ray television screen, for example, is transmitted as lines of information drawn line by line from the upper left to the bottom right of the screen by electron beams inside the picture tube. The chip receives a rating encoded in the vertical blanking interval (VBI) of a particular program's transmission signal. The invisible and inaudible signal is best known for carrying information for closed-caption text. Line 21, also known as line 21 data area, the VBI line that the rating code is transmitted on, makes text available for the hearing impaired while simultaneously and instantly denying the ability to see to the visually unimpaired. The "view," as in vision, becomes invisible, whereas the "view" as an object and practice of control remains highly visible. It is a process whereby we engage in the practice of merely watching television and using our RCD. Informational seeing to regulate content and viewers is a process far removed from our actual vision. Closed captioning, data that textually enable the deaf to "hear" television, has come to also mean the blocking of visual access.

Seeing and non-seeing: the emphasis here is a hybrid of encouragement and eradication within which visibility is the object for improvement and correction while television—projecting onto the viewer—becomes a self-monitoring, beneficent technological means to display the control over what is directly accessible to our senses and in our homes. This prompts the question: is the object of the V-chip necessarily the content of television or, as I have suggested, conduct? As stated previously, to watch television is to also watch the practice of blocking. Sightless vision would suggest the removal of the viewing subject from the responsibilities of watching and evaluating. Herein lies Virilio's humanistic fears and anxiety over the displacement of vision by new vision machines. The "televiewer," as Virilio prefers, is removed from this act of perception: "the computer would be responsible for the machine's—rather than the televiewer's—capacity to analyse the ambient environment and automatically interpret the meaning of events."[61] A viewing subject is produced by a vision machine that reduces the complexity of moral questions to an automatic blocking response: to block or not to block becomes the set of options. The act of watching is reversed and conducted away from human perception. All we observe are the effects of the V-chip: control. Television is now "watched" according to the encoded response between chip and transmission signal.

Whether or not the V-chip is adequately explained to parents by RCA and other television manufacturers, assigned a PIN and enabled via one's remote control, or regarded as a viable "quick fix" in countries like the United States with hundreds of television channels to zap through from the safe distance of a sofa is not an urgent concern. It may very well be the case, even after Ms. Jackson's performance and Bono's expletive of "fucking brilliant" at the 2004 Golden Globe Awards, or even after Michael Powell's sales pitches for digital television, that the V-chip is nothing more, as skeptics continue to assert, than a gimmick, a diversion strategy to push through a law granting megacorporate consolidation of media production and distribution, or an electronic Band-Aid for boiling-point culture wars. Yet, as I have insisted, we ought to refrain from an easy dismissal.

"Vyou Control" forces us to consider what type of control is being enabled by the televisions embedded with blocking capabilities that pepper our screenic environments. The *you* in "Vyou" is not any you. It is overdetermined by the category of parent (after all, it is "for parents only"). The eradicating block, determined by the erroneous, programmable agency of parental control, demands a mode of docile seeing that can only look where predetermined and a type of visibility premised exclusively on access. In this respect, the V-chip is horribly anachronistic despite claims of interactivity and the "newness" of viewer-centered technologies of control. The V-chip purports to improve television by means of impairing visual access to it. This presumed beneficent technology, touted as enabling, choice enhancing, interactive, the key to "winning back the living room," an active involvement in controlling televisual content entering the home through interaction with the television, puts the viewer in control (Vyou Control), and this continues to be a prime marketing point for networks, television manufacturers, politicians, the FCC, and media watchdog groups.

The V-chip furthers television as a technology for seeing, in this case a technology for administrating vision by imposing a blinding view on television. The "fantasy scenario" that Boddy insists on would be one within which the adoption of the V-chip offers a course of direct action to manage media (and the visual field) at the micro level of the personal and domestic, to manage *through* television—a means and rationality of governing the cultural formations of filtering technology and the expanding logic of television's instrumentality as a control device. Viewers are bestowed the ability to determine what information makes it into the domestic sphere and on their home screens while coming to regard consumer products as accessible solutions to the control of information and the regulation of media.

3. Filtering

Keep your family safe with our award-winning
filtered Internet.

Mayberry USA

Stop users accessing harmful Internet content by
blocking unsuitable websites, newsgroups and
search engine images. Use with time limits to take
control yet give the freedom to explore—even when
you can't be there!

CyberPatrol

The market would do the regulation of the
government.

Lawrence Lessig, Code and Other Laws of Cyberspace

Barney Fife: Armed and Dangerous

Mayberry USA, a provider of "filtered Internet access," based in
Crystal River, Florida, is a filtering service of 711.net Inc., a resource
for Christian information on the Internet (and not to be mistaken for
the heavenly home of Slurpees). Mayberry USA's mission statement
purports to make "the Internet a useful and practical communication tool—available and safe to all people, all ages, and all faiths."[1]
"All faiths" on a Christian identified and disseminated ISP smacks
of online missionary work when we consider that these services

greatly exceed the private sphere of the networked home computer to influence the connected public spheres of libraries, schools, and businesses. This is particularly so in light of legislation such as the Children's Internet Protection Act (2000) as well as company policies that implement filters on their networked computers as a protective/security/monitoring measure. "Local community standards," the benchmark for rulings on obscenity, come to frame a global network for many users. Consider the name, Mayberry USA. This past is imaginary: a town from *The Andy Griffith Show* (1960–68), where an inept deputy, Barney Fife,[2] requires only a lone bullet to patrol the staged space of reactionary midcentury rural Americana. This imaginary town now sprawls onto the computer screen not as a *TV Land* repeat but as Mayberry USA filtering software that plots and monitors the variable spaces of the Internet for its "townspeople."

Internet filtering software (IFS) aimed specifically at the concerns of parents for "online safety" began to emerge on the U.S. market in the late 1990s. Soon after the U.S. Supreme Court ruled against the Communications Decency Act (CDA) of 1996, which attempted to criminalize the display of "patently offensive" messages and transmission of "indecent" information to minors by way of the Internet, the emphasis immediately shifted from prosecuting senders and users of a "telecommunications device" to the "less burdensome alternatives" of voluntary filtering software.[3] Writing on flaws common to filtering technology, Christopher D. Hunter rightly notes that Internet filters "have been championed as *the* solution for keeping inappropriate content at the edge of cyberspace, and away from children."[4] Filtering software purports to filter, monitor, and block a range of Internet activities and content that threatens to impose on our networked computer screen: Web sites, e-mails, pop-ups, newsgroups, file sharing, streaming media, search engine images, attachments and downloads, Listservs and message boards, peer-to-peer (P2P), chat and chat rooms, IM (instant messaging), and, in some instances, any application and the entire Internet according to predetermined levels and categories set by the "expertise" of parental judgment within the home or by "experts" like school officials, school district leaders, and librarians. School officials and librarians were forced into play after the passage of the Children's Internet Protection Act significantly stimulated the market for filtering software by legally requiring schools and libraries to adopt filtering software on all networked computers or lose funding from the E-rate program, which provides discounts on classroom technology for schools and libraries.[5] We might also include in this litany of experts the "expertise" of software designers who write code for filtering programs that purport to protect children from the hazards of the Internet.

Management of access to online content through filtering software is regarded as more sophisticated than the limited capabilities of its television counterpart, the V-chip, which simply blocks out an entire television show to display its "view." Security Software Systems (executive offices in Illinois and Texas), the company that produces the "parental control software" Cyber Sentinel, describes their product as a "content monitor" rather than a URL blocker. Monitoring content can take the form of site blocking, database review of "sexually explicit" Web sites or "predatory content," and the automatic closing of an application "to get the child out of harms way."[6] IProtectYou Pro Web Filter 6.03 (produced by SoftForYou of Chapel Hill, North Carolina) takes Cyber Sentinel's ability to remove the child from "harms way" further; it shuts down an entire application (like an Internet browser) when it blocks content.[7] One "bad e-mail" results in the cancellation of all downloaded messages. SoftForYou developed its software to "help parents protect children online and to give a powerful tool to monitor and guard children from the many online dangers that exist where they have Internet access."[8] Out of harm's way is construed as access denied. In both cases the act of monitoring is automatic and based on self-selected or default settings that determine how access is configured.

Despite claims of content monitoring and "advanced" filtering capabilities, in many instances filtering does control in much the same way as the V-chip's block. An entire Web site—including all subdirectories and individual pages that make up a particular Web site—may be blocked if filtering occurs at the root level (aimed at the first address, www.amazon.com, for example). A far cry from pinpoint precision, this block is a complete eradication of all content on a specific Web page. "Granularity," as Hunter explains, is the term used to describe "the level of a Web site at which a blocking decision is imposed."[9] If blocking occurs at the root level, all linked content is blocked whether deemed "harmful," a favored expression among filtering software companies, or not. That is, all subdirectories and Web pages connected to a particular URL, regardless of content, are blocked en masse. Hunter also raises the possibility that despite the room for error and inaccurate filtering, root-level blocking may be a common occurrence: "Filter companies often block at the root level because it is too time consuming to surf through the millions of pages on such sites, looking for specific examples of off-limits content."[10] Another factor that warrants a comparison to the V-chip is that filtering companies block access to a Web site by its Internet Protocol (IP) address, a numeric address that specifies the format of packets that contain destination address information. Many Web sites rely on "virtual hosting," which allows Web sites with different domain names to share IP addresses. If a lone Web site contains "harmful" content, then all Web sites affiliated with the shared IP address, regardless of their content, are blocked as well. Internet filters do not appear to stray too far from the V-chip in their viewer-user–centered control. Upon these "safe" sites only can we navigate: our eyes may not be blinded as with the V-chip's block, but we are forced to squint nonetheless as filtering radically narrows the horizon of networked environs.

Internet filtering softwares are powerful agents, this chapter argues, in the abiding securitization of habitat and emblematic of how control attempts to manage its new freedoms through consumer choice in self-regulating online activities and Web content. While filtering software is an end-to-end technology—it focuses on the applications of individual and local network computers—the technology is increasingly designed in our online experience to foster a sense of safety and security online for all users. Filtering software does not simply affect freedoms and control made possible by the Internet's end-to-end network and increasingly regulatory operational codes, but rather functions *as freedoms and control* in managing online access, understandings of the Internet, and social relations to Web content. This furthers control's emphasis on enabling users through a social relation to and implication within media technology.

In fact, the disciplined freedoms of control are often highlighted as a sign of "good" Internet service, and reliable online security as the "instrumentality" of software is continually positioned as empowering. The common choice of "Controls On" settings indicates the presence and practice of control devices for self-regulating and monitoring online activities. IFS is designed to "filter," "monitor," and "block" access to sites on the World Wide Web whose content is considered "objectionable" and "harmful" to users, most often envisioned as children and families, per pictures on filtering companies' home pages. In these images computers are always domestic appliances around which families gather. Often overlooked in the current work on Internet filtering is the place of the computer screen in the filtering process. Screens common to the household—computer and television screens—are active technologies and architectonic elements that assist in the aims and goals of self-regulation, home security, and parental policing of the family. The computer screen meshed with filtering software performs the architectural function of the "front-door" as opposed to the "window" metaphor common to the epistemology of the television and computer screens; together they secure the habitat of the home by "screening" who and what is allowed to gain entrance and come in contact with the family. Time and movement on the Web are charted, managed, and always already regulated to ensure safe passage when we go online through filters, or at least this is the promise and protocol.

In spite of seeing the effects of filtering displayed on our screens in the form of blocked Web pages, the action of filtering is both a visible and invisible process, or what I will refer to as "visible invisibility." The Web is monitored by a technocultural complex that configures links according to the binary logic of filtering: "access" or "denied access." Users, represented by the expert category of "parent" (the "self" of self-regulation, the "you" in "your Internet"), can set levels of access through "parental control" options available from ISPs and can purchase additional software that surveys the Web for objectionable material that can be linked to opaque, proprietary lists (for accessible Web sites) stored on a software company's database. Once computer networked choice becomes facilitated by preemptive filtering software, it maps out, delimits, and denies the Internet to users based on invisible protocols that define decency and restrict access to content deemed objectionable by these services.

"A Useful and Practical Communications Tool"?

Internet filtering software, like Mayberry USA, exemplifies Lawrence Lessig's claim that market-based regulatory practices offer consumer modes of self-governance while, in relation to Nikolas Rose's work on control, rendering the practice of filtering a technology of control for the securitization of habitat.[11] Filtering mobilizes the parental function in order to further safeguard the family's domain by self-regulating Web content that can enter the home and display itself upon our familial computer screens. In the discourse of companies who produce filtering software, a filtered Internet *furnishes* a controlled experience within which parents' active regulation of their children's online activities serves as a form of security. The purported task? Protect *my* screen, home, and family: redesign the plasticity of the Web's amorphousness to abide by the machinery of "family values." This harkens back to William Boddy's claim, introduced in the previous chapter, that emerging media inscribes scenarios about how it will occupy and transform domestic space as well as rationalizes its social function and utilizations. In other words, filters attempt to make the Internet and all who come into contact with it "safe" since conduct (in this scenario going online and searching the Web) is monitored through the forbiddance of content. In relying on technological solutions to moral problems, the market surpasses the regulatory measures of government, which is not to say that the federal government does not legislate for new markets.[12]

The protocols of IFS are hardly neutral in their professed instrumentality. As François Fortier rightly notes in relation to IFS, "filters on networks can then be mounted according to commercial, regional, professional, educational, ethnic, linguistic, religious, racial, gender and class requirements."[13] IFS designs values into the Internet and displays them across computer screens in the form of inaccessible Web sites and blocked pop-ups (ones construed as threatening to children). With filtering software, this lack of neutrality is transparent because the parental function runs a monopoly on what values can structure the Internet and Web content. I draw a distinction between the Internet and Web content, as IFS affects both; content is policed as are our online movements in the form of how we spend time on online. Family, and the administration of its ever-expanding securitized habitat, orders the content of the largest repository of information ever amassed and directs its delivery to our screens (or not, in the case of blocked URLs). Mayberry USA is a testament to Fortier's claim of partisan specifications in writing code for filtering software. Political matters become an acute way to organize diverse users as discriminating consumers in the lucrative industry of filtering software and ISP subscription services.[14] In lieu of a personalized Internet organized by "cookie" crumbs that track consumer choice to make shopping at Amazon.com more "convenient" and "enjoyable," we encounter a Web charted through a technology of customized morality where we can "safely" inhabit an imaginary and solipsistic world. Imaginary because, and I rely on an analogy here, we have simply tinted our "windows" to impede the rays of online information.

Lessig and Andrew L. Shapiro both argue that the early Internet's emphasis on many-to-many communication networks—user-to-user participatory media as contrasted to the one-way, one-to-many broadcast of large-scale institutions like radio, newspapers, and television—demonstrated a transfer of power, availability, decentralization, and increased individual freedoms over the control of information.[15] Internet filters can be interpreted as beneficial technology for increased control and individualized freedom over how the Internet is accessed, and over how its content is traversed according to personally "selected" protocols for directing online behavior in the name of security and protection. Hailed as "users," we are implicated in, perhaps come to embody, the non-neutrality of filtering software through what is, in effect, an active end user redesign of the Web. I refer to the presence of Internet filters as a process of redesign because IFS defines the Internet as a hostile and insecure space that is only safe if regulated and controlled. The promise: individuals are in charge of their online mediated surroundings and govern by governing their own conduct as well as the conduct of others. They use their machines to govern their homes and its inhabitants, yelling "get off of my property" as IFS extends property lines into bits and bytes of information. The demand for filters redesigns the Internet in accordance with the twin concepts of the family and the consumer, which, needless to say, dovetail quite easily.

As the Internet's surmised radicality became supplanted by the commercial, it became increasingly clear, for Lessig, that "how a system is designed will affect the freedoms and control the system enables."[16] Many scholars of cyber law prefer to side with the end user and self-regulation over centralized authority when examining Internet governance. For these scholars, the question concerns finding ways to produce smarter filtering systems that will continue to enable the user while complying with constitutionally protected speech.[17] At the writing of this book many filtering software programs rely on the amalgamations of keyword and word pattern–based blocking, URL root-level blocking, object analysis, metadata labels, and rating systems, as well as Web site–specific blocking based on an archived "whitelist" of approved Web sites versus its "blacklist" stored as proprietary information on a company's database. Keyword blocking evaluates Web content based on the presence of text flagged as inappropriate and correspondent with ratings categories. Critics have rightly noted, on account of its inability to distinguish context, that keyword filtering is notorious for blocking Web sites related to health care (words like *breasts* as in "breast cancer," for example), AIDS awareness, sex education, gay and lesbian resources, and women's organizations. Seth Finkelstein, founder of the antifiltering advocacy group Censorware Project, stresses that "computers are extremely stupid. Talk to any computer scientists, not the marketing people. They'll tell you artificial intelligence cannot determine context."[18]

Whether or not a computer is "extremely stupid" is increasingly debatable and less pertinent to the matter at hand than Finkelstein's comment on the determination of context. One instance of the failure to recognize context was reported by a user of CyberSitter (produced by Solid Oak Software, Inc., of Santa Monica, California, whose slogan is "For A Family Friendly Internet"[19]). In response to *PC Magazine*'s review of CyberSitter 9.0, one user shared the difficulties she or he experienced when searching for the town "Cockburn." The adult user posting to PCMag.com is interpellated as the child being "sitted" when a town name is confused with male anatomy in the form of "Cock" (either slang for male anatomy or feathered fowl). CyberSitter "objected" to "Cock," the poster informs us, and instead conducted the permitted search of the keyword "burn." Despite being positioned as the willing subject whose Web access is restricted because of a forbidden keyword, the user concludes with, "I'd rather have it [CyberSitter] overzealous than load up inappropriate images to my young children."[20]

Major filtering advances are in the works that may challenge Finkelstein's claim. Already keyword filtering is being enhanced by contextual keyword patterns that categorize URLs and other protocols that increase the functionality of how content can be filtered in the name of child safety. Most IFS does not rely solely on keyword blocks but rather on what can be discerned as an integrated complex of various techniques to provide a "safe" Internet for the user. CyberPatrol, for instance, uses "layered filtering technologies" that consist of databases, lists (its CyberLIST), content submission provided by clients to update its databases (here users actively help survey the Internet by functioning as agents for CyberPatrol when they submit URLs for "review"), a combination of human content research and review as well as automatic, computer spidering technologies that seek out keyword patterns and flag them, Web analysis for the review of Web sites, and categorization.[21]

An enabled V-chip can block broadcast transmissions from reaching our eyes and ears based on FCC-approved television ratings. IFS constrains the content of the Internet for its users based on ambiguous, haphazard, sporadic, secret, or fervently prejudiced criteria. A filtered Internet is not only a technology of control but also a pronouncement on culture and technology that attempts to configure the Internet to "family values" protocols. Many researchers on the Internet have encouraged us to refrain from adopting the teleological position that the communication and information network of the Internet is simply a "tool" or "instrument." In his discussion of telematics and telecommunications in urban life, William J. Mitchell argues that the ostensible conjunction between physical and virtual spaces demonstrates that we "become true inhabitants of electronically mediated environments rather then mere users of computational devices."[22] If Mitchell is correct in his assertion and it is necessary to renegotiate the Internet as a social space rather than retain the instrumentalist position, then what type of mediated environment does a "filtered Internet" license, and how do users occupy this "safe" space?

Our example of CyperSitter's management of the search for "Cockburn" is one indicator of "how" since it emphasizes the user's willingness to endure a dysfunctional filtering system for the belief that filtering software is *still necessary* regardless of whether or not it works adequately. The software's "practicality" and "usefulness" are predicated on its presence, not accuracy. Critical investigations into the problem of filtering—these are usually concentrated on over-blocking as demonstrated by CyberSitter—have adopted a method of revealing what sites are blocked by various filters. Obviously some instances fall into the category of the comedic and absurd, like "Cockburn," while others clearly reveal the seams of ideological positions when women's health and sexuality are flagged as "harmful" or "inappropriate."[23] These efforts no doubt document and expose severe problems with IFS, and these problems ought to be taken seriously in drafting legislation and in decisions to install filtering software. Yet to be cynical for a moment, the audience for IFS is most likely better represented by the user who requests "Cockburn" and sides with a "mild inconvenience" as a necessary price to pay for a "safer Internet" and by default a "safer home." While we can debate advances in context determination by artificial intelligence, I prefer to understand the major determining context to reside elsewhere: the ethos of neoliberal self-regulation and practices of self-securitization function as the context for control devices such as IFS. The artificial intelligence of IFS is a complex intelligence governed by the parental function and is produced through and enabled by technologies of control that manage Web content, mediated inhabitance, the networks of the Internet as a mark of individualized freedom, constituted safety, and expansion of the securitization of habitat through code practiced as an end-user practical utility.

The "tool" metaphor for administering our relationship to the Internet is disconcerting when it precludes other possible ways to conceive of social relations to technology and our place within networked computing. In an argument similar to Mitchell's concern with the pervasive category of the user for defining our relationship within electronically mediated environments, James Slevin asserts that "individuals are not just *users* of communication systems, they are also participants in political communities in which the competent formation of opinion and the making of decisions depend on the availability of information and the monitoring of the differing ideas of others."[24] Mayberry USA's elucidation of the Internet as a "practical communication tool" illustrates how filtering software regards itself as a tool and its users as tool users engaged in rebuilding and repairing the Internet (regardless of whether or not they work efficiently in their repairs). Filtering software is reconstructive. It attempts to rebuild the space of the Internet according to protocols of prevention or protective inaccessibility while willfully participating in "political communities" housed deep within the public sphere of the family (and in addition there are software companies that produce filtering technology according to the marked agendas of third-party software providers). Yet filtering software companies repeatedly argue that they are, after all, marketing home security in a culture of fear, that "indecent" or "inappropriate" sites can still be accessed by changing filtering levels or simply by deactivating the filter. Is this the case for public libraries or schools that are pressured to adopt filtering software or lose federal funding? Moreover, redesign transcends usage. "User" is rarely singular in cyberspace. IFSs have power that is obscured by the way that they represent themselves as family and security. And this power impacts the very ways of conceiving of the Web; it carries repercussions of significant importance for users and nonusers alike. The "differing ideas" of Slevin's statement are not disputed or debated in a filtered Internet environment but, rather, simply kept offscreen and out of the home unbeknownst to the user despite the central position of empowerment that the parent occupies in instrumentalist views of media technologies.

The Filtered Front Door

Susan Crawford, of the Cardoza School of Law and member of the Accountable Internet Project,[25] offers the metaphor of the "front door" as a means to contemplate the effectiveness of Internet filters in determining what makes it into the home by way of the networked computer screen. In an interview with the *New York Times* Crawford alerts: "If we treat the entry to our computers the way we treat our own front doors and decide who to let in ourselves, we'll have a better online experience."[26] While I find Crawford's work on Internet governance progressive, her analogy between the computer screen and front door does warrant further consideration for the place and meanings of the computer screen in governmentality studies, in the study of control technology, and as a crucial technology in the securitization of habitat. Crawford's tone does not mirror Mayberry USA's nostalgia for one-bullet Deputy Fife. However, her analogy does proceed to reproduce the consensus shared among many IFS companies that a filtered Internet provides a type of self-administered security for the networked domestic sphere that results in some degree of increased safety. In the place of the worn welcome mat, which requires that all who enter leave "filth" outside, filtering softwares like Net Nanny, SmartFilter, SafeEyes, iProtectYou, Bsafe, Cyber Sentinel, ScreenDoor, NetMop, CyberPatrol, CyberSitter, and others suspiciously interrogate all potential visitors be they invited guests or strangers.

Crawford's analogy prompts a few mental images for me of how the mediated environment of the Internet is perceived through filtering architecture. I imagine the American parents of Powell's placid televisual environment within which a single breast can rupture the feeble "moral fiber" of a desperate and (painstakingly manufactured) fearful nation. Next, I imagine parents who have internalized McLuhan's polemics on the automobile as a "carapace, the protective and aggressive shell, of urban and suburban man"[27] to such an extent that all of their environs must become militarized and mobilized: a type of homeland security "aggressive shell" forever shielding residents from the dreaded threats of the outside; all portals into our private lives—our homes, our neighborhoods, our automobiles, our telephones (caller ID), and now our screens—must keep the outside and unknown at a secure distance. Of course, this is a total reverse of television and the Internet's promissory pledge to bring the world closer.

I also envisage this front door as one fortressed deep within Rose's gated community with deed restrictions, security guards, sophisticated home alarms, and razor-sharp fences. But perhaps my mental picture is misguided, if not totally inadequate. At the average rate of $49.95, filtering software is far more affordable than a suburban mortgage. With V-chip usage and Internet filters the accessible information points and image utilities of television and computer screens by way of user activation tighten the bolt, affix the latch, to continue with Crawford's metaphor, on the supply of information into the home. "We'll have a better online experience" is a claim that understands the Internet as a hazardous and threatening space obviously exempt from neighborhood crime watches but not immune from the technological solution of preemptive end-user controls of filtering software. The metaphorical register of the front door, therefore, must not be limited to an act of description or salient analogy. It is predicated on the changing cultural and social understandings of the Internet—its architecture and redesign. The computer screen as "front door" literally demarcates the Web and the home as a filtered space. This is recognized through the filtered networked computer within the home as well as the invocation of the front door in the structure of Internet filters and their functions.

Filtering software is marketed and consumed as "just another" tool or application for a packed tool bar to manage the unwieldiness, unpredictability, and unsecured spaces within which users may find themselves. With this development in mind, we might be prompted to ask how *filtering software as front door* changes our relationship to the information deluge of the networked computer in the home. Television's screen history provides a few answers. Television's material history has been configured along two competing design and theoretical imperatives. Lynn Spigel's argument is well known: television was hidden or placed in a remote corner of the postwar home.[28] The set was introduced into the gendered space of the domestic sphere as a new consumer technology as well as a decorative household object. While Jean Baudrillard spoke of the class status of television and its pedestal presentation,[29] Spigel convincingly demonstrates (for mid-century U.S. cultural history) how the television was camouflaged as a piece of furniture.

In the same period, television's status as furniture was challenged, an epistemological shift from a material object (box, set, furniture) to an architectonic element, an architecture of transparency best articulated as a cathode-window. Spigel situates television in relation to postwar domestic design schemes that attempted to renegotiate distinctions between the interior of the home and the outside world. The television as a "window on the world" emerged alongside the architecture of "picture windows" or "window walls." For Paul Virilio, who is less historically arduous than Spigel, the television screen becomes a "third window." In *The Lost Dimension* Virilio describes a procession of architectonic windows: coming after the "door-window" and "window" comes the "cathode-window"—"an introverted window, one which no longer opens onto adjoining space but instead faces beyond the perceptible horizon."[30] Virilio's first window was the door. The door enabled one to enter an enclosed structure. It provided direct access. It permitted the structure. When closed, it also negated access in the way that IFSs do per the companies who create them. His door-window marked an opening, "a threshold for the immediate and undifferentiated access of people, things, daylight and direct vision. . . ."[31] The television-window, a specialized window, is characterized as a "puncture," as in "the television set posted before the sofa is an object that punctures the walls."[32] Virilio's cathode-window, the framed visuality of the screen, renders the wall transparent and open to the instantaneousness of the ubiquitous television transmission. The television screen, Virilio continues, is a "mediated opening for solar light and nearby perspectives."[33] Unlike the television screen, the front door of Internet filtering architecture punctures no wall. It has the total opposite effect: the front door is a discriminating device that delimits entrance by selecting who can and cannot come in. Like the V-chip's remediation of television, the networked computer screen is remediated by IFS as a control technology. It works through strict closures (at the end of the highway, a slammed front door) rather than a mediated telepresent window to the outside and faraway.

The present state of filtering software realizes while systematically revising Manuel Castells's early prediction that "secluded individualistic homes across an endless suburban sprawl turn inward to preserve their own logic and values, closing their doors to the immediate surrounding environment and opening their antennas to the sounds and images of the entire galaxy."[34] Of course today, compared to the period within which Castells was writing, the television antenna is all but extinct, replaced by modems, satellites, mobile, wireless, and digital delivery services. Possibly also becoming extinct, or rather easier to manipulate, is the "opening" that Castells speaks of in regard to domestic telematics. The wooden doors may block out the neighborhood while the digital door of today's Internet filters proceed to screen all that passes through the electronic threshold of the computer screen and its virtual windows *into* domestication.

Following the lead of Spigel's work on the discursive construction of television (especially magazines aimed at female readers) in the 1950s, Elaine Lally's *At Home with Computers* contends that by the 1990s the home computer was "portrayed as a novel kind of domestic appliance—an 'information appliance'—which, it is implied, will soon become indispensable to the contemporary home."[35] Marsha F. Cassidy, also indebted to Spigel's research method, notes that "marketing discourse in the early 1990s redefined the personal computer's meaning at home by promoting its value in women's work—both income-producing and family-centered."[36] This redefinition marks a radical contrast from the home computer's educational, business, and hobbyist (mostly male) tradition that permeated during the previous decades. Also, it is well worth mentioning that "computers" were first introduced in the home in the 1970s and early 1980s in the form of computer games for the television screen.[37] As the computer joined the ranks of other home media like televisions, VCRs, audio equipment, and game consoles, its domestication (after all it was not that long ago that computers required huge warehouselike spaces for their physical storage), as Lally continues, was not articulated as "an isolated, individual activity, a possible threat to family cohesion. On the contrary, it is suggested, computing can be a joint leisure activity, a way of spending 'quality time' together as a family."[38]

This is a proverbial digestion of technology into the home. Hegemony turns the new, foreign, or threatening into a functional tool, a familiar as well as familial object, something easily controlled, used, and managed within existing ideologies of normalization. The doldrums of functionality quickly swallow the once novel. Roger Silver-stone discusses the consumption of new technologies as a "process of 'domestication' because what is involved is quite literally a taming of the wild and a cultivation of the tame. In this process new tech-nologies and services, unfamiliar, exciting, but also threatening, are brought (or not) under control by domestic users."[39] The home com-puter is no exception; it is rendered an appliance, as Lally argues, and its communicative capabilities are limited to that of an instrument. Her research on the domestication of the computer unfortunately did not consider the Internet in any great detail. In her engagement with the Internet, Lally highlights the relevance of the now dated (and tragically unhip) neologism for the Internet, "the information super highway." At the time of its heaviest circulation this metaphor sug-gested "a more user-friendly, familiar place, a place rather closer to home" and far, far away from William Gibson's fading neologism of "cyberspace."[40]

The "information super highway," the metaphor for networked communications, was not lost on Deleuze when he previously pro-posed the "highway" as the mode for the administration for control. In fact, his model of the highway as a decentered network, or what Galloway regards as a distributed network, predates Vice President Al Gore's well-known celebration of the "information super high-way." Freedom is already charted and produced through the paved surfaces of assurance and reactive choice. The highway also leads to the front door of the suburban sprawl discussed by Castells. One se-curity system begets, channels, travels into another. Display devices, as Mitchell attests, "bid to become the most powerful organizer of domestic spaces and activities. In most rooms, it's what most eye-balls are most likely to lock onto most of the time."[41] In the case of IFS our eyes are locked out from what we cannot see while being locked onto security.

In fact, the far away is kept so, denied proximity by electronic proxy. A filtered Internet replaces Virilio's door-window and television-window with a networked computer front door. This re-placement marks a reverse in telematics and televisuality. The once separate categories of "near" and "far," oppositional categories conjoined through telematics, are pried apart as filtering architec-ture seeks to position the user as the determinant of access and spa-tial regulation. Where Virilio claims that "telematics replaces the doorway,"[42] filtering architecture further realizes this announcement by redesigning the front door not as a "puncture"—a cathode framework—but as an urgent repair: a reinforced structure disallowing the immediacy of free electronic flow. However, unlike so many front doors, filtering architecture lacks a peephole, chain lock, or frosted glass windowpanes through which to catch a quick peek of a visitor. This door inspects on behalf of the computer owner: it is a mildly smart LCD door programmed to filter all that attempts to cross its threshold. Not only is the domestic space organized by the computer screen that our eyeballs are locked upon, the domestic space locks onto the space of the Internet as filtering technology attempts to extend the protective front door well beyond the domestic structure that it is attached to so that the Internet is an introverted experience—an extension of the domestic and private—rather than an opening forth to public space.

The imposition of a morality displayed on screen and aggressively asserted into the space of the Internet attempts to disseminate the hegemony of the family and its values of deterrence and security beyond the confines of the home. The Internet becomes an aspatial entity through which the family "spreads its tentacles" in the form of filtering software that is not just loaded onto a domestic screen but enforced in the public sphere by way of the Children's Internet Protection Act. I agree that a decentralized network with IFS located in the physical layer of end users is more agreeable than centralized administration carried out by governmental agencies. However, we should remain cautious, skeptical, if not downright derisive. Peer-production or market-led self-regulation does not function in isolation even when end users rather than the network are the controlling node. A vast and unknown space is marked as a threat, an unruly space, a source of potential harm, and an imposing danger when we keep to our tiny turf with its fixed boundaries. IFSs are loaded on our own computers and constrain the Web according to an integrated complex of parental selector (selecting settings and levels for domestic usage), nonhuman and human review, and code (in conjunction with Internet ratings that I will discuss in the next section).

I agree with Shapiro when he characterizes a filtered Web as the "privatization of experience." IFS users assume a smug sense of omnipotence when they "insulate" themselves within their own online world exposed only to information that conforms to their worldview.[43] The beneficial aspects of filters allow us to block spam and thwart damaging viruses that can erase our hard drives, and phishing programs that attempt to hijack personal data; and for those parents who feel the need, filtering software can assist in a child's online education. At the same time, however, the problem, as I see it, is that our privatized experiences are rarely private (the terms are not synonymous). We come to expect other experiences (let's just call them public) to resemble our private ones. Internet filters invert the public sphere of the Internet into a private, individualistic space: the front door shares double semantic duty with the gate of gated communities—to keep out as well as control what resides within. The front door of IFS is not simply one's private view of the Web but a call for redesign of the entire Internet to be more compatible with one's private view.

Consider a few examples of filtering software that embody the protective promise of the front door. Palisade System's ScreenDoor (Ames, Iowa) blocks access to Web pages according to its "ScreenedOut List" of categorized Web sites (in compliance with SurfControl's categories from its "Internet Threat Database"). ScreenDoor is a "network appliance" that blocks and monitors e-mails, access to chat rooms, and instant messages.[44] Similar to ScreenDoor's reliance upon SurfControl's database, to be addressed in more depth shortly, Secure Computing's (San Jose, California) SmartFilter Bess edition,[45] for which the company mantra is *"keeping the bad guys out and letting the good guys in* is what security—and Secure Computing—is all about," allows schools to determine filtering protocols, blocks based on keywords, and, if selected, bars access to MP3s and images.[46] Cyber Sentinel reports on online activities undertaken by students. It monitors the content of e-mail, chat-room conversations, attachments, and instant messages.[47] SonicWALL's Pro 100 Education Edition combines content-based filtering programs with other protective applications such as firewalls and antiviruses. St. Bernard's iPrism monitors the URLs accessed by students, provides reports on attempts to access blocked sites, and alerts schools to e-mail content. Symantec Web Security collapses antivirus and filtering software to monitor HTML pages. In certain cases school staff can override filtering levels, customize blocking based on specific categories and school policy, and disable filtering software to enable access (for student research projects, or in the case of public libraries, adult access). Totally disabling filters may, however, run the risk of violating the Children's Internet Protection Act.

I have included IFS that targets or is also available for schools and libraries here to demonstrate that the front door is not restricted to the architecture of the home. For Susan Crawford, writing with her Accountable Net colleagues, the "door" remains present and is afforded a telling context: "The Internet is becoming a major city, in which it no longer makes sense to leave one's door unlocked."[48] The Internet's trajectory articulated in such a manner invokes paranoid images of "inner city crime" that do share ideological repercussions with IFS reactionary images of "yesteryear" as exemplified by Mayberry USA. Both appear to suggest that filters are *the way,* referring back to Hunter, to protect and make secure in such a dangerous world. This "door" also appears more literal than metaphorical, akin to Mitchell's aforementioned claim that we become "true inhabitants" of an "electronically mediated environment" rather than possessors of tools, as is commonly the case within IFS discourse. As "true inhabitants," it would appear that we require sound structures within which to support ourselves as well as protect ourselves.

When McLuhan probed that the media are "extensions of man," he worked from a position of humanity, the collective extension of "our" bodies and "our" central nervous system to the "whole of human society."[49] As I stated in the introduction to this book, McLuhan's statement ought to be read as one that proposes an enabling system. The *extending* family, by way of filtering software, "affects the whole psychic and social complex" not, as McLuhan declared, as an effect on human consciousness but as an effect of a particular worldview disseminated across the "scale" of the Internet: the "message" of filtering software "is the change of scale or pace or patterns that it introduces into human affairs."[50] Change of scale demonstrates an adverse effect for Virilio, who, in *Open Sky,* declares the family is in jeopardy as "the city spreads its tentacles, the more the family-unit dwindles and becomes a minority."[51] The change of scale produced by IFS is far-reaching because it enables "family values" to "spread its tentacles" rather than recede. The front door opens out as well as keeps out. We could say that IFS guarantees "the family" a structuring presence. According to Amanda Lenhart of the Pew Internet and American Life Project, a nonprofit research group that studies the Internet's impact on social structures, "the number of children living in homes with filters has grown from 7 million in 2000 to 12 million today."[52] This is hardly a minority position for the family unit enabled by the architectonics of a filtered Internet. The "front door" of filtering architecture is structuring a large community that looks toward software as a tool to protect and secure the scale, pace, and pattern of family, the space of the Internet, and the loaded "consciousness" of filtering architecture.

U.S. courts have long defined obscenity based on the concept of "local community standards." In the era of global information infrastructures and decentralized networks, the concept of "the local" seems exceedingly difficult to pinpoint, while communication systems and their transnational corporate shareholders appear even less containable in a "free-market" economy that rarely respects borders. Throughout this chapter I provide the actual geographical locations for each software company discussed. The purpose is to highlight the geographical basis that roots IFS technology to regional headquarters. No apparent pattern of organization materializes between "blue" and "red" state cartography when it comes to IFS design. If in fact software companies are representative of standards in their local communities, how can they boast a standard for an orbital "global community"? Surely their wares exceed the geographical restrictions of their immediate community. They are, after all, sold online and neither limited nor solely dependent on regional sales in the way that a grocery store services local residents. For example, SurfControl boasts "thirteen worldwide offices and a global research team operating in 20 countries."[53] When "local community standards" become a component in the redesigned architecture of the Web, they transcend the territorial boundaries of a town, city, region, or nation. Third-party IFS companies mediate family standards as a territorialized, deterritorialized, and reterritorialized process. Mayberry USA's use of nostalgia is the most overt. "Weburbia.com," perhaps semantically the clearest testimony to the family's dissemination into cyberspace, provides "Safe for Kids" labels to mark Web sites (much like the inane "Baby on Board" placards that used to adorn U.S. automobiles).

Citizenry is premised upon access to information in order to make erudite decisions and participate within public debates and discussions.[54] Perhaps on account of filtering software, we have run the risk of becoming politically pasty from self-afflicted cyber-agoraphobia: too fearful to leave the safety of permitted Web pages, chat rooms, and the identifiable company of approved IM buddies and social networks. Don't talk to strangers has now, on account of IFS, become don't let them even near you, or totally remove the possibility of encountering them from your online world. Perhaps we have grown even more fearful of that which does not perfectly replicate our understanding of the world in HTML. Or to speak more clearly, the name "Mayberry USA" administers a preferential space through which to understand, identify, and occupy the Internet: this preferential space is increasingly being delineated by a real-time *ideological* windowed interface positioned as the guardian of the domestic threshold. Althusser's well-known proximal hail of "Hey, you there!" (which I will return to in chapter 5) is replaced by a more tacit interpellation in the taken-for-granted form of ISP "Controls On," "Parental Control," "AOL Guardian," "Google SafeSearch filtering," or the icon of a law enforcement shield like CyberPatrol's, which brusquely announces, "To Surf & Protect," or even SmartFilter Bess edition's golden retriever icon of a reassuring family pet that protects his or her master. The promise to "serve" is usurped by the drive *to screen and protect*. The computer loaded with filtering software becomes the officer whose hail is now code designed in and affixed across the traveled digital spectrum; the subject of a filtered Internet becomes an interpellated law-abiding user "signing on," "logging in" to enter this invisibly surveyed space. Sure you can disable filters or change the settings (if you are a parent, holder of the password, a hacker, or even a clever kid), but this possibility plays as the alibi for the constitution of neoliberal self-regulatory subjects while the action of filtering boisterously broadcasts the Internet as a space of danger—even cyber law studies seems to replicate this understanding by employing its front door metaphor—complete with the fearful rhetoric of porn "addicts" and sexual "predators" lurking around every corner: a virtual razor blade in every user's Halloween apple.[55]

Behind the Filtered Front Door

Acknowledging that instances of erroneous keyword or word pattern filtering are frequent and continue to bear ideological implications for the services and resources denied access in the public and private space of a filtered Internet, and leaving aside the question of whether filtering software actually works as its technology promises (or works too well in denying access to sex-, sexuality-, and sexual identity–based sites), I would like to concentrate for the duration of this chapter on the problematic of invisibility, or what I call the "visibility of invisibility" specific to filtering architecture. The invisibility of IFS demonstrates another instance of "informational seeing" in the form of stored lists of banned URLs that IFS companies build to reference specific sites within their categories for Web filtering, "stealth modes," or instant alerts that inform parents of their child's online activities via e-mail, text, or phone, and warning messages that replace the filtered content and inform the user that he or she has attempted to enter a site considered "dangerous" or "harmful" (often without stating why). Invisibility is a matter of supervision at a distance.

In supervising a child's online activities a parent will be notified by e-mail of the violation—a screen shot of the Web page that a child has attempted to access will be sent—if a child's online activities are judged inappropriate according to, for example, Cyber Sentinel's control protocols. A young person's time online, a possible form of play, communication, study, work, socialization, leisure, or wonder, is placed under constant monitoring regardless of whether she or he attempts to access a forbidden site.[56] AOL's Guardian provides "report cards" on a child's online activities directly to a parent via e-mail. The report documents behavior in the absence of a parent's watchful eye and becomes the all-pervasive "eye" that never blinks, while disciplining a compulsory regard for what an appropriate use of the Internet can be. "Appropriate use" in this scenario, a clear example of the conflation between content and conduct, is following links that do not generate a report. Act accordingly to avoid being "tattled on." Similarly, third-party filtering software can work in conjunction with Internet service providers to enable additional parental control over instant messaging. Safe Eyes (Acworth, Georgia) allows parents to monitor and store user online destinations. Information can be retrieved from its secure server via any Web browser. Bsafe (Bristol, Tennessee), the "Ultimate Online Family Protection," provides detailed reports on "good" sites that a user visits as well as blocked ones. CyberPatrol's "Chat Guard" filters words, phrases, and names designated objectionable,[57] while CyberSitter 9.0 allows parents to monitor and "archive" their child's IM conversations. Unannounced to the child user, such activities are said to operate in "stealth mode."[58] The same software that blocks Web-based content also allows parents to spy on their children in an undetected fashion. Lastly, consider Spector Pro 5.0 by Spectorsoft (Vero Beach, Florida). Like CyperSitter's spyware, this product sends e-mails to parents to inform them of their child's IM activities. Described as "the most comprehensive Monitoring and Surveillance software,"[59] Spector

Pro 5.0 informs "you," presumed to be a person in a position of authority such as a parent or employer, when an inappropriate keyword appears on a networked computer (typed at the source), a Web site, or an e-mail.

Under the supervision of IFS, online activities are monitored, tracked, documented, and presented to parents as requested. Going online carries a potential guilty verdict before anything is even accessed because a child's online activities are constantly under suspicion. The parental presence that delimits and defines the Web becomes increasingly pervasive when it structures the behavior of all users, not just children, whose online activities are monitored, recorded, reported by IFS. In asking what types of users we become through the architecture of Internet filters, it seems that this beneficent technology positions all of us at risk and in need of protection from the Internet's content. IFS does not simply block content but produces solutions to online safety through its functions. Like the V-chip, this solution results not simply in a blocked URL or individual Web pages but in the proliferation and visible evidence of the functionality of IFS as a reliable technology for securitization. Online behavior becomes classified into filtering binaries of good/bad, safe/unsafe, clean/dirty, adult/child, to render the milieu of cyberspace easily classified as an intelligibility of control.

Within the promotional discourse of filtering software, that which is rendered invisible by their products is manifestly visible in the form of omnipresent "danger" and "threat." Integrity Online, an IFS company based in Jackson, Mississippi, offers steadfast distinctions between types of Internet experiences simmered down to a puerile dichotomy: "today's filtering technology is highly effective at blocking *bad* Web sites without preventing access to *good* sites" (my emphasis).[60] "Protect kids against hate literature, pornography, pedophiles, and other inappropriate information or persons on the Internet," urges Net Nanny 5.1.[61] Rather than the conservative "lock them up," Net Nanny fully realizes the front door metaphor. When it comes to "inappropriate information or persons on the Internet," this filter "locks them out." Harsh words for a not so sweet Nanny. "Worried about what's online? Internet filth wipes away easily with Netmop."[62] Netmop places its users in a plastic bubble such that one's ambient environment becomes a prophylactic against harmful online contagions. Its filtering software is regarded as a hygienic tool for disinfecting a "dirty" or "contagious" space that threatens to "infect" families. Netmop pairs security with sanitary solutions in its attempts to protect the family by "cleaning up" the Internet.

It is vital to consider the action of filtering as producing a type of visibility that is not predicated upon the obtrusiveness of the block. In the case of monitoring a child's online activities its aim is to record and make visible their activities to the ever-present process and observational gaze of the parental function. While, as we will see, IFS requires a form of invisibility in its code and databases, the object of its visibility is not necessarily Web content but, like the V-chip, the persistent presence of filtering itself: the display of a technological solution for Internet governance and the securitization of habitat.

The paradigm of tool-user empowerment is a central faculty of filtering software. Lessig is skeptical, and rightly so, of the prominence placed on user-based blocking and the World Wide Consortium's (W3C) Platform for Internet Content Selection (PICS) protocol. He writes:

> Filtering can occur at any level in the distributional chain—the user, company through which the user gains access, the ISP, or even the jurisdiction within which the user lives. Nothing in the design of PICS requires that such filters announce themselves. Filtering in an architecture like PICS can be *invisible* and indeed, in some of its implementations invisibility is part of its design.[63]

The user (parent) who monitors other users (generally understood as children) and who is also monitored through installed software such as CyberPatrol, Cyber Sentinel, and ScreenDoor and the application of ISP "parental controls" (if enabled for a parent's online time) represents the more easily recognizable level of IFS. Here the user of a filtered Internet can see the signs of IFS at work when he or she is restricted from accessing certain Web pages. In this instance, IFS does not hide its apparatus well. Parents have access to graphic user interface control screens (that look like any other windows' toolbars with clickable boxes and adjustable bars) that allow them to set levels and select which categories they feel are suitable to monitor their child's activities. More often than not, parents do not see what Web sites actually comprise the various categories that they can select, especially if IFS blocks at the root level. Parents activate a category based on criteria they are not active in determining. Without such knowledge, both parents and those whom IFS is meant to protect are subject to the categorization devised by software manufactures. Like the reactive "voting" schema that I discussed in regards to the V-chip, where V-chip compliance with a television rating is likened to a vote for a particular rating, the parental controls of IFS require parents simply to select, highlight, adjust, or click on prepackaged options.

While invisibility is part of the design and functionality of the Internet, IFS requires that its mediation be apparent at the level of interface in the display of parental controls. After all, safety and security must be "displayed" to users to generate signs of assurance whether or not they are actually achieved: *show* users that we are indeed safe because our ability to navigate has been filtered. We may not know what a Web site's content consists of, but nonetheless we are shown messages that entrance is forbidden. We ought to be careful here. Instead of satisfy ourselves with a position that only regards this act as one of blunt censorship, we should understand the filtering process as productive as well, a formative operation in normalizing the Internet. The emphasis is not directed at content, although the voluntarism of content ratings does inform content, but on the user and his or her choice to employ IFS. The ability to access a site is cast as less restrictive; it represents a sign of empowerment premised on control.

IFS "showing," screens that display the message of denied access, is a "compulsory visibility" that makes visible—in the multitudinous forms of documented user history, instantaneous reports in the form of screen shots, alerts on "harmful" content, stored user log-ins, monitored Internet movements and blocked access to Web sites—the Internet as a network of "threats" and "harms" that can be regulated and redesigned only through the constant application of IFS. The Internet is reproduced as a threat by means of continuous monitoring, filtering, and blocking. It is precisely the Internet *as a threat* and IFS as a self-regulatory means to produce a safer Internet that are on display. A filtered Internet displays a great deal in its visible invisibility. In the problematic of invisibility, IFS regulates behavior as an automatic process without the constraint of direct human impediment, without the veritable visible evidence of the contested information. As users we only *see* a myriad of results: messages articulated as "blocking page styles" by CyberPatrol, such as "This Web Site Is Off Limits," "The Requested Site Is Not Available," "No Access," "Error," or "Blocked." Even more so than with the V-chip, a computer's "capacity to analyse the ambient environment and automatically interpret the meaning of events," to refer to Virilio's automation of perception,[64] provides a filtered Internet without involving the actual eyewitness account of a human user. IFS—its designers, databases, regulatory categories, and individual companies—becomes the expert "eyes" for securitization.

Invisibility also characterizes the relation between filtering software and W3C's Platform for Internet Content Selection. PICS is protocol built into computer browsers that, according to its home page, is a specification that "enables labels (metadata) to be associated with Internet content. It was originally designed to help parents and teachers control what children access on the Internet. . . ."[65] PICS provides specifications by which filtering software can block access to Web content. Essentially PICS is a standard. Metadata means that PICS provides information in the form of labels on Internet information (associated with URLs and IP addresses). PICS labels contain information on what type of information is housed at a particular URL. Members of the Information Society Project at Yale Law School, J. M. Balkin, Beth Simone Noveck, and Kermit Roosevelt, who have written one of the most insightful and explanatory articles on filtering systems, clarify the function of a PICS label. It is a statement that "generally takes the form of an assertion that the data has certain properties, for example, that it is a picture, that it contains guns, that it is violent, that it has been rated by a certain organization, and so on."[66] The protocol attempts to rate/label the content of the Internet via various rating systems. PICS is not filtering software; we should be clear about this. It is a general-purpose framework for categorizing the content of any Web site. Its objective is to provide specifications for its labels. A rating service can be an individual, organization (e.g., the Recreational Advisory Council on the Internet, RSACi), or company (e.g., third-party software like CyberPatrol that designs its own ratings to be PICS compatible[67]) that provides "content labels," a rating of information on the Internet, to support a "rating system." The Recreational Advisory Council (RSAC) was originally organized to rate video game content. In 1996 it began to provide ratings for Internet content. Four categories were used: "Sex," "Nudity," "Language," and "Violence."

In 1999 RSACi became a new organization, the Internet Content Rating Association (ICRA). Its mantra: "Working for a safer Internet." In December 2000 ICRA released its first "vocabulary" descriptors. They contained the following categories: "nudity and sexual material," "violence," "language," "other topics" (these include tobacco, alcohol, drugs, gambling, weapons, discrimination, and other "disturbing" materials), and "chat." As of July 2005 its vocabulary has been expanded to include two separate categories for "Nudity" and "Sex material," "other topics" has broadened into "Potentially harmful activities" (quite a distinction from "other topics"), and "User generated content" appears to have usurped "chat." While ICRA provides labels for Web content, it also provides parents with its "ICRAplus" platform, a filtering system working in accordance with ICRA ratings. Lastly, ICRA surpasses the likes of Mayberry USA to appeal to a global market. It has produced versions in French, German, Spanish, Italian, and Chinese.

Internet ratings are referred to as labels, "data structures containing information about a given document's contents,"[68] that are embedded in (the header of) HTML documents. These files, like any HTML file, are transmitted using HTTP. Labels contain information on the content of a Web site. They are associated with both URLs and IP. A Web browser enabled by a filtering program responds to the encoded information (machine readable object code) of a rating system contained within a label to process accessibility of Web content. The World Wide Consortium (W3C) defines a "ratings system" as a system that "specifies the dimensions used for labeling, the scale of allowable values on each dimension, and a description of the criteria used in assigning values."[69] Jim Miller of the W3C offers the MPAA rating system as an example of a one-dimensional system. The criterion (or measurement) is based on age and assumptions about age and filmic content. Compared to the multidimensionality of Internet ratings, the media of film, video, and DVD (and we could add the MPAA's involvement with television ratings) are governed according to this single dimension and by a single governing authority. The "dimensions" of the Internet radically differ from those of broadcast media. As such, age rating systems (those often favored by ISPs) are only a single dimension of ratings complemented by others, like SafeSurf, a parents' organization, that offers a complex rating system that consists of subcategories to those of the RSACi.[70] In other words, a Web page can have multiple ratings attached to it rather than be aligned to a single centralized institutional system.

Filtering software can work in conjunction with the ratings protocols of the PICS standard. Web browsers like Microsoft Explorer and others have adopted ratings systems enabled by PICS.[71] Software designers manufacture filtering software that is compliant with PICS's content labeling such that PICS protocol becomes the standard for filtering software.[72] Rating sites, that is, creating labels for specific sites, is a major part of PICS's aim "to control what children access on the Internet," though it does not exhaust the scope of PICS's influence. Balkin, Noveck, and Roosevelt provide a composite sketch of the additional components that work in conjunction with PICS.[73] After a Web site is rated according to PICS standards, labels must be assigned. Labels require distribution either through an end user's browser, search engine, or ISP. Once distribution is established, filtering software needs to be able to read labels (software is written to be compliant). Specifically, filtering software needs to be PICS compatible in order to be effective in filtering Web content. Lastly, filtering software must be loaded and have its settings and rating levels selected by a parent.

PICS regards itself as a neutral framework; it provides the code for content rating, not the criteria. In this scenario Lessig introduces the possibility that "software authors would compete to write software that could filter according to the ratings; content providers and rating organizations would compete to rate content. Users would then pick their filtering software and rating system."[74] Lessig's last step refers back to Fortier's discussion of solipsistic settings. In being PICS compliant, an entire architecture is set to provide the framework for IFS to offer additional ratings/categories on top of those already available. Although not confronted by the red letters of "EXPLICIT" in iTunes, the televisual bug of MATV (Mature Audience), an Entertainment Software Rating Board (ESRB) rating affixed on the artwork of video game packing, or even the MPAA rating that proceeds all films and DVDs, the Internet becomes the most "overrated" medium around.

Lastly, in addition to the filtering process and predicated on another type of invisibility, blacklists of inappropriate Web sites are established by private companies and organizations outside of the public domain. Databases of banned sites are the copyrighted property of individual filtering software companies. The protected information is actually what customers pay for: access to an updatable list of blacklisted sites that support a company's filters. Databases containing information on "obscene" or "indecent" Web pages and Web sites are regarded as "trade secrets," and the information is not disseminated to the public or the user of filtering software.[75] SurfControl's "Internet Threat Database" provides "47 Well-Organized Categories,

145 Focused Subtopics" through which its filtering technology can evaluate and monitor Internet activities.

SurfControl also claims that its database contains "2.2 Billion Web Pages" compiled by the complex that I spoke of earlier: customer submissions, "professional researchers" (how qualifications are determined remains a mystery), and automated tools that determine access free from human evaluation. In addition, customers of SurfControl can receive daily updates, which may total up to "45,000 new sites a week" added to the Internet Threat Database.[76] IFS's dual role of extraction-detraction takes away, prevents, and denies visual access to categorized information and images based on an electronic register that monitors accessibility according to the ratings/content labeling of PICS as well as the set protocols (whatever they may be) for discerning banned Web sites. Here the database is an apparatus that supports the monitoring of activities of networked users as well as information surveilled as "threatening." It targets incoming information on one's browser: it preempts the media object before it can even reach our eyes.

Mark Poster's articulation of the database as "superpanopticon," discussed briefly in chapter 1 of this volume, places the subject as active in facilitating the actions of surveillance. He writes, "The unwanted surveillance of one's personal choice becomes a discursive reality through the willing participation of the surveilled individual. In this instance the play of power and discourse is uniquely configured. The one being surveilled provides the information necessary."[77] For Poster, this supply of self-surveillance is provided through consumer transactions stored and immediately retrievable via databases in their constitution of the subject as a "sum of the information in the fields of the record that applies to that name."[78] The database compiles the subject as a composite of his or her online choices and activities as tracked by IFS. This compilation is fixed on media objects (images, text, MP3s, Web pages, IPs, URLs) across the deluge of code that can be intercepted through keyword pattern recognition and private lists of "threatening" URLs.

Databases store a list of banned sites, which the filtering software monitors and blocks for users. In this way, a filtered Internet plots the path that the subject can travel. It presents a Web that is accessible according to database information. We can move "freely" only if we avoid Web sites and pages flagged as inappropriate according to Internet rating systems and filtering software. Our movements are carefully controlled and self-selected. We choose to impose a demarcated route upon ourselves as the safest form of navigation in a space surmised as threatening and harmful. FamilyClick (Virginia Beach, Virginia) is an exceptional example of how choice attempts to enable a disciplined freedom. Its age-based categories do not provide an unlimited access option for its subscribers. According to the FamilyClick home page, its adult option, entitled "full FamilyClick access," "automatically excludes sites and content dealing with crime, hate groups, pornography, illegal drugs, promotion of non-medical drugs, online gambling and violence."[79] Adults too are controlled by a default setting that the parent is unable to disable. It seems that child and adult blur considerably in the FamilyClick universe. Settings to monitor teen online activities find "alluring or revealing attire" blocked alongside access to information on family planning and STDs.[80] The solution for "Kids Access" is to block the entire Internet with the exception of specified kid sites deemed appropriate by FamilyClick protocols. FamilyClick's CEO is Tim Robertson, son of television evangelist Pat Robertson and former head of the Family Channel. Like the entertainment industry, religion constantly seeks new ways to distribute its content. For FamilyClick, it is the user who decides which filtering software and ideological framing of the Internet is best for the home computer. The choice to adopt FamilyClick is the issue. In doing so, one chooses to be disciplined in the name of protection and freedom of choice.

Choice mobilizes the user's abilities to move freely by supporting only limited "free-way" access, to keep Deleuze's highway model active, as the only safe mode of travel. What type of choice is exerted through technology? The choice is one of discipline: a choice of disciplined freedom as the only solution for security and the maintenance of parental control and a family-friendly Internet. As noted earlier, end-user choice is preferred by many who work on Internet governance over centralized government-sanctioned regulation because IFS is considered nonhierarchal, a decentralized way for citizens to self-regulate their own Web environs. However, it is necessary to ask, who is the "self" in self-regulation, and what type of choice is being exerted? "Self" is hardly individualistic, private, or the sole property of the user who "self-regulates" his or her own domain. The self is part of a larger complex that, as Monroe E. Price and Stefaan G. Verhulst demonstrate, "encompasses a cornucopia of institutions that maintain self-regulatory characteristics."[81] "Self," in this instance, is an amalgamation of institutions, ideology, private companies, Internet protocol, and software that redesign the architecture of the Web as a space where choice can regulate content and produce a more family-friendly environment. When choosing IFS we also choose to see the Web as threatening and harmful. We make visible a threat only to immediately display a solution. Technological facilitation of choice ought not to be conceived of as a utopian notion of unrestrained freedom, as many IFS companies boast. As I have stated throughout this book, control augments freedom as a disciplined freedom. The concept of "end-user autonomy" must be carefully discerned as part of a technology of control whereby choice is a disciplinary technique enabled through control devices. All that the user is permitted to see is determined by the omnipresence of "choice" acted out on a computer screen in the form of a regulated space and controlled experience while moving "assuredly" through this space. Yet, "choice" is located less in how we decide to move through the Web than in the decision to employ filters as a mode of security: an Internet surveilled through the automatic, invisible, and immediate action of a filtering complex that produces a space that can be occupied according to the preferences set by its user in compliance with protocols of categorization.

When we go online *through* the narrow framing of IFS produced by Mayberry USA and the other companies discussed throughout this chapter, we inhabit a world without sex, sex education, and words with *sex* as a prefix or root. How can you fully navigate the Web without the "sextant" of the twenty-first century, a fully operable search engine?[82] We are left with only quiet porch swings and fishing holes to surf. As Mayberry USA attests, filtering "tools" are not neutral. In fact, the opposite is true. Their reaction is violent. Their reaction is aggressive. They repackage the Web as a safe space only if inhabited through IFS. In the case of Mayberry USA a set of meanings are issued that structure appropriate use and experience of the Internet as well as what information is deemed appropriate online.

To purchase IFS (after all home security is not free despite how "dangerous" the Internet is claimed to be) is to occupy the Internet through the strictures of a particular protocol that charts exactly what that space consists of for its users. In accessing the Web through a personal networked computer, users require assurance that their time online will be "safe" from the presence of danger like other supposedly secured spaces we frequent on a daily basis: shopping malls, chain coffee stores (dare I call Starbucks a café!), gated residential communities, private schools, office "parks," university "villages," regentrified entertainment "islands" (the Spectrum in Irvine, California, and the Grove in Los Angeles, for example), and multiplexes. Is the Internet facing the same threat of banality, homogeneity, and relentless regulation? Arguably the gated community that Rose offered to exemplify the securitization of habitat is guarded through the architecture of the securitized community: physical structures like gates, guard stations, security patrols, CCTV, walls, warning signs, home alarms, and where visible rather than camouflaged by topiary, barbed wire. The network architecture of the Internet—turned outward away from the home as an extended parameter of security—has its own types of barriers implicit in the IFS code emanating from the "physical layer"[83] of the Internet that spiders the Web in search of "objectionable" content to flag as too dangerous to enter your home through the unlocked, unprotected "front door"—a persistent metaphor for the computer screen within IFS discourses. Daily romps online can be circumscribed in accordance with a protective and prescriptive default morality, loaded onto a networked computer as a legitimate third-party authority, for only $49.95.

4. Sanitizing

It's About Choice!

CleanFlicks

ClearPlay: The Technology of Choice!

ClearPlay

In Clean We Trust

"If you're a studio that's spent a lot of money developing a *Spider Man* brand, do you want to dilute it by having a *Spider Man Lite* on the market competing with it?"[1] When asking the question why should anyone care whether a subset of people want clean movies, a number of answers quickly surface. The violation of federal copyright law and studio ownership, as voiced above, is one such charge leveled against Utah's CleanFlicks. At the time of writing this book, the company transformed from a service that reedited Hollywood films into "clean versions" or "sanitized films," as they are often referred to, to one that offers "family friendly" G- and PG-rated films to its clients without additional reedits. CleanFlicks countered the accusation of theft by stating that its reediting did not violate copyright because the company purchases the DVD each time it produces one of its sanitized versions. On August 29, 2002, CleanFlicks filed a lawsuit in the U.S. District Court in Denver to determine whether its editing practices were a violation of copyright law. This preemptive move filed against sixteen Hollywood directors was followed by a countersuit on December 13 filed collectively by the defendants, eight major Hollywood studios, and the Directors Guild of America against fifteen companies that offer edited versions of Hollywood films.[2] On July 6, 2006, in the case *Clean Flicks v. Steven Soderbergh,* a Utah federal district court ruled against CleanFlicks' claims of fair use and found the company in violation of copyright infringement. CleanFlicks now "filters" content by offering nonedited titles that endorse its new mantra of "Our inventory contains only Movies You Can Trust." This ruling has made it illegal to reedit copyrighted films for commercial use even in the name of "family values." Although deemed illegal, the process of reediting content still requires consideration when discussing new modes of censorial practice because filtering DVD players have gained legal protection under the Family Entertainment and Copyright Act of 2005. Apart from the outcome of *Clean Flicks v. Steven Soderbergh,* the "service" of film sanitizing is far from relegated to a footnote in the history of media regulation.

In continuing with the inquiry into the question of "who cares," we may alternatively venture that, copyright infringement aside, we should care for artistic integrity; directorial vision is as much compromised by clean versions as legal ownership. Jay D. Roth, national executive director of the Directors Guild of America, argues that film sanitizing is "fundamentally about artistic and creative rights and whether someone has the right to take an artist's work, change it and then sell it."[3] Directors, too, defend this position. Michael Mann, for instance, deplores "the idea that somebody else . . . can arbitrarily take our works apart and destroy them in any manner they want and represent it as still being that film."[4] "Somebody else" already does "take our works apart," as content is held under scrutiny by the MPAA and its "voluntary" submission for ratings classification, so perhaps what Mann objects to is yet another somebody doing so.

The question of whether a CleanFlicks version or any other sanitized version is a film or a series of disconnected clips resulting from deletion raises questions of the relationship between audience reception and directorial vision. Marva Sonntag, loyal CleanFlicks customer, is excited because sanitized versions allow her to watch films by her favorite film star, Tom Cruise. Her love of the actor is based on one film because she and her family do not attend films rated above PG. "PG-13 was halfway to R and it was offensive," she explains.[5] With a CleanFlicks edited DVD she can have access to the actor's work "without the profanity, graphic violence, nudity, and sexual content" from which CleanFlicks promises to shield customers. In the same article where Sonntag confesses her admiration for Tom Cruise, director John Turteltaub quickly curbs her enthusiasm: "People like Marva Sonntag are fooling themselves if they think they're watching a Tom Cruise movie. They're simply watching clips from a Tom Cruise movie."[6] Sanitized versions raise the old question of how a film's meaning is determined. Does it reside in a director's intentions, the film text, or the audience's social relation to film? Or all three? Moreover, the containment of directorial vision and artistic creativity perpetuates the myth that filmmaking stems from a single authored endeavor and by extension also limits the question to one of freedom of speech. As many film-sanitizing companies point out in defense of their actions, films already exist in multiple versions: reedited for consumption on airplanes as in-flight entertainment and reedited to comply with slotted programming schedules for television broadcast.[7] Turteltaub's retort and Mann's objection could be directed to these reedited versions that are outside of film sanitizing's purview (yet well within the purview of industry profit by virtue of licensing).

Another answer to why one might care about reedited films proffers that sanitized versions actually change or revise history. This allocation circulates within the popular realm of television and film. For example, *South Park*'s "Free Hat" episode, where the characters attempt to stop directors from "improving" their films with new digital effects, regards alterations as a violation of history. Kyle: "Yeah, what if they had modified the Roman Coliseum every year? It would just be another big douchey stadium now." In another instance of satire, Vermont Senator Ortolan K. Finistirre (William H. Macy) in *Thank You for Smoking* (Jason Reitman, 2006) turns his attention to film sanitizing after failing in his anti-tobacco campaigns. When interviewed as to his support for such technologies and questioned as to whether or not film sanitizing changes history, Senator Finistirre replies, "we're not changing history, we're improving history." One can only wonder if Reitman's "Senator Ortolan K. Finistirre" is a thinly veiled caricature of Utah's Republican Senator Orrin G. Hatch, who sponsored the "Family Movies Act" (as the Family Entertainment and Copyright Act of 2005 is often known),[8] which legalized ClearPlay's filtering software for DVD players. The assumption here, of course, is that history is static and objective. Watching a film on DVD (we could also mention cable, the VCR, and, now, the iPod) is already an instance of "changing history," as is digital remastering and the addition of DVD extras, which clearly alter our experience and memory of the "original" print.

Film sanitizing is part of a larger set of practices enabled by digital technology and digital media culture. The practice of film sanitizing is a parental function for the construction of "safe" films that, through editing software and hardware, mute speech and remove specific scenes that run contrary to ideas of family viewing. How these practices extend the processes of control in favor of the user through choice is the focus of this chapter. Sanitized versions are a means of governing conduct through the digital governance of content and management of choice. Sanitizing, no stranger to the history of film, television, and video regulation, has become a practice designed to enable consumers in their self-governance of habitat and culture through two recent measures. The first consists of DVD players and software associated with companies like ClearPlay, Family Safe Media, Family Shield, and MovieMask that digitally filter Hollywood DVDs for violence, sex, and language considered obscene *without* permanently altering the DVD, as is the case with CleanFlicks copyright violation. Prior to MovieMask's closure over "licensing issues" in 2004, its software allowed users, presumed to be parents, to download files of specific films to their MovieMark DVD players and select various level settings by which to watch "safely" by distancing the family from "dangerous" images removed by the sanitized version. In the MovieMask version of *Titanic* (James Cameron, 1997) Leonardo DiCaprio does not sketch a nude Kate Winslet as in the MPAA "unclean version"; instead her breasts are covered by a "digital corset" (even his drawing is modified in order not to represent nudity); and when Neo (Keanu Reeves) enters a building to save Morpheus (Laurence Fishburne), surrogate "green sparks" replace blood spurting from guards during *The Matrix*'s (Andy and Larry Wachowski, 1999) famous shootout scene. Similarly, RCA's DRC232N DVD player equipped with ClearPlay technology spares the family viewing audience from witnessing bullets penetrating the bodies of U.S. soldiers in Ridley Scott's *Black Hawk Down* (2001), while the deaths of Somalis are left intact. Left intact and clearly visible are religious, political, and ideological biases that come to substantiate family-friendly media according to the sanitizing policy of these companies.

The second measure concerns the reediting of Hollywood films by

CleanFlicks and other companies, like HollyGood, Edit My Movie (in conjunction with Family Safe Media), Family Edited DVDs, Clean Films (whose logo includes a halo hovering over the letter *e*), and Family Flix, all of which, prior to *Clean Flicks v. Steven Soderbergh*, deleted and erased scenes and dialogue of copyrighted material they perceived to be offensive to their select audiences (mostly identified as Christian and members of the Church of Jesus Christ of Latter-day Saints) and then rented or sold their sanitized versions through affiliated chains and the Internet. The violent brutality and suffering of war are rendered less disquieting in CleanFlicks' edited version of the World War II epic *Saving Private Ryan* (Steven Spielberg, 1998): soldiers are still pierced by bullets when storming the beach at Omaha; however, the painstaking agony of death in combat is scaled back through precise edits so that, as Ray Lines, owner of CleanFlicks, defends, teens and adults are both protected from "all that blood and gore."[9] With our consumer media technologies—either filtering DVD players or reedited DVDs—we now have the ability to choose what version of bloodshed we prefer: *Saving Private Ryan* as certified by the MPAA, or a tidier version with the gruesome ordeals of cinematic warfare paternalistically deleted for our "safety."

Reedited films and filtering software for DVD players generate a filmic world, one that unseats MPAA ratings policy, where themes such as nudity, sexual relations (and this is broadened to including a variety of queer and straight acts of affection and desire), trauma, images of violence deemed "explicit," profanity (in CleanFlicks speak, "B-words," the "H-word," the "D-word," the "S-word," and the infamous "F-word"), and "references to a deity" in a non-religious context are simply eradicated outright rather than discussed with children or debated in public. Out of sight, out of mind? Hardly. DVD players that mask certain scenes deemed inappropriate by skipping past or by muting the sound of a DVD maintain the *designed-in* principal and parental function that restructures the censorial as characteristic of control technologies like the V-chip and Internet filters. And a CleanFlicks edited DVD begins to illustrate digital editing as a formula of rule expressed by the "expertise" of self-censorial practices through retail services and sectarian policy not affiliated with any industry-recognized institution of film ratings.

In this chapter, I examine film sanitizing's role as a control technology in the service of viewer governance. While this is the prevailing intellectual frame employed to articulate blocking and filtering, it is necessary to stress this (govern)mentality since intellectual property and lawsuits by film industries continue to shape firmly the debate of film sanitizing, its legality, and, in a broader context, digital copyright. This emphasis says little about the relation of culture and governing aimed at users/viewers in the devices entering the market. It is as if film sanitizing is a debate restricted to industry (or authorship) and not changes taking place in our conceptualization of the censorial in the digital age. The ruling in *Clean Flicks v. Steven Soderbergh* was not for violations to the First Amendment but for violation of the motion picture industry's copyright. Although this outcome deserves detailed attention, it must, unfortunately, take place in another project in order to examine here and now how film sanitizing introduces a radical new understanding of viewer-centered control that exceeds the capabilities of the V-chip and Internet filtering software: content is not blocked but redesigned as a security measure for family entertainment. DVDs and DVD players join the ranks of media technologies that enable users to exert protective control over how and what they watch as a disciplined freedom of choice. Again, technology becomes control. The censorial further embeds itself in our domestic environs, media, and cultural practices.

In the next section, we will stretch beyond the "newer" technologies that debuted on the market after the Telecommunications Act of 1996 in order to cast film sanitizing in the form of "family edited" DVDs and filtering DVD players into the context of family home entertainment that emerged with the VCR and Blockbuster Inc.'s redefining and redesigning of the home-viewing experience in its consumer space. Before a direct engagement with ClearPlay and CleanFlicks, it is necessary to first consider discourses of "viewer control" that came into being via the VCR such that filtering DVD players and sanitized versions are positioned as an intensification of a larger promise of control within the domestic habitat. The self-regulation that Hollywood continues to practice in its costly productions is exceeded by the additional layers of consumer self-governing enabled by reedited DVDs and DVD players that automatically filter films according to tenets of morality encoded in software. Like Internet filters, both practices demonstrate the growing prominence of niche or customized censorial practices viewed through a specialized lens of securitization enacted as technological self-governance. In examining CleanFlicks' sanitized versions, I concentrate on its (no longer available) version of David Cronenberg's *A History of*

Violence (2005), a film where content is not easily reduced to "dirty words" and "steamy sex" on account of its subject matter: complex human emotions and the philosophical problem of free will versus determinism. "It's about choice," as CleanFlicks' slogan once announced, and its version of *A History of Violence* evidences when choice serves particular worldviews in negation of others and when choice is expressed through control technology.

Wow! What a Difference!

In accordance with Jack Z. Bratich, Jeremy Packer, and Cameron McCarthy in *Foucault, Cultural Studies and Government,* in which neoliberal forms of governing are emphasized through microlevel investigations of new practices for shaping conduct "at a distance," James Hay's "Unaided Virtues: The (Neo-)Liberalization of the Domestic Sphere" situates media for the home and communications systems emerging in the 1980s within the study of governmentality.[10] Specifically, Hay expounds upon technological developments affecting the management of the household, namely programmable features for television and VCRs.[11] "Home video hardware," Hay argues, "became a technology for monitoring and regulating access from the home of material from outside the home, for deregulating/regulating the household and the family as citizen-subjects."[12] Hay's study of a specific era that began to institute new social arrangements for self-governing through technologies being introduced into the home is an attempt to intervene in the generalized accounts of media technology frequent in governmentality studies.

The self-governance afforded by the VCR that Hay highlights can also be considered within the discourse and practices of "viewer control" that began to define relations to home entertainment in opposition to "public" experiences with film.[13] While viewer control is an implicit social arrangement in consumer technologies that promise increased management and freedom over environment, as Hay acknowledges, the practice and promise increasingly serve the expertise of the parental function in the processes of control. "Viewer" is determined to be an "at risk" social category and threatened practice in the discourses of control technology. Viewer control aligned with the parental function not only targets the immediate domestic environment in its securitization actions but also, as we will see with Blockbuster Inc., structures services aimed at the home cinema market; namely, a home video market inundated with "family enter-tainment," as consumer choice and control enables an alternative to public exhibition.

In regard to viewer control in the era of the VCR we find that home theater systems, as argued by Bill Whittington, "encourage greater agency on the part of the spectator, [while] fostering height-ened interactivity and control over programming."[14] Furthermore, Timothy Corrigan details a defining characteristic of viewer activity: "the center of movie viewing has shifted away from the screen and become dispersed in the hands of audiences with more (real and re-mote) control than possibly ever before."[15] Celebratory recognition of the VCR's relatively long-standing and only recently challenged supremacy as the home theater system claims that home viewing is the antithesis to the habitual cinema experience and that VCR use affords what public exhibition, not to mention broadcast, has tradi-tionally guarded against: viewer control and agency.[16]

Corrigan's and Whittington's descriptions of the VCR's capabilities reveal that their notion of control is largely employed as a descriptive term to further endorse the popular sentiment that the VCR enables its users and that its viewing experience differs significantly from the cinema and television. The viewer-user of a VCR is celebrated for his or her ability to express control over the material brought into the home and replayed on a television screen. Convenience, the control of televisual images and communications technology defined in favor of the viewer, the ability to view a videocassette alone or with others, to time-shift televisual programming, to view films when and how one wishes—these are the practical appeals and standard promises of home theater systems. Working on the commercial discourses that construct the idea of home theater, Barbara Klinger recalls that as early as 1980, Sony began to aggrandize notions of control into its marketing campaigns. According to Klinger, Sony's VCR was pro-moted by the telling oxymoron that, in this book, is the paradoxical logic of control: "experience the freedom of total control."[17] Whether in the form of a company's marketing slogan or as scholarship on home cinema, the consensus remains that the VCR defined control in favor of the viewer and her or his ability to manipulate visual and audio information.

Neither my account of control technology nor Hay's account of "home video hardware" in the service of self-governing hopes to dispute this promise of viewer control. Instead, viewer control is fully realized into a system of governance where domestic technologies help exert further regulation over the contents of the home and continually monitor what information may circulate within its four walls of security. Viewer control is affirmed as a practice and technique for governing conduct and, in this context, content since the expertise of the parental function manages and administers content through control technology. The VCR as a technology for "monitoring and regulating access from the home," as Hay grants, is yet another device for securing habitat through which, as Rose notes, individuals "take upon themselves the responsibility for the security of their property and their persons, and that of their own families."[18] In this instance securitization is practiced on the types of prerecorded media available for home viewing. Unlike the closed-circuit video cameras that adorn the gated community, which Rose uses to typify the architectural elements of securitization that keep "threat out rather than keep it in,"[19] the VCR, in its nascent period, was a control technology that promised management over television and films relocated to the secure space of the home. Less a contradiction than we may think, Sony's "freedom of total control" suggests the simultaneity that control depends on for the self-governing practices regarded as viewer control. Viewer control is liberating to the extent that it serves to place the user in a system for the production of new freedoms.

Hay's "(neo-)liberalized domestic sphere" identifies the home's absorption of programmable technology as governing strategies for management whereby the domestic sphere itself is a mechanism of "simultaneously freeing and governing oneself through an investment in a model/arrangement/economy of domestic space that could [be] managed at a distance."[20] The simultaneity of oppositional concepts like "freeing and governing" and "freedom of total control" serves as the power-knowledge architecture of Deleuze's highway metaphor that demarcates the multiplication and generalization of disciplinary technologies in his societies of control while proving to further intensify governing at a distance through the instrumentalization of freedom located in self-inscribed prohibitive practices with media technologies for security (be it psychological, moral, aesthetic, social, or cultural). Control technologies, as we continue to see, seek to multiply the possibilities of choice by instrumentalizing freedom of choice as a governing strategy. Personal freedom is procured only through discipline and the disciplining of media. And Hay alerts us to these processes in his engagement with domestic space emerging as a self-governing practice through the likes of programmable technology.

It is necessary to further attend to Hay's claim by drawing a distinction between the viewer control of "home video hardware" and "material from outside" in the form of software (videocassettes and, later, DVDs) provided by the then new "cinematic apparatus" known as the video store. Hay's attention is directed toward "access from the home" rather than the highly regulated state of *access to the home*. Access is played out in terms of the VCR's programmability to time-shift television broadcast as well as the personal consumption of filmic content by way of the videocassette. How content makes its way into the home and the regulatory processes that mark this passage are not considered in Hay's article. Blockbuster Inc.'s family policy, its parental function, which began to emerge in the late 1980s, also functions as a control technology in that its retail space and policy perform regulatory actions on home video and the concept of viewer control. It determines what "material from outside the home" is compliant with domestic monitoring and processes of control.

It is imperative not to regard Blockbuster Inc. as a neutral space and benign service provider for the distribution of prerecorded media for home consumption but as a control technology for asserting home cinema as a family affair. One well-known and obvious facet of Blockbuster Inc.'s family policing is its continued corporate policy not to carry NC-17 and X-rated films (adult-only or rated-"A" video games are included as well). The United States' largest home media rental company policy on NC-17 is as follows: "In order to provide a wholesome environment for you and your family, we do not carry films with ratings of NC-17 or X."[21] In the United States NC-17 is a legal MPAA rating that forbids public access to persons under the age of seventeen. Introduced in 1990, the NC-17 rating was an attempt to revamp the non-copyrighted X rating and offer a classification for more provocative films that were not porn in concept or in content.[22] However, the NC-17 rating collapses at the point of distribution. Many cinemas (mostly multiplexes and mall cinemas) refuse to run NC-17. In the mid-1990s Blockbuster followed suit.

Wayne Huizenga, former CEO of Blockbuster, who sold the company to Viacom in 1994 for $8.4 billion,[23] responded to the new MPAA rating with the following statement: "Our philosophy is family and kids and no NC-17."[24] The inclusion of NC-17 would define the existence of "family" without children and thus contradict Blockbuster's marketing rhetoric. "America's Family Video Store," as Blockbuster has trademarked itself, reserves the right to reject MPAA-approved films, and its "Youth Restricted Viewing" databases monitor renting to young people. In the 1990s this policy was instituted to soothe "parental fears that their teenagers will come home from the video store with a splatter movie or something equally offensive."[25] While NC-17 remains absent from the shelves of Blockbuster, NR (not rated) titles appear regularly. For example, the R-rated version (according to the MPAA, it was rated R "for graphic crude and sexual behavior, violent images and strong language—all involving puppets") of *Team American: World Police* (Trey Parker, 2004) shares shelf space and is available for Internet purchase or rental with the NR *Team America: World Police—Uncensored and Unrated Special Collector's Edition*. NR slides past the concern that marked NC-17 in the early 1990s. It lacks the ill-fated social stigma that places NC-17 within the domain of "un-family" and relocates the MPAA rating outside of "legitimate" home cinema.

As stated above, Blockbuster's policy on NC-17 is the obvious target for questions of regulating home viewing from outside the home. Blockbuster's film library is also available through pay-per-view with DirecTV, launched in 2001. Since 2004, to keep pace with Netflix (which does offer NC-17 films), which began offering online rentals of DVDs in 1999, Blockbuster Online DVD Rentals delivers its titles directly to your home, thus eliminating the need to travel to a Blockbuster store.[26] Never one to shy away from pithy campaign slogans, Blockbuster announced this new service as "The Movie Store At Your Door," a suggestive metaphor that, again, places the Internet in reference to the spatiality of the domestic sphere's front door. However, this front door appears more permeable than the front door of Blockbuster stores. Readers may recall Blockbuster making headlines in the late 1980s when it refused to carry Martin Scorsese's *The Last Temptation of Christ* (1988) in its retail stores despite its R-rating. The title is readily available at Blockbuster Online, whereas it is still absent from retail shelves. Why? Online rentals provide anonymity unlike physically entering and renting from a local retail outlet, where your tastes are on display. It shields against the presence of the morally objectionable physically residing in your neighborhood on the shelves of your local video store, which is most likely a

Blockbuster. Or, perhaps, it is more difficult for groups of picketers to camp out on the steps of the Internet to protest Blockbuster stocking *The Last Temptation of Christ* in its online library.

Blockbuster's access to the home through its channels of cable television, Internet rentals, and, soon to pass into obsolescence, video stores provides ways for its "philosophy" to affect viewing in the home.[27] Its policy governs access through these circuits of distribution. And these hold influence over Hollywood production on account of Blockbuster's conglomerate ties to the industry as well as its alleged reediting of MPAA-rated films.[28] These are certainly not minor influences on what can enter the home considering that Blockbuster Inc. cannibalized the video store world at a lightning-fast pace since opening its first store in Dallas, Texas, in 1985.[29] At the end of 1989 more than five hundred stores, with a strong concentration in the conservative states of Texas and Florida, were in operation.[30] Gail DeGeorge, biographer for former Blockbuster CEO Wayne Huizenga, boasts that in the late 1980s "there was a new store opening every 48 hours, then 24, then 17 hours, along with stores from acquisitions that had to be converted."[31] As of 2005, Blockbuster reported more than 9,100 corporate and franchise stores located in the United States, Europe, Asia, and Australia; its online DVD rental service has a subscription rate of over one million.[32] It is estimated that forty-three million U.S. households have memberships at Blockbuster. This is largely a result of Blockbuster's acquisition of shops and aggressive expansion strategy, which decimated the video store industry. In Blockbuster's near monopoly on the home media rental market, our access to home media is quite tightly limited to the nonchoice of Blockbuster's choosing.

The less obvious measure for regulating the domestic sphere takes the form of the control technology of the video store itself, that is, the techniques, practices, and policies for disciplining the industry and consumption of home media as a family institution. The video store does not easily fit the "closed-site" molding of disciplinary institutions that Deleuze cites as being taken over by control societies. Less confining, the video store functions as a nonplace for transient renters quickly picking a new release and returning home to watch. The disciplining of Blockbuster is less about organizing bodies in its space in the way that disciplinary technology required than about transferring its sense of order, morality, security into the renter's home-viewing experience by equating film viewing in the home with

Blockbuster Inc. and its protocols of control. Blockbuster's family policy and practices for conducting its policy attempt to shape how media is positioned in the home and how it can be managed. This transference is expressed well in Blockbuster's slogan, which reverberates like a command, *Make It A Blockbuster Night*.[33] In making it a "Blockbuster Night" we are not simply renting a movie to watch in our homes but inviting Blockbuster's ethos of family entertainment past our welcome mats as well: continuous control of the "(neo-)liberalized domestic sphere" manifest in Blockbuster's seizure of the home video industry's heterogeneity to redefine the industry in its likeness.[34]

The experience of "going out to the movies" in the middle to late 1980s became one of going out to *get* a movie on videocassette to watch within a domestic setting rather than entering into a cinema to *watch* a movie.[35] Not *drive-in* but *take-out* became the jagged rupture to the historical trappings of cinema going.[36] The video store provides an additional "destination" for how and where film can be obtained. As cinema architects and film historians have argued, the place of exhibition assists in the experience of watching a film; that is, different cinema types generate different conditions and modes of attending to the projected image. Does the video store adhere to a similar principle? Blockbuster's radical redesign of the video store and redefinition of renting protocols demonstrate a precise historical moment in sanitizing practices aimed at cultivating (as well as profiting from) the conditions of family viewing within the VCR-led home theater. In contrast, and as we will see with ClearPlay, the very medium of the DVD player, not its storage media, embeds the discourses of family protection and security directly in its enabling technology. Its parental function, like Blockbuster Inc. before it, is to redesign the DVD player as an active instrument for self-governing.

The early video store, much like the nickelodeon at the turn of the past century, endured a period of scorn and moral disrepute.[37] Porn took to video with industrial zeal. This new appeal to privacy made possible by the VCR rendered the porno theater an antiquated relic among the vehicles for sex entertainment. As film historian Douglas Gomery avers, "The porno theatre has all but disappeared because those who want to see X-rated material prefer the price and privacy that the home offers."[38] X-rated videocassettes were the most prominent prerecorded features in the beginning of videocassette sales and rentals. Porn was financially valuable for early video stores. Janet Wasko claims that the "early video stores were opened mostly in larger cities and relied to a great extent on the sale of pornographic material."[39] The inclusion of porn and the relatively minimal/functional appearance of many early video stores associated the prerecorded videocassette and the video store with "adult" interest, not with a "wholesome" place in which one could entertain the family. (I recall my "typical" neighborhood video store of the early 1980s: interior walls were either wood paneling or functional Peg-Board standing on linoleum-squared flooring or stained thin carpeting of a forgettable color. Crowded racks of the then new media of videocassette boxes [Beta and VHS] and maybe laserdiscs hugged the walls or aided in the creation of makeshift aisles. Additional decor usually took the form of video release posters tacked to any free wall or taped to store windows to attract passersby.)

This epoch of the video store changed when Blockbuster grew past its humble Dallas beginnings. Former Blockbuster CEO Wayne Huizenga was not a film aficionado. DeGeorge has even pointed out that prior to Blockbuster, he "rarely watched movies and didn't own a VCR."[40] Huizenga's financial success was in the business sphere of service. Waste Management Inc. was his cash crop. The video retail business, specifically the place of the video store of the 1980s, was likened to waste in need of management. For Huizenga, it conjured images of "sleazy joints in bad neighborhoods."[41] Bad neighborhoods, for a Fort Lauderdale mogul, were equated with urban environments, the location of many early entrepreneurial "mom & pop" video stores.[42]

The plan to rid the emerging home video rental business of these "sleazy joints" consisted of enhancing the appearance of the video store and the experience of home viewing. Like the art-deco picture palace and ornamental atmospheric before it, the existing video store was reconstructed to create a radically different "cinema experience" for the home while catering to a presumed respectable audience. The video store, as Blockbuster chain, which implies a standardized mode of operation, donned a new facade of family home entertainment, complete with a guarantee of safety.

So what does a family retail space look like? Darkness—"the pall of gloom which prevents the full visibility of things"[43]—was the first dangerous element exorcised from Huizenga's "superstore." Spaces for concealment and "danger" were illuminated. The "shadowy" area of the onetime video store was razed. In its place a new structure was erected: well lit and not absorbed by obfuscation. The contrast in lighting was not a vivid relief between light and dark but a moral separation between Blockbuster and other video stores. Blockbuster's illumination is morality lighting.[44] Critics were fast to comment on Blockbuster's brilliance. In 1990, *Fortune* magazine cited Blockbuster's illuminating appeal: "More than 1,200 'superstores'—big, well-lighted outlets with twice as many titles as most stores—are spread coast to coast, and a new one opens every day."[45] Its illumination became a consistent measure of distinction as well as evidence of notable improvement over rivals. These new stores were not always slotted into an existing unit of a shopping strip. When they were located in a strip, they were much larger than existing video stores, or they stood independently. Large windows surrounded the interior. Mirrors were used (tastefully) around the ceiling (versus the sole mirror for security reasons). The illusion of vast dimensions was managed, while video cameras monitored in-store behavior (disguised behind mirrors). Blinking lights, a touch of the cinema's "coming attractions" for its retail space, surrounded posters of new releases. Costumers could clearly see in and look out, thus reducing associations with "adult" video stores. Comparing Blockbuster with its then northeast competitor Erol's, Gomery summarizes its grand scheme: "Blockbuster planned big, brightly lit stores with ten thousand or more tapes in stock."[46] Blockbuster's then chief marketer, Tom Gruber, in his address to the 1988 Video Software Dealers Association underscored the importance of its redesign initiative when he "compared the bright, clean look of Blockbuster's stores to pictures of dirty, dingy, unkempt outlets."[47]

Mirrored walls and ceilings, young Republican "preppie" uniforms,[48] in-store security cameras, organized and spacious shelves, and a centralized return/checkout station introduced an ordered and ordering structure as a regulatory apparatus to govern both customer conduct while in the superstore and the presentation of videocassettes. Rental media accompanied by the box cover are available on the shelves.[49] This eliminates the need for a back room housing the actual rental copy. Without a back room (thus preempting the possibility of porn), all of Blockbuster is a functional space where customers decide what videocassette (DVD or video game) they wish to select while in an environment that works to maximize efficient and convenient superstore productivity. As a family space, Blockbuster is one that is meticulously controlled, or at least presented as such.

Every surface is given over to the maintenance of family entertainment. It should come as no surprise that Blockbuster's influential practices engender a standard likened to the "family" concept and service orientation of McDonald's. Gruber cut his marketing teeth for nineteen years as an executive at McDonald's prior to his position at Blockbuster. He maintains that "there are great similarities between the target group at McDonald's and the target group at Blockbuster. We're both primarily marketing to families."[50]

Blockbuster, too, provides a treatise on twenty-first-century urban planning: "families across America will spend more time together at home in the 21st century."[51] And on account of this new social arrangement, Blockbuster has developed its "Family Viewing Guide" to assist the "family's movie viewing experience." Adult (a category that does not exist at Blockbuster) and child alike are crushed into the same classification as Blockbuster's parental function collides the two in its molding of family values. Adult tastes are dictated by measures to protect children. The child-family functions as a dictatorial norm. It transforms the videocassette into a mechanism that extends the morality thought to reside in safe images and secure environments. Blockbuster Inc.'s product, I would urge, is neither 3/4-inch magnetic tape (R.I.P), digital compression technology, DIRECTV pay-per-views, online DVD rentals, nor even the sugary sweet candy that satisfies an impulse to have the "flavors" of the cinema in your home. Blockbuster sells "family entertainment" as an armed concept: a power/knowledge relation that determines private social experiences with media. Blockbuster's category of family is not limited to the content of its family-viewing policies: its mediation of family is in its design, marketing campaigns, policy, and "rentail" stores. The nostalgic torn ticket—the Blockbuster trademark and iconic signature that dots the globe—signifies an illusion of passage into its control technology. We have already entered whether we have crossed an actual threshold or not.

ClearPlay: Choose Your Filter Settings and Enjoy the Show

Following the delayed release of *Crash* in the United States (it premiered in 1997, a year after it had won the Special Jury Prize at Cannes) and in response to the storm clouds surrounding the film in the United Kingdom, director David Cronenberg, in his trademark mild manner, responded, "You don't have to watch."[52] Given that

Cronenberg uttered his statement as a response to the theatrical release of *Crash* and the limited distribution that followed from its
NC-17 rating, we should inquire how this proclamation holds up
in the era of film sanitization. "You don't have to watch" immediately crashes into corporate policy when Blockbuster Inc. refuses to
carry NC-17 or X-rated DVDs in its retail stores. The reason given is
the desire to brand itself as "family entertainment." At your "local"
Blockbuster, be it urban, suburban, or rural, "You Don't Have to
Watch" transforms into "You Won't Find It Here." This amendment,
as we have seen, demonstrates the prominence of retailers in regulatory practices and the space of retail as a technology of control.
(In spite of its "No NC-17" policy, which is stated on Blockbuster
Online's home page, I found an NC-17 version of Cronenberg's *Crash*
available to rent when searching through its online library.)

Cronenberg's remark can be amended yet again, this time by the
medium specificity of DVD. *Crash* debuted in cinemas in the same
year that DVD players were released into the U.S. market.[53] New
Line Home Entertainment's DVD of *Crash* (released in 1998), on account of the larger storage capacity afforded by MPEG compression
technology, surpasses the storage capabilities of magnetic tape and
allows for both the NC-17 and R-rated versions to be contained on
the same disc. One meaning of *v* in "DVD" does, it must be stressed,
stand for "versatile." Viewers are faced with two different viewing
options. With the DVD version of *Crash*, Cronenberg's "you don't
have to watch" becomes "you don't have to watch that version." The
preferred version decided by the in-control user can be selected at the
slight touch of an RCD interacting with the DVD interface. In addition, if CleanFlicks were to provide one of its reedited copies of *Crash*
(which it does not), I suspect the new slogan would be: "CleanFlicks
Decides What Scenes *You* Watch and Don't Watch." And lastly, "You
Don't Have to Watch Once You've Enabled Your ClearPlay DVD
player." After all, when deciding what and how to watch, all we have
to do is look to ClearPlay, "The Technology of Choice!"

Prompted by the ClearPlay filter-setting screen, parents can select
to watch a DVD with "Crude Language and Humor" deleted. Filters are customized according to fourteen different settings, which,
as ClearPlay.com boasts, provide its subscribers with "16,384 potential user combinations." ClearPlay's user combinations persist
in reinscribing how "you don't have to watch." In this case, "not
watching"—the DVD player as vision machine—is orchestrated for

you through DVD commands and filtering software. Pressing the "enter" button, the user endorses ClearPlay's identification of subject matter as "objectionable" and thus banished from a viewer's line of sight. What remains perfectly in frame are ClearPlay's abilities as a control technology. Another gesture for "enter" marks ClearPlay technology's entrance into the home. In the way that Blockbuster Inc. redesigned the video store and continues to disseminate its family policy and shape our domestic environs through its numerous circuits of distribution, ClearPlay is in the process of redesigning the DVD player, available nationwide and online at Best Buy, as an instrument for parental control and technology for further regulating the securitization of habitat. Viewer control is affirmed again; a notable difference is that Blockbuster Inc.'s family policy is limited to architecture and software whereas ClearPlay designs its policies directly into the hardware to maximize viewer control as an enabled relation to media technology and culture.

Legality is guaranteed with the passing of the Family Entertainment and Copyright Act of 2005. Title II: Exemption from Infringement for Skipping Audio and Video Content in Motion Pictures (a.k.a. the "Family Movie Act of 2005") states that

> A manufacturer, licensee, or licensor of technology that enables the making of limited portions of audio or video content of a motion picture imperceptible . . . is not liable on account of such manufacture or license for a violation of any right under this Act, if such manufacturer, licensee, or licensor ensures that the technology provides a clear and conspicuous notice at the beginning of each performance that the performance of the motion picture is altered from the performance intended by the director or copyright holder of the motion picture.[54]

As permanent alterations to a copyrighted DVD are not inflicted by ClearPlay technology (or by similar technologies), the law creates an exemption from copyright violation. Maintaining the dictum of the "Betamax Case," which supports consumer usage and does not hold manufacturers liable,[55] the Family Movie Act defends a consumer's right to use technology for "the making imperceptible, by or at the direction of a private household, of limited portions of audio or video content of a motion picture during a performance in or transmitted to that household for private home viewing,"[56] while making the production of such technology "that creates no fixed copy of the altered version" legal. The provision of a "fixed copy" renders companies like CleanFlicks liable for copyright infringement, whereas ClearPlay's services are sanctioned.

Similar to the various technologies available on the market for regulating television broadcast in the 1990s, discussed in chapter 2, filtering software had been in circulation prior to the Family Movie Act, often viewed in conjunction with CleanFlicks' preemptive lawsuit against the Director's Guild of America (August 2002) and sixteen of its affiliated directors. Major attention was bestowed on the filtering software of MovieMask (developed by Trilogy Studios of Utah) when its executives presented examples of its technology to Hollywood directors in March 2002. MovieMask is responsible for the infamous digital corset superimposed on Kate Winslet and for reequipping the PG-rated swashbuckling fairy-tale sword duel in Rob Reiner's *The Princess Bride* (1987) with digital overlays that resemble the light sabers from *Star Wars*. Rather than impressing Hollywood directors, MovieMask's presentation helped "to mobilize the directors and their organization to a find a way to put a stop to this."[57] According to Breck Rice, founder and CEO of Trilogy Studios, the addition of a digital corset or light sabers does not warrant accusations of censorship: "We're letting the consumer choose for themselves. That's the difference between choice and censorship. Censorship is when someone else decided for you. Choice is power."[58] *Choice is the new knowledge.*

Appeals to choice are an attempt to abnegate accusations of censorship, and this appeal is common to discourses on digital filtering technology. In the context of neoliberal governance, power operates as choice: choice *over* content and existing general industry ratings systems; a choice *to* self-govern, to choose how regulation is practiced within the domestic private sphere; and a choice to empower parents *through* technology rather than succumb to it. Choice limits and delimits. Choice is positioned as a utilitarian practice with consumer technology in the private sphere of the home. In his statement before the House Judiciary Subcommittee on Courts, the Internet, and Intellectual Property, Bill Aho (CEO of ClearPlay Inc.) opened his 2004 testimonial by establishing ClearPlay technology as an enabler of choice:

> ClearPlay is founded on the belief that families have the right to watch movies in the privacy of their homes any way they choose. ClearPlay

parental controls provide families the choice to filter movies of graphic violence, nudity, explicit sex and profanity. This is a choice that many families desire. Many see it as a useful parenting tool that will be beneficial to their children. We believe that it is not in the best interest of society for the movie industry, in an effort to extend its artistic control over the experience of viewers, to take actions that would eliminate this choice for families.[59]

Aho articulates ClearPlay's services as offering a solution through choice, one that does not hinder other modes of viewing for "our right to watch movies," and one that maintains an instrumentalist view so definitive to control technology. Synthesizing the instrumentalist view with securitization, Representative Lamar Smith (R-Tex.) made no haste after the bill was passed to proclaim in its defense that "there are some who would deny parents the right to use the equivalent electronic device that would protect their children from sex, violence and profanity in movies watched at home."[60]

Without ClearPlay, thus denying the rights of parents, according to Smith, we can surmise from Aho's statement that families do not really have a choice, as they will continue to be subjected to the "vile" product of Hollywood. As such, ClearPlay's brand of religious morality invests in the DVD player as an instrument that mediates choice through its sanitizing effects. As a tool, digital filtering technology can be used, or not. The decision to purchase and use a DVD player with ClearPlay technology is not influenced by ClearPlay, since the company simply offers "neutral" wares for parenting (although why one would purchase a DVD player with ClearPlay technology and subscribe to ClearPlay in order *not* to filter is beyond me). Any attempt to block such usage would not only "dictate" how technology can be used in the private sphere but also deny parents choices over their family's viewing practices. Equally, Senator Hatch's January 25, 2005, statement before the U.S. Senate to introduce the Family Movie bill asserts that it "will help to end aggressive litigation threatening the viability of small companies like ClearPlay which are busy creating innovative technologies for consumers that allow them to tailor their home viewing experience to their own individual or family preferences." Three months later Hatch's David and Goliath parable for "shielding families from inappropriate content" was passed into law.

We *must choose*. We have no choice but to choose. Choice becomes an imperative rather than a possibility. The practices of power that emerge out of digital filtering technology are social relations that come to define choice as the utilization of ClearPlay products and services for the shaping of conduct. While it is increasingly clear that consumer markets exist for additional layers of censorial practices beyond those of the MPAA and the likes of Blockbuster Inc. (where some see censorship, others see customer service), the "choice is power" adage finds families entrusting their, we may say, screenic risks to the expertise of sanitizers. Expertise exists in two locations and through two practices. The first is the parent as a responsible self-governing user, and the second is the brusque set of standards invoked in flagging material as obscene in order to encode filters.

Users become "experts of themselves" and their families when enabled through their choice to purchase ClearPlay-compliant DVD players, download ClearPlay filters for corresponding DVDs, and manage the levels so that digital filtering occurs. For the user, ClearPlay works in the following manner. The user purchases a DVD player with ClearPlay technology.[61] Next the user must subscribe to ClearPlay so that ClearPlay filters can be acquired.[62] ClearPlay filters are software filters customized to specific films that "skip or mute" content judged "obscene" by ClearPlay filter settings. Filters are then loaded to the DVD player. An interface screen prompts the user to "check" the ClearPlay filter settings that the parent deems appropriate for viewing a particular DVD to which that ClearPlay filter corresponds. The categories are "Violence," "Sex and Nudity," "Language," and "Other." Each has sublevels that attempt to specify certain types of the larger categories. Lastly, the user inserts a purchased or rented MPAA-approved DVD, and the player will proceed to play the disc according to ClearPlay's protocols for a "safe" viewing experience. The DVD player will only play scenes from the DVD that correspond to ClearPlay filter settings. In one variation of selected settings, a parent may decide to filter the subcategories of "Sensual Content" and "Ethnic and Racial Slurs." When such occasions present themselves during the course of a DVD, they will be muted if spoken, and "skipped past" if expressed in a few frames.

Pressing enter (on the RCD for the RCA DVD player with ClearPlay technology, the enter button is an amenable "OK" button) to select preordained category boxes like "Strong Action Violence" and "Vain Reference to a Deity" is a matter of reactively choosing "on" or "off" in the way that Raymond Williams dismissed interactive television of the early 1970s and in the manner that I have dismissed the V-chip as an interactive, programmable device. As with the V-chip, the user's choice is expressed through preconceived categories found in the ClearPlay filter settings. Whereas the faces behind MPAA/CARA ratings system remain a mystery, subscribers to ClearPlay purchase its hardware and related services for the transparent religious ideology directly inscribed in its filtering software. Aho is vehement that the ultimate responsibility resides in the hands of the user, not the programmer. "We really don't make a call on what is offensive or appropriate," he claims in an interview with Latter-day Saints magazine *Meridian*. Instead, "what we do is create Guides according to a ClearPlay standard. Right now, that involves removing all profanity, nudity and graphic violence."[63] The act of "guiding" charts only a single course: removal.

ClearPlay editors and executives are setting standards every time they write a new filter. Guides direct conduct by encoding options for viewing based on an ideal of safety and purity. Sure one need not abide by them, but if these scenes are truly dangerous, why wouldn't one who is concerned with security and the protection of family as articulated by film sanitizers (and we could apply this to discourse that constructs the V-chip and Internet filters as beneficent and protective technologies) fail to comply? By encoding ClearPlay filters to skip past or mute precise scenes, a "call on what is offensive or appropriate" is being sounded. Filmic material is being judged obscene by ClearPlay's experts who flag these scenes as offensive and write programs to have them removed from view. ClearPlay's "guides" are all-inclusive, thus not leaving any room for accidental exposure. The slightest hint of "indecency" or "obscenity" yields to categorization. In his *New York Times* article on ClearPlay, David Pogue argues that a great deal of inconsistency exists in how filters are applied. In *The Matrix Reloaded* (Andy and Larry Wachowski, 2003), the sex scene between Neo and Trinity reveals little, and one would be hard pressed to charge this scene with any sense of "explicitness" in the form of nudity. The ClearPlay filtered version keeps the passionate kiss between the characters "and then—blink!—[they] instantly appear, sweaty and tousled, chatting in bed."[64] The rash cut, corresponding to ClearPlay's filter settings for "Sex and Nudity," implies more than the original scene delivers. Yet, the visual representation of a sexual act is not the only form of sexual content that is filtered. Meg Ryan's famous "faked orgasm" in a public restaurant is cut from the ClearPlay filtered version of *When Harry Met Sally*

(Rob Reiner, 1989), despite no nude body parts being served. This inconsistency materializes in the service of an ideological agenda instead of hack editing: "Vain Reference to Deity" signals the muting of "God-forsaken island," while "heathen gods" persists in *Pirates of the Caribbean: The Curse of the Black Pearl* (Gore Verbinski, 2003); two gay men hugging affectionately is filtered out of *Big Daddy* (Dennis Dugan, 1999) for "Sensual Content" or maybe "Crude Sexual Content"; and, as mentioned previously, scenes of Somali soldiers being shot by U.S. troops remain, while the delicate operation of filtering "Violence" removes the bullets' impact from American bodies in *Black Hawk Down*.

The sanitized version is governed according to ClearPlay's programs and its rule structure for identifying filmic material as obscene. It identifies danger, violence, sex and nudity, language, insecurity, and "filth" to offer simultaneously technological solutions to control, manage, and secure the environs prone to occupation. Like the video store, the DVD player is redesigned in the name of security. Regardless of whether the "original version" is permanently altered or not, *the only accepted and approved* clean version comes to define that viewing experience for select audiences. ClearPlay's parental function of expertise licenses its users with an authoritative voice, through their practices of filtering, to denounce all other versions as "unclean" and potentially harmful to the family. The action of watching is augmented by the actions of ClearPlay filters. Viewers see a film through control: viewers see how easily security can be enabled through control technologies like a ClearPlay DVD player. Again, the visibility of ClearPlay is not in its "cuts" but in its mere presence as a corrective instrument implemented to maximize choice in the name of security.

Gaps in *A History of Violence*

"We are the leading provider of Edited Hollywood movies," CleanFlicks' home page once boasted. Now, in place of the moniker for film sanitizing, "Movies You Can Trust" brandishes its home page. CleanFlicks is now in the business of review versus reediting: "We have reviewed thousands of movies and have identified those which meet our standard for family entertainment."[65] The accompanying image of a bucolic large white family remains and continues to suggest that CleanFlicks is a clean and safe space for your home entertainment needs. Prior to *Clean Flicks v. Steven Soderbergh,* DVDs available at CleanFlicks' rental shops, affiliated retailers,[66] and online at CleanFlicks.com offered feature-length versions of Hollywood films with specific scenes and dialogue deliberately removed and sold or rented to the public. "Family edited movie," according to CleanFlicks, is "a popular Hollywood title without the profanity, graphic violence, nudity and sexual."[67] For example, Ray Lines, owner of CleanFlicks, offers edited copies of *Schindler's List* (Steven Spielberg, 1993) with nude scenes of Jewish concentration camp prisoners removed: "I don't think my daughters should see naked old men, running around in circles. You can watch that film and know people were humiliated, traumatized and put through hell even after we cut out what we cut out."[68] Like ClearPlay, CleanFlicks governs film content according to the noncontextual categories of "profanity," "nudity," "graphic violence," and "sexual content." Profanity also includes "references to a deity used in a non-religious context." This is the only instance of context being applied to CleanFlicks' reediting protocols. As in keyword or key pattern word spider searches for Internet filtering programs, context is ruled out by CleanFlicks' targeting of these elusive categories.

Film sanitizing in the case of reediting can be considered part of a larger set of cultural practices with digital media that I dub "versioning." The reworking of media content by amateur coproducers signals a type of "participatory culture," according to Henry Jenkins. He argues that in the production of "grassroots" digital movies fans apply "traditional practices of folk culture to mass culture, treating film or television as if it offered raw materials for telling their own stories and resources for forging their own communities."[69] The most common versioning of intellectual property is carried out on *Star Wars,* where reworked versions provide spoofs, parodies, and additional narratives, thus rejecting the very notion of a "definitive version produced, authorized, and regulated by some media conglomerate."[70] Because digital editing software like Apple's Final Cut is now more common in the consumer market, people reedit/remake their own (usually unauthorized) versions of music videos, television shows, music, and films and share their versions on file-sharing networks like Guba, YouTube, Kazaa, Google video, and Gnutella. Disapproving of the character Jar Jar Binks in the long-anticipated yet disastrously disappointing *Stars Wars Episode 1: The Phantom Menace* (George Lucas, 1999), an unauthorized reedited version by an anonymous fan, *Star*

Wars Episode 1.1: The Phantom Edit, is a version where most of the scenes dedicated to this character have been removed. The argument espoused within the *Star Wars* fan community is that the reedited version makes for an "improved" film by removing vulgar marketing schemes aimed at younger audiences.

The film trailer is a valuable source of "raw materials" for contemporary participatory culture's interaction with media content. The parody trailer *Shining* (2005), reworked from the trailer for Stanley Kubrick's terrifying film *The Shining* (1980), includes a voice-over that enunciates a "feel-good" film between Jack (Jack Nicholson), a writer in need of inspiration, and his new foster son, Danny. The upbeat tale of father and son bonding is accented by Peter Gabriel's song "Salisbury Hill." Another example of reediting, which goes further than omitting a particular character as in *Star Wars Episode 1.1,* is *Scarface Short Version* (2006), available for streaming at ifilm.com, kontraband.com, and youtube.com, which is a one-minute, thirty-four-second version of Brian De Palma's *Scarface* (1983) where everything has been edited out of the original film with the exception of the use of the word *fuck*.[71] For just over ninety seconds the viewer is bounced from one "fuck" to another. The only additional words are credited to Michelle Pfeiffer, who asks: "Can't you stop saying fuck all the time?" An entire feature film is reduced to the repetition of a one-syllable word in this popular rendition of *Scarface,* whereas in the experimental films of Martin Arnold, footage from old Hollywood movies is manipulated (through frame-by-frame edits, flashcuts, continuous replays, slow motion) to reveal subtle signatures of sexual desire (*Alone. Life Wastes Andy Hardy,* 1998), violent aggression hovering just under the normalcy the American atomic-age family (*Passage à l'acte,* 1993), and terrifying anticipation of the unknown and inevitable (*Pièce Touchée,* 1989).

The reauthoring tactics of participatory culture's digital creations and Arnold's stylized practice of filmic quoting to reveal a certain presence are distinct from the versioning on offer at CleanFlicks and ClearPlay and their cohorts. Where aspects of Arnold's work seek to reveal the most minute traces, of, say, desire, the versioning of film sanitizers seeks to totally eradicate that which is already visible and audible, already certified according to MPAA policy despite how vague and biased this may be. Homage, play, parody, fan productions, critical reception, and the making of art are far removed from the "moral" undertakings in the service of protection, safety, and sanitization in the maintenance of the parental function through family viewing measures. In versions like *Scarface Short Version* or *Shining*, not reworked for commercial usage but shared on peer-to-peer sites, the practice of versioning endeavors to widen the possibility of cultural participation and creativity via user-generated content, while film sanitizing seeks to close down access by demonizing content and offering its "D.I.Y. aesthetics" as a measure of safety and security. Film sanitizing's "versioning" is not a practice of reauthored pluralism and the maintenance of a new digital folk culture but a controlled singular affair; its reedited version is an act of replacement, the one and only "clean" version for its clientele. The sanitized version is an element of governing that precludes content in its attempts to manage and further shape conduct at the interface of televisual viewing. Reedits, like the V-chip's block or networked computer's filter, mark the presence of protection through the absence of content.

A film that shows us that just under the idyllic crust of that warm slice of small-town American apple pie lurk dark secrets is *A History of Violence,* in which themes of family, truth, and identity are neither neat nor easy to sanitize due to the film's difficult and uncomfortable content. To erase violence (sex as well as sexual violence) from *A History of Violence* denies a history of violence formative to the main character, Tom Stall (Viggo Mortensen), as well as the historical use of violence as an all-too-common means of settling disputes. Given *A History of Violence*'s explicit and implicit subject matter, we ought to ask what the CleanFlicks version does to Cronenberg's film, especially since Cronenberg's defense of "you don't have to watch" falls upon deaf ears when a CleanFlicks' version invokes certain sanitizing "repairs" so that one can watch in the security of its reediting effects.

Jane M. Gaines asks this same question of an equally violent film in a different historical period. In her eloquent discussion of the banning of D. W. Griffith's *The Birth of a Nation* in *Fire and Desire: Mixed-Race Movies in the Silent Era,* Gaines addresses "the issue of what it is that the censor's cut actually does to the film text."[72] Gaines directs this question to the NAACP's early-twentieth-century campaign to ban *The Birth of a Nation* and how exhibition and the film were "scarred" by such efforts. The question can also be applied to the control technologies that sanitize Hollywood films outside of recognized (albeit continually disputed) channels of regulation like the MPAA to service sectarian family entertainment through reedited DVDs. Unlike the film censorship boards that governed the "elimination of offending scenes" from *The Birth of a Nation*,[73] ClearPlay and CleanFlicks operate through the discourse of consumer choice to provide hardware and software to enable self-regulation aimed at the domestic sphere. "Official" institutions for the regulation of film are bypassed as certain audiences are technologically assisted and enabled as self-censors. This bespeaks James Hay's emphasis on technologies aimed at the domestic sphere for self-governance and our concentration on the continued appeal to viewer control as disciplined freedom exercised through choices enabled by digital technologies. In this instance, self-governance, viewer control, and choice are embodied in the CleanFlicks version of *A History of Violence*.

Anticipating the arrival of the CleanFlicks version and curious to see what reediting would be conducted by CleanFlicks (while it still offered its reedited versions in spring 2006), I read the review of the theatrical release by the Dove Foundation, whose "mission" is to "encourage and promote the creation, production, distribution and consumption of wholesome family entertainment."[74] Theatrical and DVD releases, ClearPlay-filtered versions, edited versions by CleanFlicks, TV versions, and video games are rated by the Dove Foundation.[75] The foundation has taken it upon itself to promote "family-friendly" films by awarding a blue-and-white Dove Seal of approval for films that meet their standards. Films that are awarded the Dove Seal can use it in all promotions. Reviewers are parents "who have been trained to evaluate each film or video based upon Judaeo-Christian ethics" (although the Judaism in this equation is questionable at best). Dove provides a synopsis of each film that its reviewers rate followed by what the foundation refers to as a "Dove Worldview," which is another synopsis produced from its moral perspective. The theatrical release of *A History of Violence* received Dove's "not approved" rating. While the synopsis provides an accurate summation of the film's plot, the Dove Worldview begins with, "This film should have been NC 17 in my opinion."[76] The full review reads as follows:

> It was so graphic in the sex and violence areas which really ruined the film for me. What could have been a somewhat interesting plot became secondary in scope and importance to the showing of soft pornographic sex scenes and gruesome violence. I found nothing

redeeming or uplifting in the film. As a matter of fact the plot was so far fetched in how the gangsters dealt with finding Joey and what they were going to do to him, that it was laughable. If you have a history of enjoying the movie going experience then you might want to stay clear of this one.[77]

It is not necessary to pit this review against the praise that has been bestowed on *the film*. Nor is it incumbent on us to suggest that all films do not have to be "redeeming or uplifting." The Dove Worldview is not interested in the type of criteria reviewers often leverage when constructing their reviews. Instead, the Dove Worldview uses this space to warn its readers that their solipsism could easily be compromised by watching the film.[78]

My copy of the CleanFlicks version arrived promptly in my mailbox. The CleanFlicks logo and its slogan, "It's about choice!" brand the Blockbuster-like yellow-and-blue envelope. Underneath the slogan, another mantra appears that is not present on the CleanFlicks home page. It reads, "We want everyone in America to have a clean entertainment choice." Overstepping its denominational boundaries for the ambitious "everyone in America," CleanFlicks seeks a much wider audience than its presumed Latter-day Saints customer base. As we should expect, profanity like *damn, bitch, shit,* and *fuck* and references to God, like "god-damn," are all edited out of the CleanFlicks version of *A History of Violence*. The R-rated version has a running time of ninety-six minutes, whereas the CleanFlicks version is eighty-three minutes long. Eighty-three minutes is well below the standard running time of a feature-length film and closer to children's films, which are typically below ninety minutes. Much more than muting and editing out of language has occurred to reduce *A History of Violence* by sixteen minutes. An immediately noticeable difference between the film and the CleanFlicks version asserts itself at the DVD interface. The CleanFlicks logo replaces the New Line Entertainment logo when a disc is inserted into a DVD player (my Sony PS2 DVD player required my secret pin number to play *A History of Violence* but not the CleanFlicks version). No trailers appear on the CleanFlicks version, since they are approved for an R-rated DVD. The DVD interface for the CleanFlicks version does not allow access to "Special Features," "Set-up options" (where the viewer could enable English or Spanish subtitles), and the "DVD-Rom/Online Features." When attempting to access these features, the message "Sorry, these features are not available" is lettered in white against a tranquil blue sky. The "Special Features" option on the *History of Violence* DVD contains a "making of" mini-documentary where Cronenberg and the actors discuss the complexities of the film. Of significance here is that Cronenberg explains why he decided to include sex scenes that were not present in the graphic novel on which the film is based. The explanation, an opportunity to examine these scenes in more detail and hear a director engage with the film's subject matter more directly, cannot be watched in the CleanFlicks version.

The sanitizer's "cut" is emblematic of the operations that multiply and generalize censorial practices to relocate them away from industry-related organizations and redesign DVD players and DVDs as solutions for regulating culture and fostering security through consumer technology. As I have insisted throughout this book, the very presence of control technologies constitutes the visibility of the censorial not as a restrictive presence but one born of choice, freedom, and control. Here, the elusive and pervasive "cut" protects and provides rather than restricts and distorts—an accusation commonly leveled against the censorial cut in its perceived butchering of films. Gaines's question proves relevant for the study of control technologies, for it requires that we consider the actual action of censorial processes and practices, thus continuing to acknowledge the non-institutionally bound multifarious workings of censoring as a network of forces (I will return to Gaines's question in the next chapter). In this case, it is CleanFlicks' mediation of "family entertainment" that governs content rather than film industry institutions.

Consider Gaines's own response to the question of the effect of the censor's cut:

> The censorial reading is a reading-with-a-purpose—the purpose of suppressing or cutting—but unlike the classical film editor's reading, which is a close analysis in an attempt to produce smoothness and continuity, the censor's reading is indifferent to the whole of the text and overfocused on the part. The censor's cut, therefore, produces discontinuity, but a discontinuity that may or may not be perceived as incoherence. Audiences, looking for the cut in the expurgated text, view the gap that can't be seen and produce their own continuity.[79]

Gaines employs similar metaphors to account for what the "cut" does to film: "injure the text," "scarred the text," "deform the offending text," "fix the text" (borrowed from Annette Kuhn), and eventually "elimination" as censorship boards understand their relation and responsibility to social order. CleanFlicks' one-time sanitizing, and this equally applies to ClearPlay's DVD players and filtering software, demonstrates a "censorial reading with a purpose"; its objective is to reedit Hollywood films by deleting "profanity," "nudity," "graphic violence," and "sexual content" from films selected to be, we may say, "fixed," that is, digitally neutered for content. CleanFlicks editors use consumer digital editing equipment in their attempt to render a Hollywood film safe for family consumption. Their "team" may be a team of one, CleanFlicks' Ray Lines, as sole counsel on what materials are ruled "offensive" and removed. This editor wields not a Steenbeck or Moviola, but a mouse interfacing with Adobe Premiere Pro, Final Cut, or some other nonlinear digital editing software.

This repair is "fixed" on content that is clearly overdetermined according to film-sanitizing sensibilities and "overfocused on the part," as Gaines would say. In the case of CleanFlicks' version of *A History of Violence*, the procedure leaves behind a discontinuous film that intentionally sacrifices narrative structure, character development, and a filmic engagement with social issues of violence, identity, and family in order to further the sanitizing objective to "repair" morality within the continually contested terrain of culture. Discontinuity is the by-product of the censor's cut for Gaines, and for CleanFlicks, it is the sign of assurance that this version is safe, free of the taint of profanity and nudity. Sanitization, while "freeing" films of moral impurity, repairs the available print to secure approval as a safe and family version.

I would like to examine a few "gaps" in the CleanFlicks version of *A History of Violence* in order to address how CleanFlicks enacts its "repairs" on the film. The two sequences, "Teens" and "Questions and Answers," discussed below correspond to the scene description titles from each version's DVD, as they are identical in this respect. I have elected to focus on these two scenes because they both contain examples of "forbidden" content from all of CleanFlicks' categories. In "Teens" Jack Stall (Ashton Holmes), Tom Stall's son, is being taunted by the high school's local bully, Bobby (Kyle Schmid), after catching him out during a game of baseball. Appearing the weaker of the two, Jack mocks Bobby's tough-guy antics through his wit. This confrontation is significantly reduced in the CleanFlicks version. Bobby angrily calls him a "little faggot," which is not edited out, and proceeds to walk away in frustration. However, what we do not see is Jack's nonviolent undermining of Bobby's aggressive macho prowess. When verbally bombarded with slurs like "chicken shit" and "punk ass bitch," dialogue removed from the CleanFlicks version for violating its content categories, Jack humorously corrects and frustrates Bobby's verbal violence by stating, "shouldn't that be little chicken shit faggot bitch."

In being "overfocused on the part," as Gaines argues, the censorial reading of the CleanFlicks version denies the full sense of the antagonism building between these two characters, and we barely catch a glimpse of a side of Jack that will unfold in violence shortly. The sanitizing of dialogue proceeds to sanitize Jack's character as well. The scene is reduced to a confusing teenage male locker-room scuffle: "boys being boys," something that CleanFlicks deems acceptable. Also, many critical reviews of CleanFlicks reedited versions touch on contradictions in terms of what content is cut and what content remains. While ClearPlay has filter settings to erase "ethnic and social slurs," CleanFlicks restricts its reediting to profanity and references to God/Jesus. Hate speech aimed at sexual orientation does not warrant reediting. However, to draw attention to the fact that *faggot* is not muted like other harmful or "bad" language does little to problematize CleanFlicks' standards. After all, it is catering to a market that may already hold similar views, views that do not regard remarks based on queer sexuality offensive.

The scene "Teens" is divested of additional footage that extends considerably beyond the pinpointing of a few moments of dialogue. Learning that their two kids will be out of the house for the entire evening, Tom and his wife, Edie (Maria Bello), dedicate the evening to sex. Eager, Tom sits on the edge of their bed awaiting a surprise. Edie enters the room dressed in her high school cheerleader outfit. "What have you done with my wife?" Tom jokingly queries. Both play at teenage sex. Tom "goes down" on his wife as she disrupts their playful narrative by commenting, "wasn't much of that in high school!"[80] The two are completely dressed. No profanity suggestive of sexual acts or body parts is uttered. The entire five-minute scene is deleted from the CleanFlicks version. The scene is pivotal to the narrative as well as the character development of both Tom and Edie. But this matters little when a "family film" is being reconstructed from an existing narrative deemed inappropriate. Edie's "dual identity" from her past is playful, a temporary performance in the context of their marriage, love, friendship, passion, and trust. Her role-playing is easily shed like the cheerleading skirt that Tom removes. The practice of role-play in this intimate scene is premised on Edie "knowing who she is" and both of them "knowing one another." When Joey begins to emerge after the violent self-protective events at Stall's Diner, the small-town family man cannot easily retreat from his identity. Tom-Joey are one in the same. The scene establishes intimacy between Tom and Edie that acts as a stark contrast to subsequent discovery of Joey's existence; this intimacy is also juxtaposed against a later sex scene between Tom-Joey and Edie that calls into question the very nature of intimacy—what it does within a relationship and how it works. Without this scene we go from Jack's scuffle with Bobby to Edie picking up Tom at the diner, then to Jack hanging out with his friend Judy Danvers (Sumela Kay) on a boring Saturday night where we see the two murderers heading into town and eventually calling upon Stall's Diner. While the pace of the plot is compromised, the bigger loss in the CleanFlicks version is the sense of endearing love between Tom and Edie and how this is soon to be disrupted by the events that unfold at the diner and by Tom's secret past.

Most of the film's scenes of violence, like the infamous diner shooting and Tom defending his family from the gangsters dispatched to bring "Joey" back to Philadelphia, where he worked as a professional killer, are carefully edited so that grisly close-up shots (Leland, played by Stephen McHattie, stabbing Tom in the foot in the diner, for example) are reduced while the overall violent tone remains, as is necessary for the film's subject. There is a great deal of care expressed in the censor's cut in these instances so that acts of violence visually persist in order to maintain some sort of narrative continuity while the removal of profanity (visually evident in the movements of characters' mouths) and sex is compelling enough to forgo coherence. This is especially so when entire scenes where sex occurs are completely removed, as in "Teens" and again in "Question and Answers."

After it is becoming apparent to Edie that Tom is not the man she married and may indeed be Joey, she lies to Sheriff Sam Carney (Peter MacNeill) when he begins to suspect Tom's past. As with the previous sex scene, where Tom and Edie enjoy a "teenage romp," the CleanFlicks version deletes the sex from "Question and Answers." After the sheriff leaves, Edie breakdowns into tears from the emotional strain of her current situation; she charges out of the room. Tom pursues her and reaches out to grab her. She screams, "get off of me," and slaps him in the face. Angered by her unexpected action, Tom grabs her by the throat and fiercely pushes her against the wall. "Fuck you, Joey," she replies, thus confirming her husband's dual identity to herself and perhaps Tom. The CleanFlicks version cuts when Tom grabs her, and the next shot we get is sometime in the future when Tom is sleeping downstairs on the sofa. This cut makes it appear as if Tom is "being punished" for his staircase violence. What we see in *A History of Violence* is a far more complex exchange than sanitizing allows.

CleanFlicks separates the categories of "sex" and "violence"; its only recourse for managing sexual violence is to erase every trace of it. The scuffle between Tom and Edie on the staircase turns into mutual sex between strangers who are husband and wife, Edie and Tom-Joey. Contradictory emotions run through both characters. The energy of violence and sex is paired in their lovemaking. Less playful than in "Teens," their actions are fueled by the turmoil that has afflicted them. They fuck hard. They fuck violently. Perhaps they try to momentarily fuck away the pain that they have suffered. Their actions are neither reconciliatory nor forgiving. Nonetheless the deep love between two people who have endured a series of traumatic events and their feelings and attraction for each other are presented in this flash of violence turned longing, desire, and passion. Afterwards, neither is comforted by their actions. Tom-Joey sleeps alone on the downstairs sofa (the shot we are left with in the CleanFlicks version) while Edie weeps in isolation in their bed, revealing the bruises on her back—a trace of the rough sex—that not long ago she sought. Here we see the human conditions of vulnerability, sadness, isolation, and anguish. We see consequences of a history of violence.

What continuity, to return to Gaines, would an audience produce for CleanFlicks' version of *A History of Violence*? The deep "cuts," as I have argued, radically alter and, we may even go as far as to say, distort, perchance destroy Cronenberg's work. This reading-with-a-purpose may indeed produce a "limp and tepid" film, as Gaines asserts of the intentional and instrumental actions of the censor. However, for a CleanFlicks subscriber, these words can be easily replaced with "safe" and "family," accepting CleanFlicks' assertion that its enabling of choice furthers freedoms for all spectators, including those for whom an MPAA rating is sufficient. Yet, accusatory cries of destruction on account of deep "cuts" do little to assist our analysis of censorial practices. For subscribers of CleanFlicks and ClearPlay (and we could easily include the V-chip and Internet filters here), this "gap" signifies security: in terms of sightless vision, a type of not seeing, not knowing what was there as an indication of control and protection. Viewers choose not to know: willful oblivion. In this instance, the censorial "gap" that "can't be seen" and the one that allows audiences "to produce their own continuity" for a technology like film sanitizing is a "gap" filled with religious and political ideology that endeavors to shape the world through its repairs to culture. And for Gaines, this equation indicates the function of film censorship as a power-knowledge relation that "actually bridges the screen-world divide and hopes that it can fix the text, and in fixing it, repair the world."[81] Control technologies work on culture and function as culture in their governing, to position their users as active agents for correcting the worlds that they inhabit (be they consumers, producers, or the intermingling of both categories). Repairing the world presents itself in this study as technologies for blocking, filtering, sanitizing, and cleaning.

In *A History of Violence*'s pivotal scene, two murderers attempt to hold up Stall's Diner. Acting out of fear for his own life and the lives of his employees, or from instinct, Tom viciously kills both men. The worldview of CleanFlicks is one where Joey is eradicated and only Tom remains. "It's about choice" for CleanFlicks when that choice is supported by its operations: when its operations leave one with no other choice other than the danger and insecurity that are professed to reside outside its worldview. While Tom is recovering in the hospital from his standoff with the gangsters at his house, Edie discusses the violent course of events with Tom, who asks her what she thinks that she's heard. Edie responds by saying, "not what I heard, what I saw." Edie's ability to confront Tom-Joey is based on her ability to *see* the events unfold: film sanitizers remove this ability for us to meticulously delimit our vision through their reedited worlds.

Just as the guard patrols the territory of the gated community, as discussed by Rose and noted in chapter 1 and this chapter, today's television screen monitored by a V-chip observes all who pass through its gates of decoded signals; parent control technology in the form of ClearPlay filters that interface with a DVD player that enables the machine to automatically skip or mute content based on the protocols inscribed by ClearPlay's film reviewers polices the space of the home through community standards enforced through technology and at a distance from a centralized community; Internet filters become additional home security systems that reinforce the new "front door" of the computer screen. Blockbuster Inc. polices how content makes it "inside" under the auspices of viewer control, while CleanFlicks directly controlled content through its reediting procedures before its services were ruled illegal. Control technologies frame their subject by filtering and screening that which must remain outside the securitized space of habitat. They enable an electronic neighborhood watch whereby television and computer screens become active agents in policing the domain of the family: digital morality machines interpret information through delimitation, the space of the home, the use of media technology, and the exercise of choice according to binaries of good/bad, safe/dangerous, clean/dirty.

Visibility resides in the very presence of a sanitized version: while we do not see what has been edited out or are left with content that has been intentionally obscured as evidenced by discontinuous "gaps," we unequivocally witness the fine-tooth workings of control. As argued previously in regard to blocking and filtering, sanitizing is the visibility produced through the likes of film sanitization and filtering DVD players. Its visibility resides in its process of enabling self-governing as a technological solution over prevailing policy for the regulation and administration of film in the domestic sphere. The "editing" produced by film sanitizers is a crosscut that pits the actions of consumers using media technology available on the market beyond the informational and regulatory actions of the MPAA as well as copyright law. Both CleanFlicks and ClearPlay "show" choice as control, "show" that viewers are in control, understood as the willful participation in the disciplining of freedom for the securitization of habitat.

We may well be on the verge of unremitting multiple versions of film content to satisfy singular belief systems. With the software and increased storage capacities of next-generation DVDs like HD-DVD and Blu-ray having debuted on the market in 2006, we may soon behold a single film, like *A History of Violence,* appearing in the cuts of Not Rated, NC-17, R, PG-13, and, perhaps, various other CleanFlicks-like versions all contained on one DVD and accessible in the same way that subtitles and extras are on a DVD's interface. Setting aside copyright and artists' rights, this fictional scenario certainly upholds the principles of choice in that all viewer values are represented and made equally accessible via a single disc containing multiple versions. However, it appears as a scenario at best. Choice as practiced through film sanitizing as well as Blockbuster Inc.'s "cleaning-up" of home video entertainment initiated in the late 1980s delimits the possibility of choice to include only those versions, or ratings in the case of Blockbuster, that preserve while further instituting family as a mandate for home entertainment. In simpler terms, the sanitized version with its orchestrated safety and protection would be tainted should it share the same digital space with NC-17 or R and maybe even PG-13, as it is "halfway to R."

5. Cleaning

All the guns have been digitally changed to walkie-talkies. And the word "TERRORIST" has been changed to "HIPPIE."

Announcer for E.T.: The Extraterrestrial *2002 from* South Park,
episode 609, "Free Hat"

I know a few ~~murderer drug dealers~~, in the hood

Wu-Tang Clan, "In the Hood" (clean version)

Fills

This chapter "fills" the censorial gap discussed in the previous chapter, on film sanitizing, by focusing on digital special effects employed as cleaning effects for purposes of content regulation and management. Having contended with control technology at the location of the viewer, end user, consumer as a "service" provided by film sanitizers, we will now cast an eye and ear toward "cleaning" practices emanating from the layer of production/postproduction for the consumption of film and music. Technologies for sanitizing generally rely on acts of removal—expressed through Blockbuster Inc.'s redesign of the video store, ClearPlay's filtering DVD player, and CleanFlicks' reedited DVDs. Cleaning operates through practices that "fill up" film and music with information to maintain their circulation on the market by governing "explicit" content. Unlike the reedit that relies solely on the removal of content deemed "explicit," digital special effects clean by masking, replacing, obscuring, and "painting over" content. Cleaning may be orchestrated to secure a film a particular film rating or to secure retail distribution and to comply with FCC regulations for radio and television broadcast of music. Overlaps between cleaning and sanitizing are bound to exist since both practices aim to repair media—to "fix the text," as Gaines ascribes to the censorial reading—for purposes of securitization and the continued maintenance of consumer choice. This is most apparent in the regulation of music because removal, the "dropping out" of lyrics considered "offensive" and "explicit," continues to be a standard approach in the production of clean versions. For example, the "graphic" life of working-class African Americans is erased since the conditions of growing up surrounded by violent crimes that result from economic impoverishment are deemed too "explicit"; this life is stricken in a blatant measure that wipes clean—through the type of removal we have seen with film sanitizing—most of the cited verse from Wu-Tang Clan's "In the Hood." Discontinuity in terms of the song's lyrical flow is apparent as sound effects mask certain raps. But this apparentness is a clear moment of continuity for a cleaning process that finds the words "murder drug dealer" intolerable.

As we will see, removal is only one option for cleaning music and film, as digital special effects enable greater flexibility and control over how content can be manipulated and modified. The censorial takes the form of a digitally composited image superimposed in a film to achieve a less burdensome rating, or a sound effect masking profanity in a clean version of popular music. Stanley Kubrick's *Eyes Wide Shut* and its utilization of virtual actors to revise the film's lengthy orgy scene for purposes of securing an R-rating is a paramount example. Film sanitizers have learned a great deal from Hollywood in that a digital corset is not far from virtual actors inserted into a film to intentionally mask scenes of simulated sex. *Eyes Wide Shut* exemplifies how cleaning moves beyond the reliance on the "cut" as its digitally composited images constitute an "effects sequence" likened to computer-generated Hollywood spectacles. The exhibitionist quality of an effects sequence celebrates and draws our attention to the artifice of technological production, whereas with *Eyes Wide Shut* its censorial practices are of a paradoxical logic: they exhibit and masquerade simultaneously. Seamlessness smoothes over the "gaps." Like a superimposed image, a sound effect has the ability to correct and smooth over offensive lyrics as heard in "clean versions" of music. RZA, of the Wu-Tang Clan, employs the "scratch" to substitute, or "scratch over," "explicit" content to assist in Sony's production of clean versions for its music catalog. Just as film sanitizing seeks to augment a repair in its practices of muting, skipping, and removal, cleaning expressed through digital effects repairs a film or song by managing what can be seen and heard.

Censorial practices manifest themselves in the twenty-first century as seamless effects as opposed to the violent "cut" of yesteryear. The celluloid "scar" is cosmetically corrected to go unnoticed, if not to look and sound convincing, or, at the very least, to be less obtrusive than a ban, bleep, and blackout. Due to digital editing and special effects in the service of control practices, the very look and sound of contemporary censorial actions exercised on and through a film and sound recording appear far removed from the "cut" that was a mainstay in film and music censorship through most of the twentieth century. These practices prompt us to readdress the question of "what the censor's cut does" within the context of digital effects to grasp how control functions as a cleaning effect. We may update Gaines's question to ask: what does the cleaned film or sound recording do and how do digital effects function as corrective and cleaning measures? In continuing to engage with Gaines—and this engagement will merge into John Corbett's work on evasive practices by artists to "get around" music censorship—it is increasingly apparent that our vocabularies for understanding film and music censorship are shifting from the habit of the "cut," a metaphor and action that encapsulates both damage and repair, to "cleaning" and "correction" where films and songs are completely inundated with digital information that effaces the "gaps" of repair that persist in film sanitizing. Both sections in this chapter, "Clean Visions" and "Clean Sounds," attend to the pervasive quality of digital effects that render the censorial *an explicit operation through its seamlessness.*

In the production of film and music, cleaning indicates a moral correction as its versioning replaces "offensive materials" to achieve a particular film rating or offer consumer choice and familial protection in the form of a clean-version CD, while it also refers to the processes that make the censorial a convincing transparent continuity as opposed to an obvious mark of regulation and discontinuity. Although we can compare prints to disclose deletions, as I did with *A History of Violence* and CleanFlicks' docile version, the censor's "correction" works best when it goes unnoticed, when the censorial action is embedded well within the film not as an action at all but simply as a part of the film—when it appears seamless to the eye and ear. When censorial actions become a convincing effect of the virtuosity of filmic and music production, emphasis shifts from encountering "gaps" to an analysis of "fills": the proliferation and perfection of what can be seen and heard.

Clean Visions

When conceiving of the "cut" exercised on and through the medium of film, a dominant metaphor quickly materializes: a pair of scissors—glistening blades open and poised to injure.[1] It is a time-honored and medium-specific metaphor, an imago for how we imagine film censorship as an oppressive evil that rests neatly alongside the gag and the blindfold. In the study of film censorship, it is a potent icon. Murray Schumach's generalist study of film censorship *The Face on the Cutting Room Floor* (1964), Baxter Phillips's coffee-table titillation *Cut: The Unseen Cinema* (1975), and Tom Dewe Mathews's *Censored* (1994), a chronological study of film censorship in the United Kingdom, all promote this ominous visual metaphor as the instrument through which to imagine the censorial process. Schumach's cover shows scissors cutting through a celluloid strip, whereas Phillips's cover illustrates celluloid cascading from the blades of scissors. Scissors are absent from the cover of Laurent Bouzereau's film case study–based book *The Cutting Room Floor* (1994), yet we view the result of their action: strips of discarded celluloid overflow a trash can.[2] In Bouzereau's discussion of films by Robert Zemeckis, Alfred Hitchcock, Ridley Scott, Brian De Palma, James Cameron, and others, the trashed strips reflect not only a censor's cut but all of the "wounds, bruises, fatal cuts, and sometimes miracle remedies that can improve or destroy a film."[3] In these depictions, the ever-present pair of scissors suggests the censorial action as authoritarian and damaging, the all-too-visible evidence of film censorship. It also suggests the technique of editing as the technological means of inflicting this injurious "gap."

Representation of scissors as metaphor of authority and technique is played out well in Giuseppe Tornatore's film *Cinema Paradiso* (1989). Censorial "gaps" abound in the films exhibited within this narrative of a filmmaker's reflection upon his childhood encounters with film in his small village and the projectionist who sparked his passion. In the film, we observe the local "advisory board" in action: during a private screening of each new film, the village priest rings a little bell to indicate what specific celluloid moments must be removed for acceptable (i.e., ordained) public exhibition. When the films are screened, the audience recognizes incongruent frames (so many missed kisses) and linear distortions within its narrative and responds with boos, whistles, and hisses. Not only is the medium revealed to the audience in the cinema by this jarring discontinuity to narrative and cinematic immersion, so too are the censorial measures evidenced by the overt absence of frames—"gaps" utterly and violently visible in their incongruity. The immediacy of the censorial, as is expected at the Paradiso, is a painfully endured part of attending cinema in Tornatore's endearing film.

The authoritarian "cut" of film censorship, represented by scissors, has been perceived as indiscriminate, often clumsy when it comes to maintaining continuity: a slovenly enterprise marked by inconsistency and idiosyncratic effect in its concentration on the part and the moment. The "gap" produced by the censor's cut in Gaines's analysis is a visual and aural reservoir where meaning settles and control is manifest. It reveals presence in its absence. We only detect the repair, the seen footage spliced to conceal. It is less a palpable moment in a viewing experience than an embedded action that courses through the film from preproduction to exhibition. It is, as Gaines advises, construed as a "compulsory" violence in the form of repair, a certain sacrifice that is a certain "there" and "not there" at once. Scissors simultaneously repair the moral through damage to the physical. When films are reedited to fit neatly into a particular rating (produced with a particular rating as an objective for distribution and projected gross), as is commonly the case for distribution, the editing style most adhered to is continuity to maintain temporal and spatial logic while making the actual series of edits as coherent and imperceptible as possible in order to hide the presence of its arrangement. For instance, this could be a disruptive factor to the viability of the narrative world being projected onto the screen, or, in the case of policing film content, a moment of awareness for the audience that a particular scene or shot has been cut.

Although the unequivocal murmuring of both instances produces a rupture, censorial ruptures remind us that the image displayed before our eyes is a by-product of a complex that inscribes and defines standards, an institution that has the "last word" on what content can reach our eyes and ears; it is an awareness where we quietly whisper, "Hey, something's been cut. I wonder what and why?" In the physical cutting and splicing of celluloid strips, prior to nonlinear digital editing, the exact frames that contain the questionable footage are cut, then the remaining shots are spliced together to give the impression that the footage is continuous in its illusion of movement. The invisible "gap" is lost in this technique as the censorial reading and rewriting, as Gaines insists, tries to smooth over the elimination. Unlike the shocks and provocations of modernist montage, continuity editing endeavors to hide its presence in its faultless movements; it requires precision to minimize the unsightly appearance of seams.

While the metaphor of sharp blades is a powerful one, it is no longer an accurate signifier for cleaning practices exercised as digital optical effects. The emblematic pair of scissors owes its powers of signification to analog electronic media and the mechanized process of traditional film editing. Moreover, traditional film techniques once kept apart have joined forces to assist in production/postproduction, and this merger greatly affects the capabilities of control practices. It is helpful to cite Lev Manovich at length to explain this union:

> Previously, editing and special effects were strictly separate activities. An editor worked on ordering sequences of images together; any intervention within an image was handled by special-effects specialists. The computer collapses this distinction. The manipulation of individual images via a paint program or algorithmic image processing becomes as easy as arranging sequences of images in time. Both simply involve "cut and paste." As this basic computer command exemplifies, modification of digital images (or other digitized data) is not sensitive to distinctions of time and space or of different scale.[4]

Time and space are large contingencies in both analog and digital editing. Camera-centered filmmaking is dependent on progression; a strip of celluloid consists of individual advancing frames. Analog's cut, while inevitably affecting the spatial relations of a particular shot, scene, or sequence, performed an eradication of time (in material form) by removing specific frames that were part of a linear order. Manipulation was limited to the process of removal, physically excising "objectionable" *material.* An editor could "cut," this we know, but the ability to "paste" prior to digital editing software was known only in terms of a fine cohesive (glue splicers) used to join perforated strips together.

In contrast, digital image manipulation works through the techniques of processing and compositing. Processing (also known as sampling) involves the digitization and storage of non-converted imagery. Compositing, more relevant to our consideration of digital special effects as censorial practice, includes the superimposition, movement, rearrangement, removal, repairing, cleaning, and smoothing of images in order to foster a seamless, continuous, and believable image. Digital compositing, as Jay David Bolter and Richard Grusin note in relation to Hollywood productions, "has as its goal to smooth over the ruptures in the raw footage by removing stunt wires and other visible traces of special effects or unwanted artifacts."[5] Along similar lines, Andrew Darley writes that digital techniques "ensure the seamless combination of the disparate source images within the frame or shot."[6] To exemplify both accounts, let's consider the following well-worn example: the "absence" of stunt wires and harnesses that allowed *The Matrix*'s Trinity (Carrie-Anne Moss) not only to "get the jump" on her pursuers in the film's celebrated opening sequence but to create one of the most memorable as well as parodied moments in recent cinema (or was it already an homage to Ralph Macchio's signature crane-style move from 1984's *The Karate Kid*?) is a highly polished indicator of digital compositing's ability to erase from the final image traces of the required equipment for orchestrating the actual stunt.

The composite allows for greater control over what is placed in individual shots and entire scenes. Yet as Michele Pierson's *Special Effects: Still in Search of Wonder* cautions, espousal of the digital's "freeing" effect and its instrumentalization ought to also consider that "digital editing not only involves the automation of many activities that were formerly accomplished mechanically (e.g., the threading, syncing, marking, cutting, splicing, trimming, and gluing of film); it also involves interpreting and responding to images in an entirely different way."[7] Modification is easier, faster, and more precise: images can be combined, recombined, inserted, erased, painted, dragged, duplicated (indefinitely as is the case with the battlefield hordes of Peter Jackson's *The Lord of the Rings* saga and George Lucas's equally crowded intergalactic battles in the voluminous *Star Wars*), distorted, cleaned (digitally remastered, "improved" *Star Wars: Special Editions*), and, of course, cut. Seamlessness, the photorealism of digital effects, or as Sean Cubitt advances in *The Cinematic Effect,* "enhanced reality,"[8] can showcase and conjure convincing cinematic moments: a crowded dock for a jubilant maiden voyage in the *Titanic* (1997); the believability of dinosaurs roaming the earth in the present in *Jurassic Park* (1993) and *The Lost World* (1997); presidential acknowledgements from Lyndon Johnson and John F. Kennedy in *Forrest Gump* (1994); an intense training program with your very own robot in *Lara Croft: Tomb Raider* (2001), and the ability to punch a shark square in the kisser in *Lara Croft Tomb Raider: The Cradle of Life* (2003); the actuality of comic-book super-heroic deeds in *Fantastic Four* (2005), *Fantastic Four: Rise of the Silver Surfer* (2007), *Iron Man* (2008), *The Incredible Hulk* (2008), the *X-men* and *Spider-Man* trilogies, and the not-so-convincing but equally comic (first) *Hulk* (2003); a revised and revisioned special-effects classic, *King Kong* (2005); the graphic novel tones of *Sin City* (2005) and *300* (2007); a mother's search for her daughter in the video game cum eerie cinematic macabre world of *Silent Hill* (2006); and transforming robots, *Transformers* (2007).

Often the Hollywood digital special effects–driven blockbuster (as a type of film regardless of box office figures) builds to several climatic scenes where a computer-generated effects sequence predominates. Drawing on Tom Gunning's "cinema of attractions" thesis, where the relationship between astonishment and credibility for early cinema audiences was based on the "star,"[9] namely the exhibitionistic qualities of cinema that fostered the fascination of attraction, Angela Ndalianis furthers this idea with respect to special-effects cinema of the contemporary period.[10] Interested in the concern among film audiences and critics alike that special effects overshadow the traditional reliance placed on the supremacy of narrative by Hollywood conventions, Ndalianis articulates the emphasis placed on the visual over the literary as a defining feature of effects cinema: "Contemporary effects cinema is a cinema that establishes itself as a technological performance, and audiences recognize and revel in the effects technology and its cinematic potential. Rather than centering the action solely around a story, this is a cinema that emphasizes display, exhibitionism, performance, and spectacle."[11] Whether audiences do indeed "revel in the effects" (in, for example, *Wing Commander,* 1999; *Star Wars Episode 1: The Phantom Menace,* 1999; *Battlefield Earth,* 2000; *Star Wars Episode II: Attack of the Clones,* 2002; *The Matrix Reloaded,* 2003; *The Matrix Revolutions,* 2003; *Star Wars Episode III: Revenge of the Sith,* 2005; *V for Vendetta,* 2006; *Snakes on a Plane,* 2006; and *Speed Racer,* 2008) is very much open to debate. While the exhibitionistic elements pervade special effects–driven films, they may not necessarily dominate or displace narrative in the way that Ndalianis concludes.

An effects sequence works differently for Pierson, and this difference will help us better understand the cleaning of *Eyes Wide Shut*. Far from being visually gratuitous, the effects sequence is a moment of cine-aesthetic technological appreciation perchance awe, framed for the audience and led by the character's reactions, which "exhibit a mode of spectatorial address that—with its tableau-style framing, longer takes, and strategic intercutting between shots of the computer-generated object and reaction shots of characters—solicits an attentive and even contemplative viewing of the computer-generated image."[12] Here we are hailed to see, guided to look favorably on the digital optical effects on display. This is played out well in comic book–based films when an unsuspecting hero discovers his or her superpowers for the first time (Peter Parker becoming Spider-Man, for instance). We watch the film. We also witness a character's amazement. It is also demonstrated unashamedly when Neo expresses a "whoa" in astonishment at his power, perhaps capturing our sentiment at the very moment when we glimpse the Eadweard Muybridge–inspired "bullet-time" for the first time in *The Matrix*. The effects sequence that Pierson discusses is an emblematic gesture in spectacular cinema, for according to Scott Bukatman, it "redirect[s] the spectator to the visual (and auditory and kinaestethetic) conditions of cinema."[13] In the instance of Neo's self-astonishment or any narrative space for the display of special effects, digital compositing attempts to serve the shot, the character's performance and actions, and a film's narrative.

In another instance, digital compositing makes it easier to modify filmic information so that an MPAA rating can be attained without disruptions to the continuity and integrity of a film's narrative per the promise of seamless digital editing. In *Eyes Wide Shut*, digital compositing collapses the practices of editing with special effects so that in this case censorial actions come to participate in the promotion of believability and continuity through the seamless operations that the conjoined practices perfect. No "gaps" mark *Eyes Wide Shut* per Gaines's description of the censor's cut for the era of her study. Instead, the digitally composited virtual actors function to clean the sequence, seamlessly masking content by "filling" the sequence with digital information.

As mentioned previously, for *Eyes Wide Shut*, a film already obsessed with seeing, to secure an R rating, digitized figures, virtual actors (or synthespians), were superimposed amid the film's lengthy orgy scene.[14] Film scholar Jon Lewis is lightheartedly dismissive in his assessment of this censorial "repair." He writes, "it's a silly little change in a silly and long scene."[15] The main premise of Lewis's *Hollywood v. Hardcore* is that film censorship serves an economic function. Film censorship, rather than remaining fixated on the image with its "gaps," only "incidentally and superficially regards specific film content."[16] While Lewis does breathe a certain fresh air into the institutional study of U.S. film censorship, I am neither convinced that direct actions taken to police the image can be easily dismissed nor led to believe that these actions are somehow easily brushed aside. Images convey valuable content for understanding and processing the world that surrounds us; visual media are our dominant forms of mediation for that world and for how we inhabit it. I find it infeasible to ignore such a curious visual event as the one found in *Eyes Wide Shut,* one, it should be stressed, that we are well aware of, as its superimposed figures have passed the new litmus test for knowledge: Wikipedia's entry on *Eyes Wide Shut* includes a sub-section, "American Censorship Controversy." I agree with Lewis that a change has occurred, but this change is far from frivolous since it rearranges and redefines the practice and appearance of film censorship. The composited figures, both nude women and cloaked men, strategically obscure our visual access to scenes of simulated sex. No celluloid has been cut, as digital effects completely "fill up" this scene, thus reversing the long-standing censorial process of eradication and removal. Therefore, can we actually refer to this operation as one of "repair" in the same way that Gaines conceives of the censor's cut? No cut and splice exists. The "fills" in *Eyes Wide Shut* do not signify an absent presence but only presence: the presence of digital special effects in the service of cleaning.

This inclusion, as opposed to removal, pervades the entire sequence. It is not a "little change," as virtual actors obscure human ones throughout the entire sequence and not in one or two isolated shots but for the duration of a lengthy scene. Often the censor's cut is revealed as time deleted from a print when a comparison is possible, as in my discussion of *A History of Violence* and its CleanFlicks version, but no such temporal reduction occurs in *Eyes Wide Shut* since cleaning invests the spatiality of the scene's "inappropriate" content enabled by digital effects enacted on the image versus the actual removal of individual cells (the European version and the R-rated version have the identical running time for this scene). Digital information is apparent and inundates the entire sequence. As Dr. Bill Hartford (Tom Cruise) gingerly steps among the masqueraded guests, the viewer, too, is taken on this journey. We share his point of view. We watch Hartford desperately envy the evening's libertine festivities in his anonymous movements. His gaze guides ours as he moves through this unfamiliar space. We observe his act of looking, and at times our gazes converge. While watching the film, both character and audience share the view of not simulated sex, but digital information in the service of censorial effects. Both the character's and audience's visual access is denied in the R-rated version. The film's orgy scene professes to display the style of the effects sequence that Pierson outlines while also exhibiting the redirection of the spectator that Bukatman assigns as a definitive element in special effects–oriented cinema. This scene in *Eyes Wide Shut* may be an effects sequence in reverse, but it is an effects sequence nonetheless: instead of displaying "a new kind of effects artifact," "new" censorial effects are "displayed" to preempt the viewer's attention. The film's effects sequence is exhibitionary in its masquerading. It is the strange bedfellow of *The Abyss* and *Terminator 2*'s presentation of their "morphing moments" without celebration, and, in its absence, seamless control is showcased as visual effects. The censorial is itself part of the technology and marvel on display—meant, of course, to be seen, though not to be noticed. Or more specifically, the digital composite transforms censorial actions from a visibly invasive action on the body of film into a special effect: *from senseless acts of violence to seamless acts of visibility.*

Convincing digital composites elude our trained film eye. Despite being right in front of our eyes on the screen, we are accustomed to computer-generated images being a statement of display and visual hyperbole, not restraint and remission. In the language of film censorship, we are trained to seek out the "gaps," not to witness plentitude whereby the censorial inscription pervades the image— is the image—rather than a means of removing the image. We have entered into another way of seeing censorial actions not predicated upon the "gap," regardless of its invisibility or visibility. The censorial is the presence of digital information in the form of images, not the repaired vestiges of a cut. An effects sequence is, as Pierson insists, a "spectatorial address"; this point must not be forgotten, in order to understand how audiences "see" the censorial special effect. The address that Pierson argues for requires attentive viewing as the effects sequence illuminates the screen and our gaze is directed to its awesome presence. Dr. Hartford's saunter demonstrates an address as well, perhaps not as magnificent as our first encounter with *The Matrix*'s bullet-time or the liquid cool of the T-1000 in *Terminator 2*, but an address all the same. The superimposed CGI bodies in *Eyes Wide Shut* are not there to obscure his act of seeing but the audience's (recall they did not appear during filming and were inserted during postproduction—the actor Tom Cruise did not gaze upon virtual actors). Hartford's line of sight directly bounces off the bodies performing various sexual acts while ours catches on the backs of anonymous virtual figures that usurp the role of active spectator from the viewing audience. They subsume the act of looking for us because we do not possess the ability and authority to see. *Eyes Wide Shut* literally edits seeing.

Like the other control technologies discussed throughout this book, digital information in the form of a figure that masks illustrates new techniques of governance. While we do not possess the ability to actively choose how this occurs, we are presented with choice in the form of access because digital compositing allows *Eyes Wide Shut* to circulate freely while the NC-17 would severely restrict distribution. Digital special effects perform a surrogate seeing, in this instance, one that displays our inability to see through a spectacle designed to be seen. On display is our inability to see. The digital effects in *Eyes Wide Shut* are, once again, an augmentation of looking, an informational rather than optical seeing, but their presence as control technology enables them to display what we cannot otherwise see with our eyes, no matter how wide open or shut.

Likened to my brief discussion of blocking and filtering technology's screenic interpellation, Althusser's "Hey you there!" morphs once again at the electronic hand of digital media technology. Nicholas Mirzoeff incorporates Jacques Rancière's revision of Althusser's proviso into his work on the U.S. invasion of Iraq and visual culture.[17] For Rancière, the everyday police officer now commands: "Move along, there's nothing to see."[18] Mirzoeff qualifies this hail not just in terms of its false assumptions but to clarify its meaning: "while there is something to see, you have no authority or need to look at it."[19] This hail is not dependent on the actual presence of a police officer instructing us to "move along" since control technologies "governing at a distance" license the decision through the expertise of the parental function. Blocking, filtering, sanitizing, and cleaning perform a similar collective hail when their governing practices delimit what can be seen and heard as both are redirected elsewhere.

Eyes Wide Shut not only asks, it propels us to move along. It ushers our eyes. Yet, this "nothing" takes the form of mise-en-scène. Our looking is acquired by synthespians that show us that we do not need to look because, in shielding us, they perform this task in our stead. Within an effects sequence, Dr. Hartman's stroll shows us that there is nothing to see, that we cannot see and ought really to move along. The strategic placement of digital information is an accommodating measure that cannot be regarded as a censorial cut since this does not occur in the manner commonly achieved. Instead, the scene is "filled up" with censorial actions that police content by their required presence. Bukatman insists that special effects "redirect the spectator to the visual."[20] This redirection in *Eyes Wide Shut* reconfigures the "gap" into the "fill"; the audience is not asked to "produce their own continuity," as in Gaines's analysis of early cinema, but is left to observe how continuity is maintained irrespective of their efforts. "Move along, there's nothing to see," in *Eyes Wide Shut* becomes "move along, you can't see."

Digital special effects need not be so grand as effects sequences generally appear to be. A discussion of "invisible effects," as less pronounced special effects are often referred to, will help us understand "fills" that attempt to "improve" and "correct" filmic content beyond the overt censorial practices employed in *Eyes Wide Shut*. The capabilities of digital special effects can stretch from the climactic to the banal, as Cubitt explains: "effects are now routinely used to brighten or darken skies, correct period detail in location shoots *(Devil in a Blue Dress)*, turn small groups of extras into swarming crowds (as in the concert scenes in *That Thing You Do*) or to airbrush in or out wanted or unwanted details in the cinematographic image."[21] This raises the question of visible versus invisible special effects. Noted earlier in my discussion of digital compositing, invisible special effects can erase the presence of the required equipment needed to choreograph and realize an impossible action like Trinity's initial fight scene in *The Matrix*. Such effects efface the "reality" of production by erasing the cumbersome equipment that would spoil the realism of impossibility made possible. Invisible special effects, like continuity editing, attempt to smooth out, clean up, and make cinematically believable everything that appears in the shot. These digital applications are meant to go unnoticed, unlike an effects sequence centered on the very visibility of special effects.

Warren Buckland's work on contemporary Hollywood film and digital technology contends that invisible special effects "constitute up to ninety percent of the work of the special effects industry, simulate events in the actual world that are too expensive or inconvenient to produce, such as the waves in James Cameron's *Titanic* (1997)."[22] And we could add that this cost-effective procedure, the sheer ease of adjusting, erasing, cleaning, correcting by way of digital technology and techniques, allows a film like *Eyes Wide Shut* to avoid completely cutting its long orgy sequence (in a film sanitizer's manner of removal) as well as saving the production team the expense of reshooting the scene in order to obtain an R rating. Digital effects in the union Manovich assigns to editing and special effects enable more control over the image in postproduction than previously possible. Control can be a measure of aesthetics and realism, reediting to ensure a distributable MPAA rating, or the intermingling of both. Digital technology can assist in a director's vision of, say, the sinking of a great sea vessel (*Titanic; Poseidon*, 2006; *The Perfect Storm*, 2000), a volcano erupting in Los Angeles (*Volcano*, 1997), tornados reeking havoc across the Plains states (*Twister*, 1996), an asteroid on a collision course with Earth (*Armageddon*, 1998), or the restaging of the bombing of Pearl Harbor as a digitally enhanced action spectacle staring beefy Ben Affleck. It also assists in making repairs and corrections for MPAA submission, a different sort of labor since nothing has to be fully excised (always a concern for directorial vision and narrative continuity) or reshot (threatening the budget) but only repaired as quickly and quietly as a mouse (click).

Manovich offers us another way of conceiving of filmmaking that incorporates digital processes into its production as well as situating actions of "improvement" and "correction" into our larger engagement with censorial practices. This involves less an adjoining circumstance than a type of transference: "cinema becomes a particular branch of painting—painting in time. No longer a kino-eye, but a kino-brush."[23] Whereas for most of its existence cinema was practiced as a recording process and medium, the kino-brush, a metaphor for digital painting programs that construct and animate images in real time, marks the return to older forms of visual production as digital practices become common to filmmaking. We could assert that censorial actions, too, adopt this technique as simulated sex was "painted over" and "touched up" by digital composites in *Eyes Wide Shut*. It appears that we are witnessing a shift from the censor's scissors to the compositer's brush as the new emblem of control, one that is softer, expressive, has the potential to blend and does not have to rely solely on the myopic cut as a direct action carried out on the material body of the film. The reel comprised of the censored films' stolen kisses left behind by the deceased projectionist for his young friend in *Cinema Paradiso* loses all of its charm when it takes up space on one's hard drive.

While Manovich's claim can take us in many directions—the implosion of film and animation, the subordination of other visual technologies to the camera lens, or definitions of digital cinema—I would like to turn back briefly to Walter Benjamin's essay "The Work of Art in the Age of Mechanical Reproduction," where he compares the relationship of painting and film to reality.[24] In this short discussion, he proposes that the camera operator manipulates reality as intimately as the surgeon handles the organs of the person on whom the surgeon operates. For Benjamin then, the surgeon's technique is credited as more significant than that of the painter, whose work does not broach the natural distance between the surgeon and the body resting on the operating table. The painter's effect on the reality that he or she represents is thus compared to the magician's approach to healing. Specifically, Benjamin argues that whereas the magician can only heal by touching the surface, "by the laying on of hands," the surgeon "cuts into the patient's body," and this greatly reduces the distance maintained by the magician.

In the age of digital reproduction, we might be inclined to suggest that Benjamin underestimated the power of the magician and by extension the power of the painter—especially the painter who wields a kino-brush as described by Manovich. With a kino-brush touching the surface in the service of censorial practices and processes, digital compositing effects a far more intimate relationship to what is presented than the cut. It remains a reading-with-a-purpose, as Gaines suggests, yet its "fills" are far from unsightly. They are for all to see. The analog cut can only be practiced on the body lying in its operating theater: strips of celluloid frames. The censor's scissors, like the surgeon's scalpel, can only perform an invasive procedure of eradication on the materiality of the body. Such cuts always bespeak a form of destruction, for no matter how precise a scalpel's incision, surrounding tissue is always damaged and requires some form of mending. Unlike digital compositing, which is capable of acting on and in the body of "film" indiscriminately without leaving evidence, analog censorship's dependence on the cut always leaves scars—minute traces of its presence and gracelessness.

How does the kino-brush clean? I would like to further our address of the invisibility of digital compositing by considering additional examples of cleaned images that demonstrate digital practices in improving and correcting film that do not function in the same ways that masking occurs in *Eyes Wide Shut*. Accompanying Disney-Pixar's *Finding Nemo* (2003) is an older Pixar short titled *KnickKnack,* which features an animated character that Pixar's Web site describes as "a disproportionate blonde from Miami." The character is described as disproportionate because of her large breasts and incredibly thin waist. It nearly goes without saying that such a disproportion expressed on the female body is nothing new to animation: it has become a standard for female characters in popular media ranging from comic books to video games. Pixar's exaggerated character, perched in a bikini on a "Sunny Miami" ashtray and appearing as a mermaid on a "Sunny Atlantis" rock, underwent what has been referred to as a "digital boob reduction," by way of digital brush rather than scalpel. While the waist remains the same, the chest has been subjected to computer-generated mammoplasty to satisfy the age restrictions associated with the G-rating.[25] This version has seemingly replaced the original Pixar image. Sander L. Gilman's *Making the Body Beautiful: A Cultural History of Aesthetic Surgery* draws several important historical distinctions between "aesthetic surgery" and "reconstructive surgery."[26] The latter's function is restoration—to restore and repair the body—while the previous term embodies a host of procedures designed to "alter the surface and shape of the body." Aided by digital compositing and like the correction effected on Michael Jackson's skin for primetime broadcast, with which we began our study, the body of the anonymous blond was not removed from the scene in order to reconstruct it, as Gilman's surgical distinction declares, but underwent an aesthetic procedure of the particular to correct her appearance cosmetically, thus rendering it "better" suited for a select "general" audience. Like special effects and editing, practices and technological camps once kept separate, censorial actions and film aesthetics have joined forces to assist in the production of both.

In framing the actions produced in *Eyes Wide Shut* as censorial, we must also attend to a barrage of cleaning practices that have become common in the early twenty-first century. Here actions associated with the censorial remain in a complex that corrects, improves, and cleans rather than being an overt censorial cut. I am referring to the phenomenon of director's reediting their films to "improve" them with digital effects and the erasure of the twin towers in films post-September 11, 2001. Like cosmetic enhancement, digital compositing can also constitute an "improvement" or "upgrade," as expressed in Steven Spielberg's rerelease of *E.T.* The physical presence of violence in the form of federal agents wielding handguns is "replaced" with walkie-talkies to express a kinder, gentler home-grown aggression in the wake of 9/11. My epigraph from a *South Park* episode satirizing this practice is less comedy than political commentary. Spielberg's decision to exchange the word "terrorist" for "hippie" is not a Parker-Stone gag, although the rerelease of *E.T.* now reads like a *South Park* script. In the reedited version of *E.T.*, Spielberg's matriarch, Mary (Dee Wallace-Stone), disapproves of her older son's Halloween costume, warning that he looks like a "hippie," whereas in the previous release from 1982 he is said to resemble a "terrorist."[27]

Scott McQuire engages with how the idea of control is expressed through digital practices and procedures for film "repair" and "restoration." He claims that "the massive returns generated by the 'digitally enhanced' *Star Wars* trilogy raises the prospect of a future in which blockbuster movies are not re-made with new casts, but perpetually updated with new generations of special effects."[28] This is the difference between what Spielberg has done in his millennial makeover of *E.T.* and, say, Wolfgang Petersen's remake of *The Poseidon Adventure* (1972) in the form of *Poseidon* (2006). Spielberg upgrades his original version by inserting computer-generated effects of the alien that he was unable to create at the time of the film's original release in 1982. Of course, this also includes a form of replacement: walkie-talkies for guns, hippie for terrorist. In the 1982 release, as Mike Ward discusses in his review of the 2002 rerelease, Spielberg has depicted federal agents not as beneficent governmental agents, as in the climax of *Close Encounters of the Third Kind* (1977), but as interfering and potentially destructive to the alien life-form. Mostly framed through low camera angles, Spielberg indicates their aggressive presence "not by searching gazes but by flashlights and key rings. In the movie's visual language, this sort of shot indicates that someone is up to no good."[29] Yet, the presence of a digitally superimposed walkie-talkie in place of a federal agent's standard-issue weapon in another shot suggests a cause for further concern. Federal violence is easily covered up by this brushstroke. Nothing is invisible in this instance, because an "original" version exists. Whereas the original pre–boob job *KnickKnack* has virtually vanished, the 1982 version of *E.T.* still resonates clearly in many people's cultural memory. The cleaning conducted on shots of federal agents in 2002 is less for reasons of digital enhancement than to remove hints of state violence, though one cannot help but witness acts of aggression in news reports on U.S. activities in Afghanistan and Iraq. The new version of *E.T.* is the one and only gun-free zone in the United States, or so it *appears*.

I do not think that we can consider this replacement as an effects sequence in the way that we have for *Eyes Wide Shut*. Shots and shot-reverse-shots do not prepare us, draw our vision, and provide an instructional response on our behalf. The walkie-talkies are simply there. They fulfill the function of invisible effects that Cubitt and Buckland discussed previously. They are meant to go unnoticed, but this is impossible (at least for the moment until our collective cultural memory forgets). They are, as Buckland advises, "visible special effects masquerading as invisible."[30] The walkie-talkies are visible in that we see them and may notice that a modification to the original *E.T.* has occurred, while they are invisible as a seamless digital composite that can easily and convincingly replace a gun for something nonlethal. I consider it a real stretch to regard this change as film censorship in the way that the "fills" to *Eyes Wide Shut* became necessary to avoid the market-based censorial policies that would have followed an NC-17 rating. However, this little action is not outside the purview of control as discussed throughout this book. A production team is enabled through new digital technologies, instrumentalizes choice as an act of replacement, and, like film sanitizing, exercises this choice as an example of control to improve (and possibly protect?).

The federal agents, who now have walkie-talkies "locked and loaded" and "at the ready," digitally perform the interpellative "Move along, there's nothing to see" when their presence comes to embody the authority to show us what we ought to see by virtue of their visibility. Likewise this showing is not limited to replacement;

it is also evident in erasure as a corrective. After 9/11, film release dates were pushed back, scripts were scrapped, scenes deleted, trailers pulled *(Spider-Man)*, and promotional materials bearing images of the twin towers altered *(Sidewalks of New York, 2001)*. Shots of the World Trade Center in *Zoolander* (2001) and *Serendipity* (2001) were erased or obscured from view, and *Spider-Man* redesigned New York City's new skyline in last-minute postproduction. *Spider Man2: Enter Electro,* a video game where Spider-Man battles the final "boss" on top of the twin towers, was pulled, and the rereleased version sets the final battle on top of a bridge instead. The digital composite that inserts synthespians to facilitate an R rating for *Eyes Wide Shut,* the aesthetic "surgery" that redesigned *KnickKnack*'s voluptuous mermaid to a sporty A cup, Spielberg's replacement and erasure display in visible and invisible manners practices of control that far exceed film censorship's concentration on the cut to assemble other actions in the production of visual effects.

The censorial action that attempts to repair an offensive scene through "fills" is the same action that treats national memory as an offense when the kino-brush paints over the twin towers not as a requirement for a rating but as an exercise in national security, erasing signs of trauma and keeping images of violence under wraps. Controlling hearts and minds, the cry of the despot extends to eyes, as ours are repeatedly instructed (by visual media) to look on, look beyond, because "this is what you should see." Digital effects, as Manovich claims in his other writings on digital cinema, may be incorporated to enhance filmic environments and the banality of the realism in spectacular cinema, yet they "aim to show us something extraordinary; something we have never seen before."[31] In films where the twin towers have been erased or even composited in, as in *Gangs of New York* (2002), this digital effect shows an edifice we can no longer see. Although Benjamin's magician has a relatively small impact on the materiality of the body that he heals through the laying on of hands, the action may effect a major change in the condition of the magician's subject for it speaks to the subject's belief in the magician's practice, expertise, and authority, the source of power. The very authority (and we could say, expertise) that purports to heal a damaged body, be it an "obscene" film or a nation, is always the source of the power that the magician expresses. The authority of the digital composite resides in convincing audiences that it is not there, that any "gaps" are "filled" with new technological abilities that render the scissors obsolete and violent while the brush smoothes away and cleans purportedly questionable images.

Clean Sounds

From the eye to the ear: move along, there's nothing to hear, as cleaning affects music content in ways aligned with film but also continuous with sanitizing's reliance on removal in the construction of clean versions. Not since the mid-1980s with UTFO's "Roxanne, Roxanne" and the response record by The Real Roxanne aka Adelaida Martinez has a lyrical battle ensued with such magnitude as 2003–04's Eamon's "Fuck It (I Don't Want You Back)" and Frankee's rebuttal rap aptly titled, "F. U. Right Back." Adopting the role of the begrudged ex-girlfriend, Frankee's verbatim answer to Eamon appears below:

> "Fuck It (I Don't Want You Back)"
> Fuck what I said / It don't mean shit now
> Fuck the presents / Might as well throw em out
> Fuck all those kisses / They didn't mean jack
> Fuck you, you hoe / I don't want you back
> "F. U. Right Back"
> Fuck what I did / Was your fault somehow
> Fuck the presents / I threw all that shit out
> Fuck all the cryin' / It didn't mean jack
> Well, guess what, Yo!/ Fuck you right back

In the now standard clean version of Eamon's song the audibility of the word/sign *fuck* is partially expunged on account of its complete pronunciation being truncated. The anaphoric of the word *fuck* is implied only by the sound of its first syllable "ef" (much like the absent "uck" in "F-you" implies "fuck you," and not the letter *F*). Bearing no connotations of a sexual act in Eamon's chorus, the word *fuck* is cleaned regardless of the context within which it is uttered. *Shit* becomes the audible sound "shh." Despite this aposiopetic reaction, we could say that the connotation of *shit* remains, suggested by the frequently heard "shh" sound, while full utterance of each letter to form the word *shit* is prohibited in a reedited version for radio play and family-values mass merchant distribution. The total word may be prohibited in a clean version while its partial utterance implies its presence and possible meanings. In fact, cleaning may even intensify the presence of profanity as a result of the measures employed to mark its absence. *F-you* masks little (only correct spelling), yet it seems to satisfy the ambiguous criteria for what constitutes a clean version. In addition, a sample of a female moan replaces *ho*, and this sound returns to mask Eamon's lyrics again in the form of "Ya played me, ya even gave him head." The reference to a blow job is masked by an identical female moan. The same aural signifier of female pleasure is employed to mask the derogatory *ho* as well as imply the pleasures of oral sex. The logic of this edit suggests that simulated sounds of sexual pleasure are acceptable as a mark of cleanliness, while semantics are ruled dirty. Sound is less suggestive than the denotative quality of words?

Unlike Eamon's song, the clean version of "F. U. Right Back" does not substitute sound effects; instead, it conspicuously drops out all profanity: "Well guess what yo, —— right back." As in the children's book game *Mad Libs,* listeners are left to fill in the blanks for themselves, left to contemplate the presence of speech in its absence. Given the context of this particular song, contemplation ought not to be a laborious task. The words *fuck* and *shit* are dropped out twenty-three times total, such that the clean version is riddled with this corrective procedure, completely "filled up" with the presence of control in a more overt manner than the way that visual digital information inundates particular film scenes to fix and improve them for certification, directorial preference (or the supervision of national memory). Marked as "clean," labeled "clean version," all other versions, ones that we might have simply referred to by their "pre-reedited" title instead of, say, "F. U. Right Back (dirty)" or "F**k It (dirty)," are deemed "explicit" and automatically made "dirty" by this new counterpart: a song's state of being, that is, *not being clean,* let alone its actual content, becomes the dangerous abnormality that only the clean version can correct in its promises to protect. Clean versions make all other versions dirty. They are more formative than they are reactionary, oppositional, and repressive. The clean version requires the "explicit" one so that its normalizing operations are not judged an aggressive replacement or censorship but a practice in choice and consumer self-regulation. As with a cleaned DVD, consumers are given another version, a clean one, as an instrument of choice and a measure of security.

John Corbett's *Extended Play: Sounding Off from John Cage to*

Dr. Funkenstein is one of the few texts to address critically contemporary policing procedures for regulating popular music. Similar to Gaines's questioning of the censor's cut, Corbett's brief address questions the "cut" for music since its "gaps" are preemptively filled with provocative practices that occupy this rupture on an artist's own terms rather than succumbing to external ("limp," to stick with Gaines) censorial scars that, as is often the case in music, are utterly absurd. In policing content in the form of what we now regard as a clean-version CD (and this extends to radio versions and MP3 downloads), he cites procedures like bleeping out words, deletion, substitution, and backwards masking. Bleeping out words, to consider only one practice for the moment, is a long-standing practice to reedit versions, and until digitally edited clean versions became routine, constituted one of the most applicable manual methods of managing the content of lyrics before (as well as during) mass dissemination across the airwaves. "At one time this was done at the radio station," Corbett explains, "with time delay being the narrow margin-of-error window through which censors had to work their magic."[32] After Janet Jackson's 2004 Super Bowl half-time exposure, enhanced time delay brings to mind not the censoring of songs on radio but its utilization on "live" television events like the Oscars to smite potentially "offensive" speech by politically conscious upstart actors speaking out against the U.S. invasion of Iraq.[33] Rapper Kanye West's off-script criticism of the mismanagement of Hurricane Katrina aid, stating, "George Bush doesn't care about black people," went out live to the East Coast and Midwest, but his statement was censored when rebroadcast on the West Coast.[34] Pointing Judith Butler's analysis of hate speech from *Excitable Speech* in a different direction,[35] we could say that these utterances are "injurious speech" to a regime whose use of freedom as marketing strategy does not include U.S. citizens broadcasting their voices in opposition. Opposition to the U.S. invasion of Iraq and this administration's utter failure to address domestic poverty are treated like a mild annoyance such that U.S. audiences come to despise politically active celebrities for disrupting their "entertainment"—be it the Oscars, Grammy Awards, or a Dixie Chicks concert.

A number of diverse measures, systematic and nonsystematic, emanating from official, state, local, industry, and market-based processes, attempt to regulate music content and performance. Before returning to Corbett's argument in relation to the state of clean versions since the publication of his text, I want to provide a gloss of the different practices and processes that have governed, and in some cases continue to govern, the distribution, content, production, and consumption of music. The most steadfast general measure is banning and forbidding access to music and its performance. This, of course, has taken many forms over time.[36] In the midcentury United States the electronic delivery technology of the jukebox, for example, was highly regulated. Legislation was passed to delimit its hours of operations. The storage medium of vinyl has been subject to police seizure and set ablaze by religious zealots (the burning of Beatles albums by church groups and radio stations in 1966 on account of John Lennon's claim that they were "more popular than Jesus" is one well-known example; another is the burning of Dixie Chicks CDs by pro-war Louisiana country-western radio station KRMD-FM following mild comments singer Natalie Maines made while performing in London; she confessed, "we're ashamed that the president of the United States is from Texas"). Certain acts and performers are banned from performing in select cities (be it black and white artists performing together in the 1950s, concerts being called off or raided for alleged obscenity, permit denials for reasons of "public safety," or artists like Marilyn Manson being barred from performing in certain cities). Last but not least is the banning of specific songs and music videos and their artists from radio and MTV rotation for far too many reasons to list (after the attacks on the World Trade Center, Clear Channel issued a list of potentially "offensive songs" to its affiliates that included peaceful pleas in the form of John Lennon's "Imagine" and "Peace Train" by Yusuf Islam, formerly Cat Stevens; neither contains references to explosions, death, or air disasters). The FCC remains diligent in its threats to revoke licenses should "obscene" songs receive airplay.

Visual representations of music are not exempt. The wearing of rap, goth, punk, and rock T-shirts is regularly banned from schools in the United States, while album cover artwork is altered for retail distribution. The latter is a visual clean version. In the United States, alternative cover art has long been implemented as a replacement for "offensive" work. For example, the original cover of Jimi Hendrix's *Electric Ladyland* displayed twenty nude women, one of which holds a picture of Hendrix; the U.S. release offers a photo of the artist performing live. A standard photograph of the band replaces the image of a presumably young nude girl on Blind Faith's self-titled album of

1969, while sales of John Lennon and Yoko Ono's *Unfinished Music No. 1—Two Virgins* (1968) that originally contained front and back images of the couple nude was sold in the United States in a blanketing wrapper. The blocking of direct visual access to album cover art continued in 1993 when Chumbawamba's *Anarchy,* which features a close-up of childbirth, was sold in a plain sleeve in the United States. Rather than replace cover art or hide it behind a plain sleeve, an album cover, like the lyrics etched in vinyl or encoded on a digital disc, accords with the politics and practices of clean versioning. For retail distribution at Wal-Mart, the naked male infant swimming on the cover of Nirvana's *Nevermind* (1991) was castrated to produce a clean cover art version. In the original cover art and those sold outside of Wal-Mart and now online, the infant's penis is spared. Like the digital corset superimposed on Kate Winslet's breasts by MovieMask film sanitizers, a similar censorial accessory is imposed on White Zombie's *Supersexy Swingin' Sounds* (1996). The original cover and interior art for the CD contains photos of four nude girls whose nudity is never fully visible (intentionally obstructed by other body parts). The clean version superimposes bikinis on each image. Both are readily available. Nothing is banned. Instead competing versions circulate freely within their restricted domains.

Cleaned art and graphics are not restricted to the materiality of protective card stock. Apple's iTunes displays cleaning elements on its download interface. The "Parental Advisory: Explicit Content" sticker agreed upon by the National Parent Teacher Association (NPTA), the Parents' Music Resource Center (PMRC), and the Recording Industry Association of America (RIAA) in 1985, but not launched until 1990, is now an online icon inscribing releases on iTunes, as does a similar-looking "Clean Lyrics" icon. Accompanying the name of each downloadable track, the word "CLEAN" appears to indicate a clean version while "EXPLICIT" appears in red to signal . . . what exactly? Neither icon is displayed next to the 2006 releases The Flaming Lips' *At War with the Mystics* and Morrissey's *Ringleader of the Tormentors,* whereas The Sounds' *Dying to Say This to You* brandishes the "Parental Advisory" icon next to the "buy album" button. The Vines' *Vision Valley* and Bubba Sparxxx's *The Charm* immediately don a "Clean Lyrics" icon. "Clean Lyrics" does not seem to apply to an album that contains no profanity or sexually suggestive lyrics (the Flaming Lips rely on allegory and humorous spacey babble) but to one that *has been cleaned.* I will return to this point below. But first I would like to point out that the iTunes interface also deletes profanity (this includes "nigga") in titles of songs and in album titles. It controls the textual graphics that, for many, are today the only visual document of a music object as MP3 files replace the tangibility of a vinyl record and the plastic and aluminum of a CD. However, the visual production qua evidence of control through censorial practice remains when individual letters that construct swear words are replaced by asterisks that signify the absence as well as presence of profanity. One example will suffice: as is well known, Atlantic Records changed the Rolling Stone's song title "Starfucker" to "Star Star" on the band's *Goat's Head Soup* (1973). "Star fucker" remains in the chorus (no "explicit" warning appears next to the song on iTunes). Peaches' second album, *FatherFucker* (2003) appears on iTunes in the following manner: "F*********r." Oddly, even the word *father* is replaced (whereas the Dwarves' "Motherfukker" remains in iTunes' track listing in intentionally misspelled form). Each track title of *FatherFucker* contains Apple's "EXPLICIT" red-lettered warning. (Color theory isn't required here.)

The "Parental Warning: Explicit Lyrics" sticker (and online icon) has become synonymous with the meaning of *explicit* understood as depictions of nudity and sexuality rather than the word's other definitions: to be unambiguous in expression, clearly expressed, plain, and distinctly stated. The explicit is equated with the obscene (the RIAA states that the warning accounts for strong language, depictions of violence, sex, and substance abuse). This meaning is rather recent considering that in Latin *explicatus* means "clear," "regular," or "expounding," while the French *explicite* refers to "definite." Neither the Latin nor French definition makes any reference to nudity, sexuality, or obscenity. Explicit content could pertain to virtually any recording of music according to the word's more long-standing definitions. However, the "Parental Warning" sticker and its connotations of obscenity inscribe the music object by its dictatorial presence whether or not this was the original intention. The RIAA has repeatedly insisted that the label affixed by music companies ought not to be utilized to refuse sales to minors or to oust music from retailer stock. Like Blockbuster Inc. in its decision not to carry NC-17 rated films, shortly after the RIAA released its warning label, Wal-Mart, the United States' largest retailer, refused to carry CDs inscribed by the parental warning label on account of its "family values" marketing ideology.[37] Given the enormous market commanded by Wal-Mart, music companies responded by producing clean versions that would still be able to reach the retail giant's lucrative shelf space, as it does not ban these versions from its stores or Internet commerce.

Yes, as in Jon Lewis's argument about film censorship's economic imperative, clean versions anticipate access to valuable mass markets and attempt to provide high revenues even if, as Hilary Rosen, former RIAA president, claims, "unedited versions of titles outsell their clean counterparts by a 10-to-1 ratio."[38] And this is the case even though certain retailers like Wal-Mart rebuff parental warning versions (a huge area in popular music). Stickering, as a preventative and enabling practice, alters the surface of music reception. Either affixed to a CD's wrapper or printed directly on an album's cover, the "Parental Warning" standardizes the music object as dangerous for the implied supervisory audience and policing function, the parental. An "explicit" element in an album's cover art, the sticker is now part of the experience of music, part of how we visualize sound and lyrics as content marked obscene. Displayed on the cover, a part of the actual design and image of the music, the sticker is an enactment of power: its presence inscribes the surface of music as simultaneously unsafe and made safe; the sticker is an assurance that protective measures are at work to identify a possible threat and place risk in the enabled sphere of self-governance. Persistent visibility builds control in as a regular application in the consumption of music: like the invisible "cut" or seamless "fill," it is already there. Unlike the "cut," it requires direct visibility in order to be effective as a deterrent; informational address, and interpellation, the distinct graphic warning resounds loudly. Its surface resonates protection, security, and freedom of choice. Its smooth texture marks an acceptance of regulation as a necessary measure for more efficient control that is less burdensome and more productive than an all-encompassing ban. The "Parental Warning" may only be a little sticker, yet it marks music objects as sufficiently dangerous to elicit regulation and management. Today the sticker is normalized as part of music consumption (a "mark of authenticity," for Corbett, that proudly evidences a music object's street credibility to listeners), while its counterpart, the clean version, circulates more freely as a correction, a solution, to the need for any warning whatsoever. Again, expertise of the self is enacted when music producers are employed as "voluntary" self-regulators and consumers are called on to choose between versions, purchase a reedited version already made safe or take the unknown chance of explicitness. The fact that clean versions, despite their unpopularity among listeners, have become a mainstay in music production, a technological solution to complex issues of cultural and social meanings, power knowledge relations, and an economic measure to maintain product circulation (be it retail or airplay), further intensifies regulatory practices by making that which has not been cleaned, that is, reedited for broader commercial networks, "dirty."

Where the sticker has become a normalized signifier of security, we are prompted to ask, what is the current status of clean versions? Have they too become a normative measure to police music content and enable securitization through choice? Corbett provides us with an answer to this question, although, as we will see, it exists on an altogether different register than he originally imagined. In his incredibly brief chapter titled, "Bleep This, Motherf*!#er: The Semiotics of Profanity in Popular Music," Corbett inventories strategies like bleeping and deletion as examples of artistic and innovative measures employed for "getting around censorship, be it legislatively explicit or economically controlled."[39] As evidence of these procedures in hip-hop of the early 1990s, he cites KRS-1's live performances where he raps swear words backwards and radio edits for NWA's "Straight Outta Compton" as examples of backwards masking, House of Pain's radio edit for "Get Out Your Shit Kickers" in which the now standard "shhhh" masks the word "shit," and the replacement of the word *fuck* by *forget* in Tim Dog's "Fuck Compton," also reedited for radio play. Novel to the ear at that time, these sounds forge an intelligibility that both materializes the presence of censorial applications in the policing of popular music while demonstrating sonic maneuvers to eclipse the suppression of a reedited song. Even with the early ascendance of the parental warning sticker, artists like Ice-T retooled their alert to reflect back upon those who demand such measures. On the cover of *Freedom of Speech . . . Just Watch What You Say* (1989), underneath a warning that cautions parents as to the suitability of this album for younger listeners, follows the caveat: "Some material may be X-tra hype and inappropriate for squares and suckers."[40] For Corbett, these examples and others demonstrate self-imposed, perchance self-styled, proactive evasive strategies for responding to market pressures over "obscene" content and family-values merchants like Wal-Mart and Kmart that pose a detriment to the distribution of music. Ulterior signifying practices that reverse words, intentionally misspell (or respell) words, and vary pronunciation all attempt to carry connotations of expletive lyrics beyond the PMRC's (then much more vocal before the RIAA accommodated its concerns) and other pressure groups' concentration on literality in popular music while trying to preempt censorial measures on their own terms.

What Corbett would regard as self-stylin' strategies persist, although they frequently appear more in the service of censorial practices as opposed to a marked evasion. The "clean" and "dirty" versions of Missy Elliott's "Work It" from *Under Construction* (2002) includes the lyrics: "ya gotta big (elephant sound) let me search ya / find out how hard I gotta work ya." The sound of an elephant roar replaces what we might suspect to be *penis*. *Bitch, ass,* and *fucking* are dropped out, while Elliott employs phrases like "ratatatatatatatatata," the Betty Boopesque, "BUBOOMP BUBOOMP BOOMP," and "VOOMH" (the same in both non- and reedited versions) to comment on body movement and gestures used within the context of sexual liaisons. Perhaps Elliott's choice of performative onomatopoeia over the literally explicit in Eamon's pissed-off tale of loss further evidences Corbett's reading of "a new generation of obscenity, a provisionally stabilized code of masked obscenity."[41] Here we witness how *bitch* morphs into *biotch*, the aged slang *weed* becomes "izzle"—fo' shizzle, as Snoop Dog and his multitude of middle-class wannabes might chime in. Yet, cleaning procedures are quick to catch on to neologistic connotations while broadening definitions of what is considered offensive. For example, CleanFlicks even sanitized the now embarrassingly uncool *skank* from its version of *A History of Violence*. Procedures employed on "Work It" are not necessarily representative of the majority of clean versions in the period of Elliott's release. Da Brat's 2003 song "Boom" from her album *Limelite, Luv & Niteclubz*, relies upon replacement, where her track "Boom! I fucked your boyfriend" is *returned* to "Boom! I got your boyfriend." I say "returned" on account of Da Brat basing her version upon M.C. Luscious's "Boom! I Got Your Boyfriend" (*Boom!* 1992). In this instance the replacement restores Da Brat's version to its former configuration while, possibly, treading on copyright infringement in order to be clean. Other replacements consist of *nigga* being replaced by *him*. "I'm a fuck him" is replaced by the more timid "I'm a touch him," and *dick* is exchanged for the childlike ambiguity of *thing*.

Adult lyrics redesigned for younger ears? A certain perversity exists when adult sexual desire is reencoded through puerile euphemism.

Where replacement cleans Da Brat, Khia's electro party rap "My Neck, My Back (Lick It)" (off *Thug Misses*, 2002) is rewritten in its clean-version form. A song dedicated to the "toasting" of female pleasure by way of cunnilingus (and not much more), the verse "your pussy," like with Da Brat, is replaced with "your thing," while "lick my pussy" and "suck this pussy" are replaced with Elliott's elephant roar technique in the form of "ahhhh": "My neck, my back ~~Lick my pussy and my crack~~, (ahhh just like that)." To illustrate the extent of the replacement that occurs in Khia's song, I have isolated a verse and have inserted clean-version lyrics in parentheses among the songs original content:

> First you gotta put your neck into it
> Don't stop, just do it, do it
> Then you roll your tongue, from the ~~crack~~ back (up) to the front
> then ~~suck it off til I shake and cum nigga~~ (ya get it up,
>   keep me up on ya)
> make sure I keep ~~bustin nuts nigga~~ (my eyes on ya)
> all over ~~your face~~ (the club) and stuff
> ~~slow head~~ (real clear) show me so much love
> the best ~~head~~ (love) comes ~~from a thug~~ (so slow 'n' long)
> ~~the dick good dick big and long~~ (knows how to stay down on ya)
> ~~slow fuckin~~ (all night) til the crack of dawn
> ~~on the edge makin faces n stuff~~ (real good, keep it coming strong)
> Through the night, makin' so much love
> Dead sleep when the sun comes up

The clean version of Khia's "My Neck, My Back (Lick It)" not only replaces but also rewrites and relocates. Events portrayed in the song are no longer confined to the body of a person but now (oddly enough) occur in the public sphere of the token "club," which is substituted for "face." A sexual act is forcibly equated with personal emotions when *head* is deleted and replaced with *love,* while an imagined sexualized being in the form of the "thug" is usurped by an action that is equally sexually suggestive, "so slow 'n' long." In fact, where profanity is deleted and hip-hop's stylized meanderings denied (the song is not that "good," I will say, Khia is no Salt-n-Pepa, Missy E., or MIA), tired pop music euphemisms (mostly associated with rock male vocals and R & B) are inserted: "all night" and "real good, keep it coming strong." Thus the song is reauthored away from its classed, sexed, and raced experiences as articulated by the song's black female rapper, Khia.

The extent of cleaning can even rewrite the subject matter of an entire song in the way that digital compositing "improves" Spielberg's *E.T.* or redesigns the New York City skyline. Consider the case of Eminem and D12 posse's "Purple Pills" from their album *Devil's Night* (2001). A song about experiences with drugs (so much so that at one point in the song Eminem seems to lose track and mumbles "something," "something," "something," as if too high to remember his own lyrics) in its "dirty" version is transformed to the clean release "Purple Hills." Extensive dropouts and replacements delete profanity and most references to drugs in a song dedicated to drug use. In co-rapper Bizarre's verse the lyric "Drugs Kill (yeah right)" is revised to become an antidrug slogan, "Drugs Kill." His "Looking like a slave" becomes "Looking like a babe!" Slavery or slave to addiction is equated with affectionate or derisive slang for an attractive girl? "With a couple of Valium inside her palm," rapped by Eminem, is cleaned by replacing *Valium* with the somewhat improbable *lawsuit.* These replacements are not just trivial substitutes but notable warnings, where a punishment ensues for enjoying the activities described within the song. In one of my most unusual encounters with replacement, the line rapped by Kon Artist and Kuniva, "Who's upstairs naked with a weapon drawn" becomes "Who's upstairs wrestling with Elton John." Displaying homophobia, if not barefaced bigotry, this verse is approved, used as a replacement, for a clean version. The inoffensive prescription drug Valium is deleted while a derogatory statement on homosexuality is inserted? One may wonder if clean-version editors possess similar agendas to CleanFlicks since verbal abuse aimed at sexual orientation ("faggot") is acceptable while "damn" is profane.[42]

Lyrics have long been replaced in recorded music, live performance, and airplay. This practice stretches back from Cole Porter through Frank Zappa and the Rolling Stones to Michael Jackson (Sony did not take kindly to Jackson's antiracist song "They Don't Care about Us" and demanded that he replace "Jew me" and "kike me" with "do me" and "strike me"—anti-Semitism out, masochism in?) Today, however, it is far more common to "hear" the sonic vacancy of a dropped-out word, encounter sound effects masking "offensive" lyrics, or endure the heavy-handed reediting that machine-guns just under forty deletions through Eminem's "Kill You," discussed in this book's introduction, or Frankee's "F. U. Right Back." The precise excision that isolates a word, rendered unacceptable within the discourse of clean versions, attempts to remove its literal meanings (seemingly isolated in the lone word and not a series of traces in other words) from a larger social and cultural network of interpretative acts on account of meaning's deferral and persistent modifications.

How would Corbett's investment in the noted strategies for evading censorship account for the blatantly literal approach offered by Eamon? Corbett positions the strategies that he discusses as part of a history in popular music (especially black cultural production) that has had to rely on double entendre, clever innuendo, and what he regards as "cultivated techniques" such as humming and musical instrument masks that stand in for a profane aural moment. "F-you," rapping backwards (*kcuf* for *fuck*), and even the sound produced from an elephant's trunk can all be said to follow in this tradition of "getting around censorship." Yet, Eamon, himself hailing from a doo-wop background, does not employ any of these evasive maneuvers. No "kcuf you right backs" appear in his rap of personal torment. And he opts not to employ a series of metaphors to express himself. Consider *Los Angeles Times* writer Baz Dreisinger's account of "Fuck It (I Don't Want You Back)" with respect to clean versioning:

> Instead of toning down his blunt style of speech to write music, Eamon lets his verbal improprieties run free. His track is a triumph of literal-mindedness, a radical departure from the litany of classic songs that . . . cloak explicit or illicit messages in metaphor or code. The Beatles eschewed overt drug references in favor of covert ones ("Lucy in the Sky with Diamonds"); Shaggy slyly suggested he was the "cheese" to his lady's "bun"; Eamon, however, replaces simile and symbol with straight-up speech.[43]

For Nietzsche and Derrida, the idea of "straight-up speech" held in opposition to metaphor would deny language's metaphorical structure while reasserting the literal as a truth claim. Eamon's "triumph of literal-mindedness" is less a will to truth in our context than a challenge to Corbett's advocating of "semiotically tricky techniques."

Far from thwarting censorial practices, clean versions are the full realization and intensification of the practices Corbett once recognized as evasive. When the inclusion of sound effects becomes an example of a creative act while serving the dual purpose of concealing (cleaning) a reference to male anatomy, as in Missy Elliott's "Work It," the enterprise of creativity and principles of control become synonymous. It seems that the quality of cleaning is a matter of artist participation in the process instead of artistic evasion. Hilary Rosen laments this evasion in her plea, "I wish more artists would take the edited versions seriously and make them more compelling artistically so people didn't feel the only choice was some garbled words or the original version."[44] As does Nelly in the clean version of "Country Grammar" (from *Country Grammar,* 2000) when the word *fucking* in the verse "fucking Lesbian Twins" is substituted by sound effects of a female sexual moan (a real lesbian moan, we may query?). Also, the verse "Smokin' blunts in Savannah" substitutes the word *blunts* with the sound of turntable scratching, another method of reauthoring and rearranging lyrics. At the same time, however, substitution is practiced through word replacement. Lil' Flip's "Game Over" (*U Gotta Feel Me,* 2004) replaces *fucked up* with *messed up, ho* is equated with *girl, niggaaaaa* is translated into *playaaaaa,* and *rap shit,* in an unflattering move to Flip's professed genre, is conflated with *rap music.* Lastly, deletion remains the most formidable approach, where words beyond the "explicit" are dropped out: 50 Cent may profess to be bulletproof; however, his music in clean-version form is not so fortunate; his hit "Candy Shop" (*The Massacre,* 2005) contains glaring holes from the deletion of *nympho,* ordinary slang for *nymphomania.*

Rosen urges artists to take clean versions "more seriously" and make them more "compelling artistically" so that the censorial does not sound like policing, regulation, or actions of power expressed on and through cultural production but rather resounds with the same lyrical style as the unaltered track. The actual process gravitates between two poles. Neil Strauss's *New York Times* article on the subject reports that for an executive at an unnamed major label, it is a "haphazard process with no rules and that it was usually done by an unsupervised junior staff member at a computer."[45] Furthering this notion and describing a less haphazard method, Kevin Lines of Def Jam and Def Soul Records explains how his label manages clean versions: "there was one employee whose job was to pore over lyric sheets with a red pen, circle explicit lyrics, show them to him and then sit at a computer covering up all offending words with sound effects to create a clean version."[46] Both instances are a far stretch from the ideal scenario urged by Rosen. However, artist involvement, perhaps a placation for Rosen, who could claim "quality" clean versions as a feasible alternative to increase sales, maintains a reading-with-a-purpose that targets the explicit as a contained entity neither reliant upon context nor introducing evasive measures but embodying them as corrective practices to achieve clean status. According to Skip Miller (senior vice president of black music at RCA in the mid-1990s), RZA of Wu-Tang Clan fame "supervised the rewording and bleeping of tracks."[47] Nowhere in Miller's discussion is concern over music censorship raised. Instead, as Miller notes, "our goal was to find a way to satisfy the masses without tampering with the integrity of music."[48] Yet as we have seen, the "cut" and "fill" are never neutral actions in their repairs and replacements.

Inviting the artist to "oversee" reediting is an attempt to lend a voice of authenticity to the clean version. It also shifts attention away from the "censor" to the artist as the creative agent responsible for the clean version (here music censorship becomes a commonplace creative act instead of external oppression). However, this voice duplicates existing censorial practices as the artistic effect constitutes the censorial despite how it sounds. For example, RZA replaces profanity with an actual "bleep" and "backspins" over *fuck* and *nigga*. The aesthetic of the scratch lends its capabilities to the cleaning process as part of this production rather than resistance to it. The artist identifies similar content as warranting cleaning. The warning moniker "Wu-Tang Clan Ain't Nothin' to Fuck Wit" from their debut *Enter the Wu-Tang: 36 Chambers* (1994) is "scratched" as "fuck" dissolves in the sound of vinyl spun in reverse. The scratch, an aesthetic technique to expose layers of embedded sounds, snag them, resound them through the physical action of tactile manipulation, becomes an aesthetic-censorial technology that covers up rather than sets free.

In the elephant's roar or scratch, the censorial sounds. The corrective erasure becomes a trite cleaning effect; the more obvious "bleep" is what is lost. In this sense, the clean version does fit the challenge of invisibility enabled by censorial effects in the digital age. In these "fills" resides the aesthetic production of standards and moral values, as we have seen, in what words are replaced and by what. Clean edits, like Gaines's censor's cut—and we should include blocking and filtering as well—are always full of information. They not only illustrate choice in their acts of versioning but also indicate securitization's persistent subject: consumers who abide by the clean/good and dirty/bad poles for managing the conduct of consuming music and reduce the complexities of culture to these simple binaries. A version must be declared "dirty" so that the action of active cleaning can be witnessed and normalized as an acceptable and tolerable solution. This is precisely why a clean version is never unique and always refers to a process of *being cleaned*. It requires the act of repair (as witnessed in the painter-magician analogy discussed previously) in order to compel choice: "clean" or "dirty." Likewise, it requires the unclean to pronounce the need for security.

The onetime creative gestures employed to circumvent, undermine, camouflage and sound out against music censorship circulate today as standard procedure for eliciting clean versions. This is less a jilting of Corbett's analysis than an attempt to account for censorial practices as they persist. Incorporating bleeping, deletion, and substitution into the production of clean versions marks the censorial sound of the early twenty-first century not as an exception—evasive techniques—but as a strategy of rule for manufacturing and maintaining choice as a regulatory practice. Butler posits the matter in the following way: "the question is not what it is I will be able to say, but what will constitute the domain of the sayable within which I begin to speak at all."[49] For Butler and her focus on injurious speech, the censorial is less about that which is stricken than the determining power of censorious actions as a normative effect. As a control technology the clean version (its various editing practices resultant from various hands as well as the surface strictures that display the safety of a clean version) conducts the possibility of conduct to achieve harbored results. Government, as Foucault reminds, "structure[s] the possible field of action of others."[50] Our practices with control technology are a structuring process that attempts to realize possibility as an expression of choice that is delimited, in this case, to clean versions as instruments for governing content and the larger social aims (racial expression, sexuality, youth agency, ideas of identity, decency, cultural expression, and culture itself) this form of governing hopes to effect. Again, the parental function prescribes a protective measure over culture, across airways and bandwidth, on the surface of music objects, and in the very grain of the cleaned voice. These "structures of possibility" are flexible, the choice between "clean" and the pronounced "dirty," as generative freedoms as opposed to harsh forms of suppression. Even "bans" are cleaned since control makes these actions appear primitive, reactionary, if not "extreme" and "intolerant." Why "ban" when a quick reedit job secures markets, maintains access, shrugs allocations of censorship while keeping music content perfecting *in* control?

Eamon's diction, his explicit rap, does not require the extra work of covert references or double entendre when clean versioning does this work for the artist via partial deletion. The "means of control are multiplied," as Deleuze insists, when restrictive barriers are pushed aside. Eamon can incorporate even more *fucks* into an already jam-packed refrain as long as the clean version marks the original "dirty" and provides alternatives for distribution and consumption. The song still achieves radio play and major retail distribution, while listeners have the choice to make do with aural edits (already in heavy rotation via radio play and music video) or seek out the original version. No major policy initiatives were launched as with "Parental Warning" stickers in the mid-1980s; clean versions are a response to retail boy-cotts and the threat of FCC fines and license revocation. The implied parental function of clean versions is incidental while furthering a versioning that equips consumers with choice.

The metaphor and action of the censor's "cut," be it in film or music, have mutated. We have seen how television and networked computers are technologies for blocking and filtering, DVD players and DVDs sanitize film content, and now digital special effects as-sist in cleaning film and musical content. Even the idea of a censor's cut—whether in the form of "gaps" or "fills"—increasingly demon-strates a reassignment as media technology enables producers and any user to embody this social position and author their own "censorial reading" through the designed-in control protocols at their disposal or licensed as a consumer who chooses to purchase control in the form of reedited media designed for purposes of security. Procedures forced to abide by continuity editing are, however, no longer the gen-eral practice of the censor's "overfocused" gaze. This procedure—marked by the presence of incongruent frames—is historically con-tingent and fails to adequately account for the operations of control that, as we have seen, are played out on media objects today. The seamless censorial effects sequence in *Eyes Wide Shut* attests to this as do the various "improvements" that act through digital aesthet-ics to maintain old ideologies that shape the notion of appropriate content. If the censorial techniques exercised on media have changed, then so too have cultural understandings of censorship as we work to come to terms with the censorial as part and parcel of practices and processes of control. The seamless digital composite comprises a radically different relation to the image; total removal of a celluloid frame is only one option when alterations, modification, and manipulation can be carried out on computers rather than analog editing machines. And digital effects employed for the production of clean-version music demonstrate that the "drop out" can easily be replaced with the "fill up" as sound effects work to mask and replace "explicit" content.

Cleaning is not an after-the-fact process. Today the market demands a clean version upon release. The clean version is far from an abnormality. An unsightly earache previously likened to poor cell phone service, this "noise" remains as much a part of our musical terrains and encounters with music as the "version" we once pronounced by its album's title free from the prefix or suffix of "clean" or "dirty." Think about your radio commute, music video viewing, the pumping soundtrack while on a treadmill at your local gym: these spaces, too, are cleaned as the clean version resounds in these proximities. The clean version with its "filled gaps" acts on our actions of listening and seeing (recall the surface encounter) so that these experiences are rendered safe before we are even exposed. No risk. More choice. Wu-Tang Clan Ain't Nothin' to —— With.

6. Patching

> You know, no longer is something like the v-chip
> the "one stop shop" to protect kids, who can expose
> themselves to all the rest of this media at one time.
> And so parental responsibility is crucial but we
> also need to be sure that parents have the tools that
> they need to keep up with this multi-dimensional
> problem.
>
> *Senator Hillary Rodham Clinton, speech to the Kaiser Family Foundation*

> Damn—This shit's fucked up.
>
> *Lance "Ryder" Wilson, Grand Theft Auto: San Andreas character*

Hot Coffee Gone Warm

"The disturbing material in 'Grand Theft Auto' and other games like it is stealing the innocence of our children, and it's making the difficult job of being a parent even harder,"[1] derides onetime presidential hopeful Senator Hillary Rodham Clinton (D-N.Y.) speaking about the much publicized hidden interactive sexual scenarios in Rockstar Games' *Grand Theft Auto: San Andreas*. Rockstar's hugely successful title for the 2004 holiday season became the target of legislators, media watchdog groups, Christian groups and activists,[2] and retail policy after it was revealed that a downloadable modification for its PC version allows the player who controls "Carl Johnson"—a young African American character who returns home to avenge the murder

of his mother to find his old stomping ground in gang-related chaos—
to engage in interactive simulated sex ("lewd," per Senator Clinton[3])
with female "girlfriend" characters. "Hot coffee" is a "mod" (game
code modification) and a euphemism for sexual liaisons between Carl
and the game's various "girlfriends" who roam GTA's mean-street
environment of Los Santos, San Andreas (modeled on Los Angeles).
The downloadable mod, posted online by Dutch programmer Patrick
Wildenbourg (or at least that is one version of the story), enabled
interested gamers to unlock mini-games in the PC version of GTA:
San Andreas (the mod is still widely available online). It is significant
that the hidden mini-games were first made visible on the PC version
and not on game consoles such as Sony PS2 or Microsoft's Xbox.
Computer games account for 10 percent of the gaming market and
are not necessarily representative of game types for other platforms
such as console games.[4] Games aimed at the computer platform often
consist of historical simulations, first-person shooters, strategy, fantasy, as well as massively multiplayer online role-playing games (or
MMORPG for short); they constitute a different gaming experience
and attract a different gamer than console games or handheld games
like Nintendo's Game Boy series and DS that appeal to younger gamers (GTA: San Andreas is not available for any of Nintendo's platforms). Senator Clinton's "family values" charge of sexually explicit
content in video games fuels the notion that all players download
codes to access graphic scenes and that "hot coffee" is standard
GTA: San Andreas game play.

The next installment in the GTA universe was released on April 29,
2008, for both PlayStation 3 and Xbox 360. Grand Theft Auto IV
swaps coasts as its Serbian protagonist, Niko Bellic, experiences life
as a new immigrant in "Liberty City" (modeled on the boroughs
of New York City). Take-Two Interactive Software, Inc., publisher
of Rockstar's games, reports that its title generated $310 million
in first-day sales worldwide. First-week sales are estimated at $500
million, and GTA4 is expected to do over $1 billion by the close of
2008.[5] Prior to its release, rumors began to circulate across gaming
Web sites and blogs that Rockstar Games was planning its revenge
on Senator Clinton for her congressional attacks on its previous title
by including prostitutes that resemble her. If killed in the game, the
Hillary-prostitute would utter the following statement in her dying
breath: "Now I'll never get to be president!" This does not occur in
the game (or is not unlocked at the time of writing). In addition, the

sex "mini-games" that drew national attention to *Grand Theft Auto: San Andreas* are equally absent. Instead, Niko arranges numerous dates—via his cell phone and the use of an Internet café—throughout the game. These include going to bowling alleys, pool halls, bars, clubs, and restaurants. Niko must dress (and drive) to impress, and part of the game play is to act in ways that may lead to a "successful date"—that is, receive an invitation back to a girlfriend's apartment. Dates are "side-games" within the narrative of *GTA4* and can be a time-consuming and an arduous affair! Niko's first date is an actual "mission" in the game, and this can unlock the "warm coffee" achievement. An overt comment on its own hot coffee mod, warm coffee seems equally aware of the political climate within which its latest title is released. While portrayals of sex remain—mostly in the forms of strip clubs, lap dances, and cutaways of interaction between Niko and his various dates—the warm coffee achievement is satirical (even the Statue of Liberty's torch is replaced by a to-go coffee cup) and highly conscious of the game's history and legal matters confronting its parent company, as well as persistent calls for further regulation of game content and access.

Discourses on "media effects" (always couched in terms of harm) and the "loss of innocence" rhetoric embraced by Senator Clinton that reveals the threatened "vulnerability" of children are overriding tropes in narratives of moral panic and proposed legislation that seeks to cordon childhood from the rest of the world, manage social meanings and experiences, and define the ontological status of and access to media. Video games, like film, comic books, television, and music, are opined as detrimental to children's well-being (or young people in general when video games are commonly blamed for school shootings such as at Columbine High School and Virginia Tech University) and in grave need of new regulation beyond existing age-based ratings and accompanying restrictions at the point of sale. Solely equating video games with children as well as capitalizing on a surmised helplessness of parents (a tiresome and disrespectful attempt at empathy), as do Senator Clinton, Senator Joseph Lieberman (I-Conn.), Senator Evan Bayh (D-Ind.), Representative Mary Lou Dickerson (D-Wash.), and Representative Joe Baca (D-Calif.),[6] is misleading and yet another measure to invest control into new electronic devices so that all emergent cultural interfaces further the parental function of security and empowerment. Narratives of victimization and breaches of securitization continue to facilitate the proliferation of technological solutions for governing culture such as blocking, filtering, sanitizing, and cleaning.

The Entertainment Software Association (ESA), which conducts business and consumer research as well as assists federal relations with the entertainment software industry, finds that the average player is thirty-five years of age, whereas the purchaser of video games is reported to be, on average, forty. For 2008, the ESA purports that 96 percent of computer game consumers and 86 percent of console game consumers are over the age of eighteen, thus legally classified as adults in the United States.[7] According to the ESA, game play is not exactly restricted to the realm of childhood, as adults comprise the largest market for video games. In 2005, shortly after *GTA: San Andreas*'s October 24, 2004, release, ESA reported that 85 percent of console game buyers and 95 percent of computer game buyers were over the age of eighteen. The bodies that constitute the statistics are able to purchase games rated M for mature and AO for adult only, and this age group seems to fall short of the expansive "threat to the innocent" currently spun by congressional lawmakers. We might wager that a gamer who downloads "hot coffee" could just as easily download other types of pornographic material from the Web and that *GTA: San Andreas* is neither unique in its modified game code nor somehow a lucrative source for interactive porn. (Adult video games are not new by any means. Mystique produced its "Swedish Erotica" series cartridges for the Atari 2600 nearly thirty years ago,[8] and Digital Picture's CD-ROM game *Night Trap* (1994) starred Dana Plato as a scantily clad member of a slumber party.)

In light of attempts to prosecute the sale of video games to minors in California, Louisiana, Illinois, Kansas, Maryland, Massachusetts, Michigan, Minnesota, New York, North Carolina, Oklahoma, Pennsylvania, South Carolina, and Washington, the ESA reports that 85 percent of the games sold in 2005 were rated E for everyone by the Entertainment Software Rating Board (ESRB).[9] In 2003 the ESRB reported that 57 percent of games were rated E, while 42 percent consisted of games rated T for teen or M for mature.[10] Games rated E for everyone are on the increase. Moreover, Senator Clinton's reference to the difficulties facing parents ignores the actual presence of parents when children under the age of eighteen purchase video games. The ESA estimates that 94 percent of purchasing children are accompanied and supervised by a parent (possibly due to the expense of new titles). Perhaps parents *choose* to allow their kids to purchase games rated M for mature in the way that a parent or guardian can escort a person under seventeen into an R-rated film. This sense of choice remains outside the technologically enabled choice of control where choice is confined to the enablement of securitization.

Similar to the MPAA/CARA age-based ratings for films and DVDs, a nonprofit voluntary ratings system was established in 1994 for certification of video games, following senatorial debates around violence in video games like the fight game *Mortal Kombat* and first-person shooter computer game *Doom*. Game producers submit video/DVD footage (demos), as opposed to actual games, of new titles to the ESRB in order to have their products awarded an official ratings certificate, which is displayed on the game's packaging much like the Parental Advisory sticker for music. The ESRB "watches" game content rather than plays games in determining its rating. Current rating schemes include EC (early childhood), E (everyone), Everyone 10+ (everyone ten and older), T (teen), M (mature), AO (adults only), and RP (rating pending) for use in advance advertising. Should a particular title contain content not made available for review at the time of the initial rating, the ESRB can impose sanctions that result in the pulling of advertising until an accurate rating can be awarded, require a restickering of products to adequately reflect game content, and possibly recall a game if it is found to violate ESRB's rating criteria.[11] Games that receive ESRB's AO rating are treated much like an NC-17 film and Parental Warning CD in that major retailers of video games like Wal-Mart and Best Buy refuse to stock titles designed for an adult market (the majority of gamers in the United States according to the ESA). And rated-M games often require proof of age to purchase and are kept out of reach of younger gamers. In addition, the Federal Trade Commission, the same commission that investigated Rockstar's *GTA: San Andreas*'s game mod, applauded the Video Software Dealers Association in 2002 for their "Pledge to Parents" program, which encourages retailers and parents to join forces in managing young people's access to video games.[12] Once it was revealed that the PC version of *GTA: San Andreas*, as well as versions for game consoles like PS2 and Xbox, contained sexual scenes that exceed the ratings criteria that originally warranted a mature rating, the ESRB re-rated the game as adults only, and retailers who refuse to carry AO titles unanimously removed the game from their shelves. Regardless of these efforts, all of which have been approved by the Federal Trade Commission and make *GTA: San Andreas* more difficult for young gamers to purchase, legislators insist that more regulation is required in order to protect children who are not meant to play the game in the first place according to the ESRB original rating of M for mature.

Aside from Senator Clinton's lobbying of the Federal Trade Commission to resolve the issue of the *GTA: San Andreas* modification, the ESRB launched its own probe into Rockstar Games to determine whether the hidden scenes were originally programmed into the game or were a result of hackers rewriting the prevailing game code, as claimed in defense by Rockstar. Take-Two Interactive Software, publisher of Rockstar's game, originally denied that the hidden scenes where programmed into their game when they insisted that any simulated sex scenes were the result of hackers who "created the 'Hot Coffee' modification by disassembling and then compiling, recompiling and altering the game's code."[13] On July 20, 2005, five days after Take-Two's statement, the ESRB raised the game's rating to AO, thus restricting sales, as the scenes were found to be already present yet unverifiable without a mod to unlock them. Take-Two reneged on its previous statement that the scenes were the work of game modders, who modify and reauthor game code. On behalf of Take-Two, Rodney Walker draws an analogy between designing games and painting: "the editing of any game is a highly technical process, . . . [W]e liken it to a painter who paints one painting and paints over it on the same canvas."[14] Whereas the kino-brush, discussed in the previous chapter, in the service of cleaning corrects and improves the image through its seamless brush strokes, video game's painting in the case of *GTA: San Andreas* reveals rather than removes. Modders had previously claimed that the scenes were already embedded within *GTA: San Andreas*'s program code and that the downloadable mod simply unlocked what was already present. Walker continued by stressing that these scenes, while in the PC game's final form, were not meant to actually be seen: "the mod community scratched the painting, revealing the earlier work."[15] Whether or not "hot coffee" scenes were "meant to actually be seen" is a moot point since they remain intact and with game modding are accessible, hence able to be played.

It was not until rumors set in that "hot coffee" could also be accessed on Sony PS2 and Xbox that Rockstar's defense involving hackers fell apart. Console games are stored on unmodifiable DVDs, and as such no content can be added. When cheat codes began to circulate on the Web, it became apparent that the mini-games were in fact present since cheats serve to unlock preexisting code already encoded on the disc. The activation of cheats for PS2 and Xbox are far from a user-friendly affair. Running a test to see whether downloadable cheat codes would actually unlock "hot coffee" on the PS2 version of the game, *GameSpot News* found that it "cannot be accessed without entering a long string of cheat codes, and takes several hours of effort to access."[16] When Carl Johnson does have sex with his various girlfriends in *GTA: San Andreas*, should the player not balance his or her "excitement meter" correctly, the message "Failure to satisfy a woman is a CRIME" appears on-screen. Despite the tedious labor to glimpse at pixilated sex for those interested in the first place and for those who can purchase or rent a rated-M game, Senator Mary Lou Dickerson responded by stating that the country's top-selling modified video/computer game "is in the hands of thousands of children who can practice interactive pornography."[17]

Representative Joe Baca, founder of the Sex and Violence in the Media Caucus and leading proponent for legislative rehaul of the current ESRB games ratings, made the following statement on April 26, 2006: "Parents want clear, accurate information that they can understand. They need to know what is actually in a video game in order to make informed, responsible decisions about what is appropriate for their children."[18] The notion of "in" a video game cannot account for content in ways similar to film, television, and music. Players of a console game are different than viewers of film or television in that they occupy the screenic space through the game interface and interactivity. Consider the physical scale of *GTA: San Andreas*: a player can navigate Carl Johnson through the game's environment by performing tasks required to advance in the game's narrative. In these instances tasks most likely will result in some form of action necessary to complete an objective, and more often than not this will involve some type of violent action given generic conventions. Unlike a violent scene in a film, violent or sexually explicit scenes "in" video games do not have to be initiated for the game to be experienced. The *GTA* series is a good example: the player does not have to actually perform any of the game's tasks in order to play the game. *GTA: San Andreas* players can explore the interiors of the rich digital world, talk to pedestrians, trick on a BMX bicycle, fly around the city on a jet pack, swim, cruise around listening to music, turn San Andreas pedestrians into Elvis impersonators, or spend hours customizing the appearance of one's avatar. As a recent arrival to Liberty City, Niko of *GTA4* can spend his time exploring the urban environment via car, subway, or taxi. And a player can dedicate hours to selecting Niko's clothing for his various dates—not to mention, surfing dating Web sites at the Internet café to actually meet someone. In other words, a video and computer game can be played in a variety of different ways that may not subscribe to the game's violent elements and themes. Therefore, regulating what is "in" a video and computer game is a difficult, if not an incorrect, conceptual approach that fails to consider how game content is played, the game interface, online social networking through gaming (where ratings may vary), and simply spending time in the immersive screenic environment. To see games only in terms of ratings to "protect" against violence and sex is to understand games in static terms that reduce their interactive spaces to celluloid strips cut for "safety" or a television program blocked by the V-chip.

While members of Congress are still aiming to have their bills voted into law, which would increase fines and prosecute retailers who sell M-rated and AO games to underage consumers, Rockstar's response to allegations of its awareness of "hot coffee" was to issue a downloadable "patch" for *GTA: San Andreas*. A patch is designed to repair a program bug. It is object code introduced into an executable program. Customers of the PC version of *GTA: San Andreas* can download the patch in order to block access to its "hot coffee" scenes. Patches are common downloads in computer gaming. In general, patches update game versions and add new features to existing game play.[19] These can include new control options, different game modes, new game elements and environmental effects, and repair of game bugs and server problems for online multiplayer games. Patching demonstrates a viable technological solution to the concern about sexually graphic content in computer games: paint over it again, so to speak, so that gamers cannot interact with the embedded scenes. But why would one who has taken the time to download the "hot coffee" mod in the first place then want to download a patch to purposely not interact with the game, especially if he or she is over the age of seventeen? Rather than regard Rockstar's gesture as absurd, and bear in mind that it was a temporary solution until its new versions with the hidden scene removed from the programming were placed on the market, we could argue that the patch is reminiscent of other control technologies that have won congressional favor: the

V-chip, Internet filters, and filtering DVD players. All regulate content at the additional layer of the end user's active involvement in self-regulation. Gamers could have "patched" and "unpatched" versions of computer games. "Patched" could be the new "clean." Despite its similarity, the patch proves ineffective in quelling calls for further legislation and higher fines.

On March 8, 2005, Senator Clinton gave a speech to the Kaiser Family Foundation to endorse their recently published report titled "Generation M: Media in the Lives of 8 to 18 Year Olds." Her speech addressed the "concern" of children and media and the challenges facing parenting today, especially from video games like *GTA: San Andreas,* which she mentions to her audience. Reminding the audience of her involvement in helping enact the V-chip into law and that she too is a parent, Senator Clinton sees, as the epigraph to this chapter states, that this control technology is no longer the "one stop shop to protect kids" given that parenting now faces a "multi-dimensional problem" from media.[20] Game consoles must keep pace if control is to circulate freely across our electronic media technology. The effect of "sexually explicit images and graphic violence" on children, according to Senator Clinton, is an issue of health care likened to the dangers of junk food and childhood obesity as well as an "infectious disease" and "silent epidemic" where all children are "vulnerable" due to excessive "exposure" to such imagery. Senator Clinton goes so far as to suggest that "what we are doing today, exposing our children to so much of this unchecked media, is a kind of contagion."[21] The solution for iGeneration latchkeyism? Federal sunscreen to protect against the violent UV rays of media? A proper media diet of filtered and blocked calories? Media education to inform parents, higher fines, and end-user parental control technologies remain the solution for "parents who work long hours outside the home and single parents, whose time with their children is squeezed by economic pressures," parents who "are worried because they don't even know what their children are watching and listening to and playing."[22]

Senator Clinton's statement reminds us of Marjorie Hein's frustration with V-chip legislation, as referenced in chapter 2, which drove her to denounce the parental control of filtering technology as absolutely useless against racism, classism, and homophobia. Whereas Senator Clinton in her empathy with parents trying to raise children "in today's media saturated world" (a type of classism unto itself) opts for the parenting-at-a-distance model of governance, this does little to address pressing issues facing all citizens, namely, the conditions that constitute the absence of parents in the scenario that parental control technology is meant to rectify. A reduction in the long hours that keep parents away from their children; higher-paying jobs that provide health care, child care, and retirement guarantees for all employees; longer paid holiday leave for all U.S. citizens so that more time can be spent together with loved ones; and federal investments in education seem like better solutions than fining a shop owner for selling *GTA: San Andreas* and entering into yet another long-winded election-time debate about media ratings.

June 8, 2006, the day that the Federal Trade Commission announced its settlement with the companies responsible for *GTA: San Andreas*'s "hot coffee" scenes, is the same day that *all* U.S. major news sources paraded violently graphic photographs of the United States' killing of Abu Musab al-Zarqawi in close-up for all to see on unrated television news programs and across the Internet (unless a parent blocks its ISP). And this action against media violence does not even begin to consider the huge gaming market and active recruitment of young people through imperialistic war video games like *America's Army* and *Call of Duty 4: Modern Warfare* that allow players to photorealistically combat "terrorism" from the safety and security of their sofa.

Enable Parental Controls

The *designed-in* premise of control technology is a stalwart element in today's emergent media. In being designed-in, control redesigns media technologies to go beyond their capabilities to send messages, receive broadcasts, store content, play back, record, process, play, communicate, and display. Our media are now machines for protection, security, and resolution. Not restrictive, but freeing. Not detrimental to freedom, but productive, freeing, and regulatory. Not disabling, but enabling. The multilayering complex of federal, retail, industry, and privatized efforts rationalize and instrumentalize regulation across culture and put it into the hands of consumers, who govern over themselves as "policy" becomes a personalized governing practice at the touch of many buttons and the new posture for the reconstitution of censorial practices across media. This is not the big hands of the federal government interfering with the little hands of citizens in negotiating strategies of rule, but both actively working simultaneously to cover more ground. Control technologies are mediators of neoliberal governmentality. In this instance, the federal government's role is to pave the "highway," so to speak, in order for free-market, deregulatory "governing at a distance" to have a smooth modus operandi in the form of beneficent technology designed not to inhibit but professedly to empower through choice.

Not long ago it would have been an absolutely absurd action to purchase a television or acquire computer software to intentionally disable its capabilities, whereas today's media technology is marketed for what it *does not contain* and what it *will not deliver*. Control is the ability to disable. Like a low-cal diet, to echo Senator Clinton's analogy, control technology promises healthier and better living in its conduct management (this is most obvious when Microsoft's Xbox 360 includes its parental control features as part of its "Healthy Gaming Guide," prescribing good body posture and the need for breaks during game play). Media technology is increasingly required to include controls as free-market legislation secures more markets to enable and empower consumers through practices of self-regulation for neoliberal processes of governance positioned as parental controls despite user status. The pervasive state of being *designed-in* is the success of control as governance becomes a standard component in further developing and redefining media technology through the parental function. Media technology becomes increasingly "family friendly" as self-governance is seemingly equated with parental control and practiced through measures to maintain and safeguard "family values" by determining consumer media like television, networked computers, DVDs, DVD players, music, and video games as the quotidian tools responsible for disciplined freedom.

At the end of chapter 4 I paused to consider the possibility of next-generation DVD technology offering consumers multiple versions of a single film that could even include film sanitized versions (or something equivalent). Can we extend this idea to video games? Why not release a version for each ESRB rating, thereby managing content for different gamers rather than condemning game content and seeking standards that do not necessarily gel with actual gamer ages? While this certainly appears feasible and the games industry may welcome the opportunity to avoid fines for possible ratings violations,[23] we ought to keep in mind that the operation of control technology is less about maximizing choice than narrowing it to select options deemed

safe while enabling disciplined freedoms for purposes of securitization. In the modulations of control it is choice that is instrumentalized. Not unlimited choice, but delimited choice constitutes our relation to control technology. For film sanitizers, "choice is power."
CleanFlicks and ClearPlay offer their editing services as a form of
corrective replacement, so it is doubtful that competing versions can
coexist on the same storage medium. Choice is an imperative for control technology. When Senator Clinton likens unregulated media to
a "contagion" (in her speech, "unchecked media"), the clear implication is that control is required to maintain safe perimeters and ensure
security, as Deleuze would say, by "spreading out the treatment": generalizing and multiplying the effects of control as a matter of choice.

Next-generation video game consoles are the latest media technology to assist in the securitization of habitat in that the parental
function administers the game console as an empowering device
for regulation. When pending legislation targets software sales,
Microsoft, Sony, and Nintendo implement parental control solutions
directly in their hardware. As discussed previously, my PlayStation 2
parental function was inspired by the V-chip to monitor access to
DVDs based on my personal security code PIN that either allows or
disallows a DVD to play according to the DVD player's built-in security levels. It has no blocking effect over the games that it is designed
to play. It acts only on DVDs, a secondary feature for this gaming
console. Microsoft's Xbox 360 and Sony's PlayStation 3 contain parental controls that enable users to manage DVDs *as well as* video
games in a manner that approximates blocking technology. In anticipation of the PS3's new features, online magazine *PS3 Today* reports
that "Sony appeared determined to provide self-regulatory functionality to its hardware devices, putting the decision over content firmly
back in the hands of the parents and drawing the decision away from
developers and retailers."[24] This sentiment shares former President
Bill Clinton's praise for the V-chip, discussed in chapter 2, as a successful venture that "hands the TV remote back to America's parents." Not an expansion of the long-accustomed RCD but another
controller—the Wii Remote, Xbox 360 Wireless Controller, Sony's
SIXAXIS Control and Blu-Ray Remote Control—the game console
proves equally valuable in regulating televisuality, DVDs, game content, and online communication as next-generation game consoles
extend beyond offline gaming. Another cultural object is inscribed as

a control technology. Parenting at a distance is expanding to include the game controller on the same coffee table as the RCD.

DVDs can be set to play on the Xbox 360 and PS3 in compliance with MPAA ratings (the next model Wii, it has been reported, will contain a DVD player, a feature not possessed by the first model). Parents can select what ratings are appropriate for their children through the Xbox's "Family Settings Features," its name for its parental control capabilities. In managing game play, "Family Settings Features" allow parents to "program" access on the game console based on ESRB ratings. Only games that correspond to select ratings can be played. The rest are "locked out" unless the family settings are disabled. Games designed for Microsoft's Xbox 360 have encoded data, like DVDs, so that the console can read ratings in order to determine whether a specific title is permissible for play. Software, while already displaying an ESRB rating on its surface, also carries metadata encoded into its programming so that ratings are literally part of game play rather than external information for advisory purposes. The PS3 has an elaborate "Security System" with various parental controls to manage its multiformat DVD features. Its Blu-ray playback capabilities are monitored by "BD Parental Controls," and this extends to "BD/DVD Parental Control Region Code," which allows parents to set levels of restrictions for U.S. and world regions Blu-ray discs. "DVD Parental Controls" organize access according to levels between eight and one. "One" roughly corresponds to the MPAA's "G" rating. "Parental Control" levels can be selected to allow game play based on set levels of access between eleven and one. The lower the value, the higher the restriction.

As online gaming is now a common feature for game consoles, Xbox 360's "Family Settings" police both off- and online content in ways similar to Internet filtering software. "Xbox Live," its online gaming function, allows players to game online with players that span the globe, communicate in real time with online gamers, download new game mods, and establish a social network for game play. "Family Settings" for online game play allow parents both to "approve" online gamers that their child can connect with and "block" all online communication. The content of downloadable items is also monitored. "While no security tools are foolproof," Microsoft explains, "the new Xbox 360 Family Settings are powerful tools to help protect your kids while they game."[25] Wii's online access is restricted by the holder of a four-digit PIN that allows the operator to restrict or allow access to its Shop Channel (to download Wii software) and to disable the ability to send or receive messages from other Wii consoles. PS3 online settings allow parents to restrict chat and restrict a gamer's online game play to ESRB ratings deemed acceptable. The child's birth date is entered, and the console allows online game play in conjunction with ESRB age-based ratings. The PS3 automatically monitors access to online games by tracking a child's age. A device to play games in the era of control is also a tool for regulating these activities.

The securitization of habitat and the parental function knows no bounds as family becomes a ubiquitous agent for determining media technology's functionality and capabilities. To possess a game console, any television, ClearPlay DVD player, networked computer, clean-version sound recording is also to be configured as a self-regulating user. "No kids? No problem! You can turn off Family Settings any time you like," Microsoft assures its adult consumers.[26] Yet as I have insisted, actual usage of parental controls matters little for managing conduct via content when its strategies of rule become normative conditions and their inundating presence proceeds to inscribe and demarcate our social relations to media technology. This is best witnessed when computer parental controls no longer reside in the form of an ISP or third-party software but are now part and parcel of an operating system's general management protocols. Microsoft's new operating system, Windows Vista, includes parental controls as a standard feature, located, where else, on its "control panel." Mac OS X Tiger likens the need for parental control to other domestic responsibilities such as keeping sharp objects out of the reach of children: "You wouldn't think twice about keeping dangerous household items out of your kids' reach; Mac OS X Tiger helps you do the same with the information on your Mac."[27] Mac OSX Leopard locates parental controls in its system preferences. Redesign and continued redefinition reaffirms William Boddy's claim that helped initiate our engagement with the V-chip, for with every new media product come ideal visions of its domestic consumption, social functions, and ontological status. In the case of computer parental controls, they cease to be optional software and are now computer-embedded architecture. Whether we use them or not, controls are designed in our media technology, and their presence reshapes the expectations we assign to them and how they mediate our world and enable governing through their technical capabilities.

Scenarios for domestic consumption are apparent in discourses of control technology regardless of actual usage. They ring out in congressional statements and speeches that define the home as a family space and declare that all who enter or emanate from such a heterotopic space must abide by this scenario. Family togetherness, "quality time," and safety are fostered by control. The domestic settings produced by Internet filtering software companies depict families huddled around computers in images reminiscent of nostalgic depictions of post–World War II families viewing TV. Film sanitizers' images of their customers' engagement with their edited DVDs or filtering DVD players evoke similar nostalgia, as do the images of children safely gaming with Microsoft's Xbox 360's Family Setting Features. The laptop computer seems to have failed to register with Internet filtering companies (but not the OS); their image of the computer is of a family desktop located in the study or living room, where each member of the family shares screen time equally.

Consider another example of mobility that will inevitably spur congressional outrage and reconsiderations of policy: "mobisodes" of television, mobile wireless videos for cell phones that offer news and sports updates, music videos, movies, as well as downloadable television episodes for Apple's iPod (Classic, iPod Touch, and iPhone). The V-chip is legally required to be incorporated into U.S. televisions with screens over 13 inches. The iPod screen is not a television and measures 2.5 inches; many portable handhelds and cellular phone screens are smaller still. Ought we to expect an amendment to existing legislation should wireless video prove to resemble television (or better yet, exceed it), thus necessitating that it abide by television ratings? Or if Apple TV and the iPod prove to be the "new" screen for televisual consumption, will some type of end-user regulatory technology accompany this experience? Television ratings have simply "carried over" to the iPod regardless of its exemption for the Telecommunications Act. "TV Shows" purchased on iTunes carry the same television ratings that we find on our television screens so that a V-chip can be activated (television ratings were originally designed to work in conjunction with the "programmable" V-chip). But no V-chip exists in our iPod. So what purpose do these ratings serve, or do they take on the function of the parental warning that is brandished on music, the ESRB ratings that mark video game content, and the MPAA ratings that "inform" cinema audiences and DVD viewers? This is a convergence of control where the governing protocols of television merge with mobile devices like the iPod, where parental warnings found on iTunes and televisions ratings sync with networked computing, where the processes of blocking, filtering, sanitizing, and cleaning know no limits as techniques and practices are reoutfitted, reapplied, and remade across media.

In terms of content for downloadable video, the Vivid Entertainment Group and other porn companies provide wireless content compatible with the iPod. Apple does not provide porn through its iTunes downloads (the major cell phone carriers, T-Mobile, Cingular, and Verizon, refuse to carry porn on their networks). Instead porn content providers have simply adopted Apple's video format in order to mesh their product with the iPod.[28] Pornographic portable digital video is also produced for Universal Media Discs for use with Sony's PlayStation Portable. While devices such as these provide new ways to distribute porn content in ways similar to the VCR and the Internet, this book closes at a moment when control technologies will soon have to undergo a redesign to stay competitive in a market no longer resigned to the home and the media of television and film. The next generation of control technology will concentrate its efforts on such questions and is already under way.

As Deleuze's highway metaphor "multiplies the means of control," we ought to look to wireless devices as technologies to further enable their users as self-regulators if a neoliberal ethos continues to define and augment how we are governed and govern. Cell phone services, for example, already provide parental control features that allow parents to monitor call lists, filter, and block. Some wireless providers design phones specifically for children. Firefly Mobile's phone for kids allows parents to set the phone to reject calls from numbers not in the programmed phone book.[29] Parental controls on cellular phones that filter call lists and block numbers can be regarded as an extension of existing control processes embedded in newer devices, whereas cellular services coming onto the market in 2006, like Sprint's "Family Locator," Disney Mobile, and Verizon Wireless's "Chaperone," introduce a new control technology into our existing lexicon: "tracking." Using global positioning satellites (GPS), these services allow parents to track their children's location as a basic feature. Verizon Wireless's Chaperone furthers the "governing at a distance" principle with its mobile leash, which "lets parents enclose up to 10 areas in virtual fencing, and to receive a text message if their children breach a boundary."[30]

AT&T Wireless's "Smart Limits for Wireless" is a pay service launched in 2007 that allows parents to place limits on the phone calls that their children make. While the service emphasizes the control of minutes to assist in monitoring expenses, the service also provides the ability to block numbers. Phone numbers become "allowed" and "not allowed," and the Web-based parental control tool also functions as an Internet filter for Web content. Smart Limits could not be used on the Apple's iPhone to filter the Internet on account of not being compatible with Safari. At the time of writing this book the new iPhone is not yet available. As always, Apple has kept tight-lipped about its new device scheduled for launch in July 2008. One piece of leaked information that has trickled online is the inclusion of parental controls on the new iPhone. According to AppleInsider, the "Enable Parental Controls" feature will block applications like Safari and YouTube.[31] Users will be able to block access to chat buddies, e-mails, and specific phone numbers. In addition, the playback of music tracks marked "EXPLICIT" by iTunes can be disabled. Enable Parental Controls furthers this book's assertion that the censorial can no longer be studied as a medium-specific pursuit. The *designed-in* practices and process of blocking, filtering, and even cleaning are converged actions when the iPhone enables its users to govern across modes of mediation via its toggle switches. Control is now a matter of gently sliding our finger across the twenty-first century's sleekest designed mobile interface.

While I have skeptically suggested that digital storage capabilities for DVDs and games can provide numerous versions for customized control, this may not prove viable for all control technologies. Internet content is already moving well beyond filtering capabilities as video content is not searchable by filtering software.[32] User-generated video content hosted by Google Video and YouTube circumvents the keyword and keyword pattern blocking to which most Internet filtering software adheres. The New York State Consumer Protection Board issued a warning to parents on June 13, 2006, about video content and the ease of access. Jon Sorenson, for the New York State Consumer Protection Board, claimed that "if Google does not police its own content, it makes the job of parents even more difficult."[33] We are continually told how difficult parenting is today, yet when we play a CD, watch television, go online, touch an iPhone, play a video game or DVD, we cannot forget how enveloping parenting is in its control practices and processes. Google already issues warnings to visitors based on video content, yet blocking proves difficult unless video content is labeled according to the Internet Content Rating Association. This responsibility is not shouldered by Google as it only provides the platform to upload and share video. Rating is the voluntary action left to the discretion of uploaders. Should Google decide to adopt a preventive policy, it would require that all video content be rated and be reviewed by Google "experts" prior to posting. No doubt an arduous task for a company continuing to refuse to hand over information on its users to the federal government, it would further restrict democratic exchange online as "speech" succumbed to the binaries of "approval" or "disapproval." With present filtering software available on the market, the only way to block access to video content on Google is to block at the root level. In the case of Google, this seems highly unlikely since it is a search engine and is relied on by billions (including Internet filtering software companies for advertising) to navigate the Web. Internet filtering software was first introduced as a solution to police the Internet in the mid-1990s, a period when Internet content was still dominated by text. Internet filtering software will have to find ways of filtering video content in order to secure the front door from letting in drafts.

While next-generation control technologies are already preset, another success of control consists in the dissemination of an ethos for regulating media. This ethos requires citizens to govern themselves and, as Rose suggests, to become "experts of themselves" for their own self-governance. Control now accompanies media technology with the inclusion of parental controls as standard features. At the same time, the authority of expertise regarding the parental function has broadened its scope to include non–family values institutions. Just as Blockbuster Inc. and Wal-Mart have imposed structures at the layer of retail to regulate content, Playboy Enterprises Inc. has recently joined the parental control market. Playboy has launched an initiative to educate parents on blocking and filtering technology as well as ratings systems for media content on its cable-based video-on-demand networks. Playboy is calling for education about its own adult-oriented content. It is informing parents how to regulate access to its products in the name of protecting children. Granted Playboy prides itself on soft-focus "tasteful" middle-class porn as opposed to the raunchier fair of, say, *Juggs* magazine, yet it may set a precedent that other adult-content producers may have to follow beyond the

"18 Enter" or "Not 18 Leave" screen that greets all visitors to porn Web sites. Jim Griffiths, president of Playboy Enterprises Inc., does not regard this venture as a contradiction: "What's important to us is that people understand that we are supporting our programming, but also supporting a person's right to choose not to see our programming."[34] Does supporting this right to choose now require that companies enter into the control industry in order to enable choice? Is it not the case that this decision can be made by not purchasing *Playboy* magazine or by not subscribing to its cable services or www.playboy.com, where members can download videos and pictures? Or is this sense of choice now an impossibility when choice is instrumentalized as a formula of rule for disciplined freedoms? Playboy's enthusiastic entrance, spearheaded by Hugh Hefner's daughter, Christie Hefner, into the parental control market demonstrates quite strongly how pervasive self-regulation has become while furthering the plurality of control effects multiplied on, in, and across culture.

Playboy's "educational" initiative (one does begin to wonder if parents will ever learn, considering that V-chip information has been circulating for close to ten years) is supported by www.takeparentalcontrol.org. The Web site provides information for parents about control technologies ranging from the V-chip, Internet filters, and parental controls in gaming consoles, cellular phones, and portable devices as well as about ratings. Providing a glossary of media-related terms and statistical information on media effects on children from the Kaiser Family Foundation, National Cable and Telecommunications Association, and various media researchers, takeparentalcontrol.org is a smorgasbord of technological securitization outfitted in red, black, and white. When visiting the Web site, we are instructed to be patient as parental control "will be at our finger tips in a moment." A cross-section of speakers explains how vital parental control is to protect your family. Parental control has gone from being a designed-in component and a choice to a right, according to the Web site: "Parental Control—It's our right and our responsibility."[35] Will the Second Amendment of the U.S. Constitution soon have to be amended as parental control becomes an electronic writ of defense for the securitization of habitat?

Acknowledgments

Early traces of *Edited Clean Version: Technology and the Culture of Control* were set in place during my graduate studies at the Center for Cultural Studies, University of Leeds. I thank Adrian Rifkin, Griselda Pollock, and Barbara Engh for their mentoring and scholarly grace.

Portions of this book were completed in fall 2005 while in residence at the Humanities Research Institute, University of California, Irvine. I thank David Theo Goldberg, Kevin D. Franklin, and Amelie Hastie for inviting me to participate in the "Object of Media Studies" seminar.

I am indebted to Jane Arthurs, head of the School of Cultural Studies at the University of the West of England, for supporting my research leave in 2005–6.

Much appreciation is extended to Anne Friedberg, Anna Everett, Akira Lippit, and Mark Poster for their support of my academic pursuits. I hope that our paths continue to cross.

Thank you, Richard Morrison, of the University of Minnesota Press, for taking on this project and for helping me see it through. This book would most certainly not have seen the light of day without our various pub meetings.

Adam Brunner, Mary Keirstead, and Alicia Sellheim have assisted me greatly during the production of this book. Thank you for your time, guidance, and patience.

Friends and colleagues who have assisted with this book through conversation, drinking sessions, cinema jaunts, and meals include Fiona Candlin, Kay Dickinson, Anna Beatrice Scott, Mark Bould,

Katrina Glitre, Estella Tincknell, Yvonne Zaragoza Garcia, Eddie Zaragoza, LeRoy and Jacque Hockensmith, Suzanne Buchan, Julia Hall, Ira Livingston, Robert Harvey, Robert Arnett, Avi Santo, my fellow editors with the *Journal of Visual Culture,* and my sister, Ashley Guins.

From my heart, my tears, my tired hands, my sore back, the muscles in my arms, my empty stomach, the strain in my eyes, and my soul (I'm referring to Stax and Motown, of course), I owe my deepest gratitude to Marquard Smith, Joanna Morra, and Heidi Cooley. They provided so many insights and invaluable suggestions along the way.

Ellis Cashmore, longtime mentor and friend, I learn so much from your sunny holiday osmosis.

My family has been a mountain of support. Those simple telephone questions of "How's the book going" always remind me that you are thinking about me, that you are there for me, and that you care. I especially thank my parents for inspiring this project at a very young age: they took me to R-rated movies as a kid, and I never felt the censorial restrictions that young people are forced to experience today. I feel nurtured by their parental guidance and greatly admire their understanding of family values. Also, my mother was totally cool for buying me a copy of the Dead Kennedy's "Too Drunk to Fuck" record in my early teens.

A cliché: this book could not have been written without the extraordinary support from Omayra Zaragoza Cruz. Something closer to the truth, closer to my heart, perhaps: you are my bombers, my dexys, my highs.

Notes

Introduction

1. The film is rated NC-17 (or "slapped with an NC-17," as John Waters spells out) by the Motion Picture Association of America for "Pervasive Sexual Content." Pervasiveness takes the form of "talking about sex," as nothing like the blow job scene from *Pink Flamingos* (1972) is anywhere to be found in *A Dirty Shame*.

2. Andrew Ross suggests a similar inquiry when he doubts the effectiveness of "censorship" to account for the policing of cultural expression in the early 1990s during the Bush-Quail administration. Ross opts for the term *regulation* to account for state practices and self-censoring of culture. See his "The Fine Art of Regulation," in *The Phantom Public Sphere*, ed. Social Text Collective (Minneapolis: University of Minnesota Press, 1993).

3. For most of the twentieth century, media censorship was premised and practiced on a broadcast model of communications whereby censorship is said to emanate (down) from specific institutions and governing organizations. A minority of media producers and executives managed images and sounds for a consumer majority of the mass media of film, television, and radio. The projected image and distant signal brought closer to listeners and viewers were a scrutinized product regulated and licensed by the FCC, internal broadcast standards and practices departments, the Production Code Administration, the Motion Picture Association of America, the National Association of Broadcaster's Code of Good Practice, and other boards, codes, and divisions that attempted to impose industry self-regulatory measures (mostly out of fear of governmental censorship and fines). The media-rich environment of the digital age, characterized by multiplicity, mixed media, convergence, digital logic, mobility, dispersion, flow, decentralization and distributed networks, dislodges and bypasses the centrality and institutionalization of the broadcast model.

4. Nikolas Rose, *Powers of Freedom: Reframing Political Thought* (Cambridge: Cambridge University Press, 1999), 240.

5. Annette Kuhn, *Cinema, Censorship and Sexuality, 1909–1925* (London: Routledge, 1988), 8.

6. Ibid., 3.

7. Kuhn is correct to point out that the prohibition/institutions model treats the object of film as passive and external to the institution of censorship. The model, she writes, "constructs film censorship basically as a one-way street, something that is *done* to films" (4). Jane M. Gaines, who I will return to in detail in chapter 4, draws from Kuhn's work and its critique of the institutional approach to ask "what it is that the censor's cut actually does to the film text." Jane M. Gaines, *Fire and Desire: Mixed-Race Movies in the Silent Era* (Chicago: University of Chicago Press, 2001), 230.

8. Given this book's insistence that time-honored modes of conceptualizing censorial practices require rethinking when digital technologies restructure the intricate process that produces audiovisual media, cinema studies texts firmly devoted to censorship's relation to legality, genre, film history, and the film industry, like Francis G. Couvares, ed., *Movie Censorship and American Culture* (Washington, D.C.: Smithsonian Institution Press, 1996); Matthew Bernstein, ed., *Controlling Hollywood: Censorship and Regulation in the Studio Era* (New Brunswick, N.J.: Rutgers University Press, 1999); Thomas Doherty, *Pre-Code Hollywood: Sex, Immorality, and Insurrection in American Cinema 1930–1934* (New York: Columbia University Press, 1999); and Jon Lewis, *Hollywood v. Hardcore: How the Struggle over Censorship Saved the Modern Film Industry* (New York: New York University Press, 2000), are much less pertinent to this project on account of their investment in documentation of the institution of film censorship within the history of U.S. cinema.

9. Heather Hendershot, *Saturday Morning Censors: Television Regulation before the V-Chip* (Durham, N.C.: Duke University Press, 1998), 2. In addition, Monroe E. Price, ed., *The V-Chip Debate: Content Filtering from Television to the Internet* (Mahwah, N.J.: Lawrence Erlbaum Associates, 1998) is another exception. However, the book appeared prior to the V-chip's official launch onto the U.S. market. A second edition that accounts for television filtering since 2000 is in urgent need.

10. Eric Nuzum, *Parental Advisory: Music Censorship in America* (New York: Perennial, 2001); Martin Cloonan and Reebee Garofalo, eds., *Policing Pop* (Philadelphia: Temple University Press, 2003); and Marie Korpe, ed., *Shoot the Singer: Music Censorship Today* (London: Zed Books, 2004) are a few examples of texts on music censorship.

11. Scholars of cyber law studies like J. M. Balkin, Susan Crawford, Marjorie Heins, and Lawrence Lessig have all moved the study of media

censorship into new areas not immediately accounted for by film or television studies' approaches to the subject.

12. I agree with Stephen Vaughn when he states that many expressed an excitement about the possibility of digital technology for filmmaking and other forms of cultural production via emergent technologies. He also points out that this excitement was shared by "critics of film morality [who] saw powerful new tools for censorship." Robert Vaughn, *Freedom and Entertainment: Rating the Movies in an Age of New Media* (Cambridge: Cambridge University Press, 2006), 258. Vaughn briefly cites the V-chip and the sanitizing practices of CleanFlicks and ClearPlay as such examples. Vaughn's text is one of the few books on film censorship that begins to address new media within this history. However, the "new media" given the most attention is the videocassette and the MPAA's battle with the then new medium of the VCR. His chapter titled "Television" shows no interest in the V-chip, the regulation of video games played upon its screen, or DVD players that reedit films for its screen. The Internet, when invoked, is in the limited capacity of "illegal downloads" and film piracy. Vaughn's text does not really get at the manner by which digital technology has transformed censorial practice despite his book's title. What Vaughn dubs the "The Digital Future," in the form of a concluding chapter, is actually our digital present, and any study vested in asking questions pertaining to how emergent media change our understanding and relation to censorial practices as well as the institution of film censorship ought to begin rather than end here.

13. Jack Z. Bratich, Jeremy Packer, and Cameron McCarthy, eds., *Foucault, Cultural Studies, and Governmentality* (Albany: State University of New York Press, 2003), 4. In their introduction to this text, the editors clarify their collection's aims and intentions: "We seek to assess cultural practices in the United States, where the State is not as central a player in organizing the relationship between 'culture and governing.' Instead, culture is more deeply inscribed in a privatized, corporate set of conditions. The issues of State cultural policy, then, are not the only, or even the primary, way of thinking about culture and governing in the U.S. context" (7–9). It is too difficult to position the subject of media regulation in complete agreement with this claim. Recent media law has a direct effect on how our cultural practices can be administered and self-managed. It is also responsible for smoothing the terrain for both user-centered technologies to be a legally required component in hardware such as televisions and networked computers and for retailers to provide software for reediting Hollywood product. What is valuable for this study is that, as Bratich and company rightly point out and as noted previously in my introduction, legal appraisal can only be *an element* in a much larger analysis of modes of governing, and as such micro, banal practices that may be under the radar of studies of policy or governmentality are equally vital for gaining an understanding of culture and governing.

14. Bratich, Packer, and McCarthy, eds., *Foucault,* 8. In his essential "Putting Policy into Cultural Studies," in *Cultural Studies,* ed. Lawrence Grossberg, Cary Nelson, and Paula Treichler (London: Routledge, 1992), Tony Bennett returns to Raymond Williams's seminal definition of culture as a corrective venture. For Bennett, Williams ignores culture's transformation in the eighteenth and nineteenth century as both "object and instrument of government" (26). This is the subject of his study on the exhibitionary complex whereby visual culture of the said period enacts a power-knowledge relation through industrial protocols of seeing; namely, the reorganization of the museum as a popular educational institute and civilizing technology along with the emergence of the industrial fair as imperialistic spectacle and complex for seeing and displaying national identity, power, and citizenry. See Tony Bennett, *The Birth of the Museum: History, Theory, Politics* (London: Routledge, 1995). For Bennett, then, the instrumentalization of culture sounds of Foucauldian mechanisms of power and government when culture is conceived as a "historically produced surface of social regulation whose distinctiveness is to be identified and accounted for in terms of (i) the specific types of attributes and forms of conduct that are established as its targets, (ii) the techniques that are proposed for the maintenance or transformation of such attributes or forms of conduct, (iii) the assembly of such techniques into particular programs of government, and (iv) the inscription of such programs into the operative procedures of specific cultural technologies" (27). Bennett returns to this address more directly in relation to "governmentality studies" in "Culture and Governmentality," in *Foucault,* ed. Bratich, Packer, and McCarthy. What is of significance here is that the editors seek to identify relations of culture and governing outside of policy. They turn to ways of identifying and working through modes of policing played out across culture and as culture. Although not addressed by Bratich, Packer, and McCarthy in their introduction, cultural studies has historically been unashamedly guilty of investing heavily in how groups utilize cultural commodities as signifying practices within the space of the everyday. Acts of usage framed in the, dare I say, "canonical" vocabulary of counterhegemonic strategies through "poaching," "resistance," "bricolage," "reappropriation," "retrieval," and "semiotic guerrilla warfare" are often not studied within a larger context of governance. Cultural studies looks to usage when it is couched in oppositional terms. Perhaps, the "governmental turn" will force those of us invested in cultural politics to readdress how we research and teach these cultural practices by positioning them into a larger discussion of policy, legal, and governmentality studies. One such text that addresses the study of law within the field of cultural studies is Jerry Leonard, ed., *Legal Studies as Cultural Studies: A Reader in (Post) Modern Critical Theory* (Albany: State University of New York Press, 1995).

15. Michel Foucault, "Space, Knowledge, and Power," in *The Foucault Reader,* ed. Paul Rabinow (New York: Pantheon, 1984) finds Foucault responding to changes in the relations between space and power throughout history. Foucault first provides an exegesis on the dangers of urban space in the nineteenth century. He then moves into a discussion of the railroad as a technological triumph that augments new spatial techniques to power and territories. The railroad is said to have "established a network of communication no longer corresponding necessarily to the traditional network of roads . . ." (243). Foucault then goes on to inform his readers about the German military's mass mobilization of its war machine in opposition to the expense of the French belief that the railroad would "render war impossible" (243). The last aspect of new relations to space and power is shyly asserted, then completely abandoned: "The third development, which came later, was electricity" (243). The question of electricity, the potential foray into media technology, is left in the dark like the inhabitants of the dungeon.

16. See Alexander R. Galloway, *Protocol: How Control Exists after Decentralization* (Cambridge, Mass.: MIT Press, 2004); and Mark Poster, *Information Please: Culture and Politics in the Age of Digital Machines* (Durham, N.C.: Duke University Press, 2006). Chapter 9, "Who Controls Digital Culture?" is especially valuable. Wendy Hui Kyong Chun employs the phrase "control technologies" in her *Control and Freedom: Power and Paranoia in the Age of Fiber Optics* (Cambridge, Mass.: MIT Press, 2006) to account for the workings of power at the conjunction of control and freedom. Also building upon Deleuze's work on control, Chun explores relationships between identity, sexuality, and fiber-optic networks. For our interests, Chun acknowledges the challenges of regulating the "mass medium" of the Internet in her discussion of online pornography. However in chapter 2, "Screening Pornography," which provides an excellent engagement with debates on cyberporn in the mid-late 1990s, Chun does not consider filtering as a sustained regulatory practice. While the sheer volume of Web content does make regulation a daunting task, we ought to concentrate on those technologies in place that promise to manage and administer the Internet.

17. Gilles Deleuze, "Postscript on Control Societies," in *Negotiations,* trans. Martin Joughin (New York: Columbia University Press, 1995), 178.

1. Control

1. Michel Foucault's "Governmentality" was originally presented as a lecture at the Collège de France in 1978. Its first English translation appeared in 1979. Its most well-known version is the 1991 republication and revision by Colin Gordon that appears in Graham Burchell, Colin Gordon, and Peter Miller, *The Foucault Effect* (Chicago: University of Chicago Press,

1991), 87–104. See their acknowledgments for complete details on various translations of the lecture. Originally published in *L'Autre Journal* no. 1 (1990), Gilles Deleuze's "Postscript on Control Societies" first appeared in English in *October 59* (1992). It has since appeared in the collection of conversations, commentaries, and interviews published from the French *Pourparlers* (1990) as *Negotiations,* trans. Martin Joughin (New York: Columbia University Press, 1995). The short essay has since been anthologized in *October: The Second Decade, 1986–1996* (1997) and included in the edited collection/exhibition *CTRL [Space]: Rhetorics of Surveillance from Bentham to Big Brother* (2002).

2. Gilles Deleuze, "Control and Becoming," in *Negotiations;* and Gilles Deleuze, "Having an Idea in Cinema," in *Deleuze and Guattari: New Mappings in Politics, Philosophy, and Culture,* ed. Eleanor Kaufman and Kevin Jon Heller (Minneapolis: University of Minnesota Press, 1998). Traces of Deleuze's formulation of control can also be found in Gilles Deleuze, *Foucault,* trans. Seán Hand (Minnesota: University of Minnesota Press, 1988); and Gilles Deleuze and Félix Guattari, *A Thousand Plateaus: Capitalism and Schizophrenia,* trans. Brian Massumi (Minneapolis: University of Minnesota Press, 1987).

3. Deleuze, "Control and Becoming," 174.

4. Foucault, "Governmentality," 102.

5. Nikolas Rose, *Powers of Freedom: Reframing Political Thought* (Cambridge: Cambridge University Press, 1999), 234.

6. Michael Hardt and Antonio Negri, *Empire* (Cambridge, Mass.: Harvard University Press, 2000), 330.

7. Michel Foucault, *Discipline and Punish: The Birth of the Prison,* trans. Alan Sheridan (New York: Vintage, 1977), 215.

8. Deleuze, "Postscript," 178.

9. Foucault, *Discipline and Punish,* 143.

10. Deleuze, "Postscript," 178; original emphasis.

11. Mark Poster, *Foucault, Marxism and History: Mode of Production versus Mode of Information* (Cambridge: Polity, 1984), 103. The concept of the "superpanopticon" is further elaborated upon in his subsequent writings on critical theory and digital media: Mark Poster, *The Mode of Information: Poststructuralism and Social Context* (Chicago: University of Chicago Press, 1991); and Mark Poster, *The Second Media Age* (Cambridge: Polity Press, 1995).

12. Deleuze, "Having an Idea in Cinema," 17.

13. Michael Hardt, "The Withering of Civil Society," in *Deleuze and Guattari,* ed. Kaufman and Heller, 31; emphasis added.

14. Hardt and Negri, *Empire,* 23.

15. Deleuze, "Having an Idea in Cinema," 18.

16. Ibid., 18.

17. Most notably the seminal Burchell, Gordon, and Miller, *The Foucault Effect*; the collection on governance, Andrew Barry, Thomas Osborne, and Nikolas Rose, eds., *Foucault and Political Reason: Liberalism, Neo-liberalism and Rationalities of Government* (Chicago: University of Chicago Press, 1996); Paul Rabinow, ed., *Foucault, Ethics: Subjectivity and Truth* (New York: New Press, 1997); Mitchell Dean, *Governmentality: Power and Rule in Modern Society* (London: Sage, 1999); Nikolas Rose, *Inventing Ourselves: Psychology, Power, and Personhood* (Cambridge: Cambridge University Press, 1998); and Rose, *Powers of Freedom*; as well as Jack Z. Bratich, Jeremy Packer, and Cameron McCarthy, eds., *Foucault, Cultural Studies, and Governmentality* (Albany: State University of New York Press, 2003).

18. Barry, Osborne, and Rose, *Foucault and Political Reason*, 2.

19. Nikolas Rose, "Government, Authority, and Expertise in Advanced Liberalism," *Economy and Society* 22, 3 (1993): 287; hereafter cited as "Government." A second version of this article, slightly more expansive than its precursor, appeared as "Governing 'Advanced' Liberal Democracies" in *Foucault and Political Reason*, ed. Barry, Osborne, and Rose; hereafter cited as "Governing." I draw from both essays and cite each accordingly.

20. Rose, "Governing," 295.

21. Foucault, "Governmentality," 103.

22. Deleuze, "Having an Idea in Cinema," 18. Roads and highways are a topic in a discussion of the spatialization of power between Foucault, Deleuze, and Félix Guattari conducted by François Fourquet in 1973 for *Recherches* 13 and republished as "Equipments of Power: Towns, Territories and Collective Equipments," in *Foucault Live: Collected Interviews, 1961–1984,* ed. Sylvère Lotringer (New York: Semiotext(e), 1996). Foucault cites the roadway as an "element of crystallization of state power" (106), while Deleuze concentrates on its "channeled nomadism" (107). Prior to *Discipline and Punish* as well as Deleuze's essays on control, we can already catch a glimpse in 1973 of disciplinary logic transfusing into control.

23. Rose, *Powers of Freedom*, 234.

24. Tony Bennett, "Culture and Governmentality," in *Foucault*, ed. Bratich, Packer, and McCarthy, 56.

25. Rose, "Government," 295.

26. Rose, "Governing," 59.

27. The "art of distributions" proposed in *Discipline and Punish* concentrated on the marshalling of space comprised through the techniques of enclosure and confinement, the composition of an analytical space through partitioning, the generation of functional space, and hierarchical structuralization to engineer a panoptic principle. As is well known, discipline's "political anatomy of detail" invested bodies in the institutions organized according to architectural configurations that endeavored to mold the effects

of normalizing power relations. Foucault offers the example of the school as a disciplinary institution and mechanism for power-knowledge relations. As a pedagogical machine the school expressed its modes of conduct in its very architectural organization: "the disciplinary institutions secreted a machinery of control that functioned like a microscope of conduct; the fine, analytical divisions that they created formed around men an apparatus of observation, recording and training" (Foucault, *Discipline and Punish*, 173). The home too is an institution given over to meticulous assemblage of arrangements ("simple instruments") to produce certain effects and modes of conduct in bodies within its specified and functional architecture for the prescription of morality. See Foucault's discussion of the home in *The History of Sexuality Volume 1* (New York: Vintage Press, 1978).

28. Rose, *Powers of Freedom*, 274. Aside from insurance policies and elaborate home security systems, we could also add an entire systematic ethics of lifestyle that strategizes space in terms of the "right" schooling for children, "safe" areas to play, "good" friends, convenient shopping areas, and SUV-carapaces to shield and transport inhabitants from one protected domain to another across a community whose collective task is the preservation, conservation, and maintenance of safety through a network of security.

29. Ibid., 249.

30. Ibid., 247.

31. Rose, "Governing," 73.

32. Rose, *Powers of Freedom*, 74.

33. Rose assigns the family a specific task, one that accords with Foucault's technologies of bio-power. The family becomes a "chief agent" or "anchoring device" along with a cast of other "experts" in what Foucault calls "life-administering power." In *The History of Sexuality Volume 1*, Foucault sees a new mode of power emerge that displaces the sovereign's supreme right to take life. "The old power of death that symbolized sovereign power," Foucault writes, "was now carefully supplanted by the administration of bodies and the calculated management of life" (140). Bio-power's "power over life" is produced by power-knowledge technologies that involve the poles of the body and species. Bio-power centers on the body as an object of power. The other pole of bio-power is the "species body," the "body imbued with the mechanics of life and serving as the basis of the biological processes: propagation, births and mortality, the level of health, life expectance and longevity . . ." (139). The duality of subjugating the body in a disparate regime of confinement, distribution, and meticulous control along with the management and policing of populations coalesced in a power-relation that "invest[s] life through and through" (139). Life itself, managed by the disciplines of the body and bio-politics of the population,

becomes an object to develop, morally propagate, and generalize strategies of rule in a manner beneficial to the "taking charge of life."

34. In programming language the term *function* refers to a type of procedure or operation. In user parlance *function keys* perform specific operations like the *delete function* to remove undesirable text. My pairing of *parental* with *function* is an attempt to move beyond specific human (i.e., parent) actions to account for a larger governmentality that, while expressed through parents, is not restricted to their domains and is a mode of operations implicit in other practices of regulation. In other words, parental function is a normalizing practice and process for the governing of culture that is not restricted to the incarnations of parents but is a power-knowledge relation expressed through media technology in the name of parenting.

35. I would like to revisit Deleuze's claim that the family is an "interior" that is in the process of breaking down like other disciplinary institutions. The family, for Deleuze, is "transmutable," and this position is at odds with Paul Virilio's understanding of the family in *Open Sky,* trans. Julie Rose (London: Verso, 1997). Virilio mourns the family's transmutability on account of an acceleration of telecommunications "tools" that redistribute our relationship to space and time. The family's domain is not exempt from redistribution since, as Virilio contends, "the more the city expands and spreads it tentacles, the more the family unit dwindles and becomes a minority" (12). Virilio's own disdain for contemporary mediated and networked societies with their erosion of space through the acceleration of time as well as his liberal humanistic critique of technology that maintains a staunch opposition between the human body and the technical fails to consider how new technologies enable the family to "spread its tentacles" for purposes of securitization. Family's regulatory machinery is no longer reliant upon the calculated use of disciplinary strictures such as the school, the home, or the reproductive micro-space of the bedroom for the deployment of bio-power strategies for normalizing and civilizing the subject and species. Virilio still proves invaluable for articulating the workings of control and will be relied upon throughout this book (particularly in chapters 2 and 3). His shortsightedness with respect to the family's diffusion of itself through control technologies allows one interested in such a process to articulate these qualities in detail.

36. Examples of consumer choice that Rose (1996) draws from include services of health, education, and finance; Rose, "Governing."

37. Rose, "Government," 285.

38. Deleuze, "Postscript," 180.

39. Aside from book-length studies that I have mentioned previously, I would also include articles such as Fiona Allon, "An Ontology of Everyday Control: Space, Media Flows and 'Smart' Living in the Absolute Present," in

Mediaspace: Place, Scale and Culture in the Media Age, ed. Nick Couldry and Anna McCarthy (London: Routledge, 2004); Catherine Liu, "A Brief Genealogy of Privacy: *CTRL [Space]*: Rhetorics of Surveillance from Bentham to Big Brother," *Grey Room* 15 (2004); Raiford Guins, "'Now You're Living': The Promise of Home Theater and Deleuze's 'New Freedoms,'" *Television and New Media* 2, 4 (2001).

40. This is in spite of Gilbert Simondon's influence on Deleuze as well as the importance of Jean Baudrillard and Bruno Latour for work on media and technology in the 1980s. Deleuze does acknowledge Paul Virilio in "Postscript on Control Societies"; however, Virilio's entrenched humanism is at odds with Deleuze's post-disciplinary networked regime perspective.

41. Alexander R. Galloway, *Protocol: How Control Exists after Decentralization* (Cambridge, Mass.: MIT Press, 2004), 4.

42. Ibid., 13.

43. Deleuze, "Control and Becoming," 175.

44. The subject of "new media" runs a risk of instilling a dangerous hierarchy in its object of study. Far too often the study of new media is equated with "Internet studies" or "information studies." If this equation persists, it will continue to turn a blind eye to other technologies imbricated in strategies of control, especially technologies similarly constitutive of control's emphasis on the democratization of our daily practices and lives.

45. Deleuze, "Postscript," 180.

46. See, for example, William Bogard, *The Simulation of Surveillance: Hypercontrol in Telematic Societies* (Cambridge: Cambridge University Press, 1996); and David Lyons, *The Electronic Eye: The Rise of Surveillance Society* (Cambridge: Polity Press, 1994).

47. See Sally Wyatt's discussion of "non-users" in "Non-Users Also Matter: The Construction of Users and Non-Users of the Internet," in *How Users Matter: The Co-Construction of Users and Technologies*, ed. Nelly Oudshoorn and Trevor Pinch (Cambridge, Mass.: MIT Press, 2003).

48. Jay David Bolter and Richard Grusin, *Remediation: Understanding New Media* (Cambridge: MIT Press, 1999).

49. Marshall McLuhan, *Understanding Media: The Extensions of Man* (New York: Signet, 1964), 274.

50. Foucault, *Discipline and Punish*, 136.

51. Deleuze, "Having an Idea in Cinema," 18.

52. McLuhan, *Understanding Media*, viii, 19.

53. Ibid., 24.

54. Ibid., viii.

55. Lewis H. Lapham, "The Eternal Now," in *Understanding Media: The Extensions of Man* (Cambridge, Mass.: MIT University Press, 1994), xiii.

2. Blocking

1. "Apologetic Jackson Says 'Costume Reveal' Went Awry," *CNN.com*, 3 February 2004, http://www.cnn.com/2004/US/02/02/superbowl.jackson/ (accessed 3 February 2004).

2. While MTV issued an immediate apology, prior to the Super Bowl its Web site boasted: "Janet Jackson's Super Bowl show promises shocking moments." And after the "shocking moment" MTV's Web site proudly ran this headline: "Janet Jackson Got Nasty at the MTV-Produced Super Bowl Halftime Show," 4 February 2004, http://www.mtv.com/news/articles/1484644/20040128/jackson_janet.jhtml?headlines=true (accessed 4 February 2004).

3. The commission decided not to fine the two hundred-plus CBS affiliate stations that aired Super Bowl XXXVIII on the evening of February 1, 2004. Instead, only the CBS stations owned by parent company Viacom Inc. (who runs a monopoly on music video by owning MTV, MTV2, VH1, and BET) were targeted and received the largest fine against a television broadcaster in U.S. history. In the immediate wake of the Jackson-Timberlake incident, the FCC fined Clear Channel's Bubba the Love Sponge and Howard Stern for indecency. A time delay was quickly adopted for the 2004 Grammy Awards ceremonies to preempt further "accidents."

4. Imagery of breasts is not absent from television. Advertisements for Victoria's Secret and the latest exercise equipment display women's breasts in their sheer fashion. Breasts are visible (but not fully exposed) in televised gymnastic and swimming events. Have we already forgotten Brandi Chastain's monumental celebration and Nike endorsement after winning the Women's World Cup in 1999? Her breasts were not exposed, yet on account of removing her jersey to celebrate in her sports bra, she was quickly covered from view. Cable and satellite television programs like *Nip/Tuck* cut into breast tissue on a regular basis. Trash talk shows like *The Jerry Springer Show* quickly pixelate exposed breasts when a rehearsed skirmish breaks out. In the 1990s breasts regularly drifted across television screens, tossed to and fro during Pamela Anderson's famous slow-motion jog for the opening credits of the global phenomenon that was *Bay Watch* (1989–2001). Erect nipples are increasingly noticeable in prime-time sitcoms. Premium channels run R-rated Hollywood films, where nudity is classified according to MPAA ratings guidelines. MTV is certainly fond of breasts, especially as jiggly props in the assembly line of "bling-bling" stardom and masculine fantasies of material wealth and 9mm entrepreneurship. Lastly, anyone who has suffered from insomnia is no stranger to *Girls Gone Wild* infomercials, where breasts, eagerly revealed to the accompaniment of requisite spring-break hollers, are pixelated to deny full visual access.

5. "FCC Chair Vows to Investigate Halftime Flash," *MSNNBC.com*, 4 February 2004, http://www.msnbc.msn.com/id/4131637/ (accessed 4 February 2004).

6. "Statement of Chairman Michael K. Powell," *Complaints against Various Television Licensees Concerning Their February 1, 2004, Broadcast of the Super Bowl XXXVIII Halftime Show*, 22 September 2004, http://www.law.umkc.edu/faculty/projects/ftrials/conlaw/FCCjackson.html (accessed 17 October 2004). Janet Jackson's exhibition was crafted for prime-time audiences accustomed to partially obscured televisual images. Like the various "bugs"—inanimate or animated electronic watermarks—used for network recognition, television ratings, sponsorship and corporate logos, and announcements for upcoming broadcasts, the broadcast image of Jackson's breast was marked and shielded from total view by her strategically placed nipple shield. It was not completely visible, and Powell's gasp at witnessing a prime-time "burlesque show" suggests this: burlesque harbors the anachronism of partial nudity, unlike its modern counterpart, the fully nude strip show. Jackson's nipple shield actually covered her entire areola, and the brief flash of her breast revealed a partially visible breast and nipple ornately decorated with jewelry worn in conjunction with a nipple piercing. This was a nipple *made* for prime-time broadcast: a nipple blocked from total visual access like so many body parts, gestures, words, scenes, and programs masked by regulatory procedures and control technologies designed in media of the twenty-first century.

7. See Adam Thierer, "The FCC as Surrogate Parent," *National Review Online*, 25 June 2004, http://www.cbsnews.com/stories/2004/06/25/opinion/main626208.shtml (accessed 1 July 2004).

8. FOX, in particular, has greatly stepped up its V-chip promotion campaign since 2004. A few of its efforts include an ad campaign for the V-chip in major U.S. news periodicals, the creation of a public service announcement for its prime-time slot, a news special on the V-chip for its Fox News Channel, and the redesign of a larger ratings depicter to appear for fifteen seconds at the beginning of each show and after commercial interludes. In addition, prime-time schedules that appear at www.fox.com include television show ratings.

9. J. M . Balkin, "Media Filters, The V-Chip, and the Foundations of Broadcast Regulation," *Duke Law Journal* 45, 6 (1996): 1143.

10. Ken Belson, "Helping Parents Lock the TV Remote," *New York Times*, 30 August 2004, sec. C. Tobe Hooper's *Texas Chainsaw Massacre* (1974) has never aired on network television. Despite its allegorical subject matter of normality as monstrous, it has very little profanity (if any), no nudity, and very little gore. Walsh's reference is purely a scare tactic to illustrate the "horrors" that lurk in the realm of possibility.

11. Another measure employed by television stations is simply to pull pro-

gramming out of fear of FCC fines and licenses being revoked. This was the case with the broadcast of Steven Spielberg's *Saving Private Ryan* scheduled to air on Veterans Day, 2004. ABC affiliates in cities like Dallas and Phoenix opted not to air the film, which was played on network television previously, in 2001 and 2002. The concerns: graphic violence and profanity—two categories covered under the new television ratings code, two categories that prompted ABC to air a disclaimer prior to its broadcast in select cities, two categories that were covered by the MPAA-approved R rating for the film's original cinema release and for the film's cable, video, and DVD releases. Even Hollywood versions of casualties of war are deemed indecent for an administration and Bush-appointed chair of the FCC, which works hard to keep body bags on foreign soil and away from homeland eyes.

12. William Boddy, "Redefining the Home Screen: Technological Convergence as Trauma and Business Plan," in *Rethinking Media Change: The Aesthetics of Transition*, ed. David Thorburn and Henry Jenkins (Cambridge, Mass.: MIT Press, 2003), 191.

13. Much to my disappointment, Lynn Spigel and Jan Olsson, eds., *Television after TV: Essays on a Medium in Transition* (Durham, N.C.: Duke University Press, 2004) neglects governance when citing the various ways that television has reinvented itself over the past decade.

14. *Telecommunications Act of 1996*, Title V, Subtitle B., Sec. 551. C(x). Networks like ABC, CBS, and NBC employed standards departments early in their histories of broadcast. The networks in conjunction with the National Association of Broadcasters maintained standards for broadcast. The deregulatory aims of the Reagan-Bush era found that the National Association of Broadcasters inhibited free trade (the NAB restricted advertising time aimed at children. See Heather Hendershot, *Saturday Morning Censors: Television Regulation before the V-Chip* [Durham, N.C.: Duke University Press, 1998]), and standards divisions were reduced. Debates concerning how to regulate televisual content after television deregulation in the early 1980s and the pervasive viewing options posed by cable, satellite, pay-per-view, and video streaming to account for programming containing themes, images, or dialogue discerned as violent or indecent and the possible introduction of devices to block specific programming have been continuous within Canada since the early 1990s. For example, the Report to the Canadian Radio-Television and Telecommunications Commission (CRTC) was issued in 1997 to publicize the findings about the V-chip's performance as well as the development of the Canadian Television Rating System. In the early to mid-1990s, the United States began to conduct V-chip test trials and introduce new legislation. This took the form of the Television Violence Act, which allowed broadcasters to work together to manage violence on television without fear of violating antitrust laws, and the Television Decoder Circuitry Act, which required television to become

capable of decoding signals for closed captioning. In 1995 Senator Edward Markey attached a V-chip provision to the House telecommunications reform legislation.

15. "Consumer discretion technologies" is a term introduced in the mid-1990s to account for the variety of technologies developed "for increased consumer control over the content of media transmissions entering the home"; cited in John Federman, *Media Ratings: Design, Use and Consequences* (Studio City, Calif.: Mediascope, Inc., 1996), 43.

16. Such devices are described in detail in Federman, *Media Ratings,* 43–62.

17. For example, in my personal oppositional use of my Sony Trinitron's channel-blocking capabilities, I have programmed my television to block out PAX, Spike TV, the Nashville Network, ABC and the Disney Channel, CNN, MTV, MSNBC, ESPN (and ESPN 2), and other channels that carry "indecent" programming (especially reality shows, fishing and hunting shows, golf, NASCAR, and American football).

18. Cable operators are required by law to offer subscribers "Lockboxes" and "Set-Top Boxes" that block programming based on various criteria.

19. The Telecommunications Act of 1996 also stipulated that if the television industry did not provide a ratings system to correspond with the V-chip within one year of the new law, then the FCC would be granted the right to select a committee to design its own television ratings system.

20. Jack Valenti, cited in "Jack of All Trades: The Man in the Middle of the V-Chip," *Broadcasting and Cable,* 18 March 1996, 26.

21. Motion Pictures Association of America, http://www.mpaa.org (accessed 12 May 1999). In 1999 Jack Valenti's voice was the authorial presence on the MPAA Web page. His first-person narrative provided a history of the MPAA and explained its ratings system to visitors. This narrative no longer appears on the current MPAA home page. Yet, the presence of parent persists, as visitors can "click" on the "Information for Parents" menu-bar option to learn about PauseParentPlay.org, an organization that provides online information on media regulation for parents.

22. The category of parent is more than a target group for information. It is also a requirement for members of the MPAA board (a violation in hiring practices?). Members must have a "shared parenthood experience" in order to subjectively impose their decision on a film (and now television). Members are required to "put themselves in the role of most American parents so they can view a film and apply a rating that most parents would find suitable and helpful . . ."; Motion Pictures Association of America, http://www.mpaa.org/Ratings_HowRated.asp.

23. Cited in Paige Albiniak, "Ratings Get Revamped," *Broadcasting and Cable,* 14 July 1997, 4.

24. Ibid., 6.

25. Matthew Murray, "Technological Thresholds: The V-chip, the Family, and Media Regulation," *Convergence* 3, 1 (1997): 31.

26. Early scholarly work on the V-chip could only offer skeptical considerations of the legal rhetoric responsible for the V-chip, cite problems with the proposed ratings, and question the implicit ideologies of "family values" and choice through which the V-chip is promoted. David Kopel, "Massaging the Medium: Analyzing and Responding to Media Violence without Harming the First Amendment," *Kansas Journal of Law and Public Policy* 4, 17 (1995); and Matthew L. Spitzer, "A First Glance at the Constitutionality of the V-Chip Ratings System," in *Television Violence and Public Policy*, ed. James T. Hamilton (Ann Arbor: University of Michigan Press, 1998) concentrated on the V-chip in regard to whether it and its ratings were constitutional. Robert Corn-Revere, "V Is Not for Voluntary," *Cato Institute Briefing Paper* no. 24 (1995) found the voluntary component of the new television ratings to be suspect. Greg Makris, "The Myth of a Technological Solution to Television Violence: Identifying Problems with the V-Chip," *Journal of Communication Inquiry* 20, 2 (1996) undertook a study of the legal, technological, and economic problems facing the new technology to determine whether the V-chip would be a viable solution to concerns over television content. Matthew Murray challenged the view that the V-chip is an empowering technology. The new television ratings and media filters were the subjects of Monroe E. Price, ed., *The V-Chip Debate: Content Filtering from Television to the Internet* (Mahwah, N.J.: Lawrence Erlbaum Associates, 1998). Raiford Guins, "The V-Chip: Seeing Eugenically," *West Coast Line* 31–34, 1 (2000) positioned the V-chip into the theoretical projects of Deleuze's writings on control and Virilio's concept of eugenics of sight. And, more recently, Marjorie Heins, director of the Free Expression Policy Project, included the V-chip in her book on censorship, youth, and indecency laws: *Not in Front of the Children* (New York: Hill and Wang, 2001).

27. Lobbying for three hours a week of educational television for children, Vice President Gore claimed: "Anybody who's ever seen a young child after they've watched the show understands why . . . shows like the *Power Rangers* project an image of violence that is simultaneously sugary and sociopathetic"; cited in Cynthia Littleton, "Gore Seeks 3-Hours Kids Programming," *Broadcasting & Cable*, 8 July 1996, 24. I guess after watching *Buffy*, one is even more confused as to whether one should slay or sleep with vampires.

28. Paul Levinson, *The Soft Edge: A Natural History and Future of the Information Revolution* (London: Routledge, 1997), 158.

29. Heins, *Not in Front of the Children*, 195.

30. Dick Wolf, cited in Michael Schneider, "Bored Lips Sink Chips: After All the Fuss, Net Content Is Relegated to the Back Burner," *Variety*, 17–23 December 2001, 29.

31. Figures provided by Schneider, "Bored Lips," 29.

32. Littleton, "Gore Seeks 3-Hours Kids Programming," 25.

33. Thorburn and Henry Jenkins, eds., *Rethinking Media Change*, 2.

34. Raymond Williams's *Television: Technology and Cultural Form* (London: Fontana, 1974) was composed while serving as a visiting professor at Stanford in 1972. His concept of "flow" accounts for television's total sequence of programs, commercials, and news. For Williams, flow is the "central television experience" (95). Our desire to watch a single program often gives way to the flow of content. This flow of televisual information constitutes the general experience of watching television. The significance of flow is not only Williams's analysis of the mode of programmed content in the early 1970s but also his assertion that any combination of flow demonstrates the meanings and values of the culture from which it emanates. In addition to Uricchio's rethinking of Williams's notion of flow for the post-network era, see Amanda D. Lotz, *The Television Will Be Revolutionized* (New York: NYU Press, 2007).

35. William Uricchio, "Television's Next Generation: Technology/Interface Culture/Flow," in *Television after TV*, ed. Spigel and Olsson, 170.

36. James R. Walker and Robert V. Bellamy Jr., eds., *The Remote Control in the New Age of Television* (Westport, Conn.: Praeger, 1993), 4. The edited collection is an excellent dedicated study of the history and theory of television remote control devices.

37. Raymond Williams, *Television: Technology and Cultural Form* (Glasgow: Fontana/Collins, 1974), 26.

38. Ibid., 139.

39. Marjorie Heins, "Three Questions about Television Ratings," in *The V-Chip Debate*, ed. Price, 51.

40. Amy Jordan quoted in Lynn Smith, "Indecency Feud Could Bring V Back to TVs," *Los Angeles Times*, 22 March 2004, sec. A1.

41. Ibid., A1.

42. RCA, "The V-chip puts you in control," http://www.rca.com/content/viewdetail/1,2811,EI700584-CI700353,00.html (accessed 24 February 2005).

43. Murray, "Technological Thresholds," 31.

44. Heins, *Not in Front of the Children*, 197.

45. Balkin, "Media Filters," 1145.

46. Cited in Leo Bogart, "Should the V-chip Fall Where It May?" *Television Quarterly* 28, 3 (1998): 47.

47. *Oxford English Dictionary*, s.v. "View," http://dictionary.oed.com/cgi/entry/50277423?query_type=word&queryword=view&first=1&max_to_show=10&sort_type=alpha&result_place=1&search_id=F0rk-3P8eoP-9293&hilite=50277423 (accessed 9 September 2004).

48. Brian Lowery, "The Eve of Uncertain V-Chip Era; Television: Creator

of the Device Wonders If It Will Be Fully Used," *Los Angeles Times,* 30 June 1999, sec. Calendar; part F; my emphasis.

49. Heins, *Not in Front of the Children,* 197.

50. Michel Foucault proclaimed, perhaps forewarned, that the "judges of normality are present everywhere"; *Discipline and Punish: The Birth of the Prison,* trans. Alan Sheridan (New York: Vintage, 1977), 304. I would add that technologies of control reveal that normality's indices are increasingly *in everything* as well.

51. John Johnson, "Machinic Vision," *Critical Inquiry* 26 (1999): 29.

52. Paul Virilio, *The Vision Machine,* trans. Julie Rose (London: BFI Press, 1994). Paradoxical logic is the third order of Virilio's logistics of the image. In the first order, formal logic, the production of the image is associated with "painting, engraving and etching, architecture" (63), and in the second, dialectic logic, is marked with the reproductive qualities of photography and film. The order of the paradoxical logic belongs to video and the computer in the production of digital imagery that Virilio defines as virtual. This order comes to dominate and replace that which it sought to represent, hence the paradox.

53. For many of Virilio's books, a considerable amount of time passes before his work appears in English translation. *The Vision Machine* first appeared as *La Machine de Vision* (Paris: Galilée, 1988). We must take this into account when consulting his work on media and technology matters, as digital objects will differ radically from the period of his original address. Moore's Law renders translation of works on technology a decrepit affair.

54. Virilio, *Vision Machine,* 59.

55. See Anne Friedberg, "Virilio's Screen: The Work of Metaphor in the Age of Technological Convergence," *Journal of Visual Culture* 3, 2 (2004): 183–94, for an excellent pinning down of Virilio's slippery usage of the metaphor of the screen in his various projects.

56. Cited in John Armitage, "From Modernism to Hypermodernism and Beyond: An Interview with Paul Virilio," in *Paul Virilio: From Modernism to Hypermodernism and Beyond,* ed. John Armitage (London: Sage, 2000), 49.

57. Ibid., 48; author's original emphasis. In the same edited collection that contains Virilio's interview, James Der Derian addresses Virilio's concerns over the mechanization of vision when he states that "with the appearance of a global view comes the disappearance of the viewer-subject: in the immediacy of perception, our eyes become indistinguishable from the camera's optics, and critical consciousness goes missing"; "The Conceptual Cosmology of Paul Virilio," in *Paul Virilio,* ed. Armitage, 216.

58. Virilio, *Vision Machine,* 65.

59. Johnson, "Machinic Vision"; and Sean Cubitt, "Virilio and New Media," *Theory, Culture & Society* 16, 5–6 (1999): 127–42. Gilles Deleuze references Virilio on two occasions when he writes of control. The first

appears in *Foucault* (trans. Seán Hand [Minnesota: University of Minnesota Press, 1988]). Deleuze demonstrates that Virilio is not in disagreement with Foucault as Virilio believes when he writes, "the problem for 'police,' is not one of confinement but concerns the 'highways,' speed or acceleration, the mastery and control of speed, circuits and grids set up in open space" (42). Later, in "Postscript on Control Societies" (*October* 59 [1992]), Deleuze briefly mentions Virilio as a figure whose theoretical interests are locatable within the analysis of the passage from disciplinarity to control. Deleuze is far too generous in his assertions. Virilio's study of crisis (crisis of perception, crisis of time, crisis of architecture) locates itself in histories of communication technologies and information and as such crosses currents with Deleuze's mapping of control societies' "third generation of machines." However, Virilio's statement on control in *Speed and Politics* (New York: Semiotext(e), 1986) that "we only need refer to the necessary controls and constraints of the railway, airway or highway infrastructure to see the fatal impulse: the more speed increases, the faster freedom decreases" (142) seems to disallow Deleuze's notion of disciplined freedom. Virilio's formula is the converse of Deleuze's usage of the highway metaphor in expressing "the freedoms" of control. While Virilio is more attuned to the history of dromology and studies modes of transportation and mobilization within their historical registers (well sometimes) rather than metaphorical currency, it nonetheless remains that Virilio has not necessarily accelerated completely into Deleuze's theory of control society.

60. Paul Virilio, *Polar Inertia*, trans. Patrick Camiller (London: Sage, 2000), 59.

61. Virilio, *Vision Machine*, 59.

3. Filtering

1. Mayberry USA, "About Us," http://www.mbusa.net/about_us/ (accessed 3 March 2005).

2. Barney Fife seems to be an enormously popular figure for certain Christian identity groups. For example, www.BarneyFife.com draws heavily from *The Andy Griffith Show* to teach "inspirational studies" in Christian morality. Lesson plans and faith-based pedagogic practices are available on its home page. I do wonder if those so inclined to teach "Fife-moral lessons" are aware of Don Knotts's other memorable television character: the late-1970s swanky Casanova in the form of the lecherous "Mr. Furly" from *Three's Company*?

3. The CDA was repelled in 1997. "In essence, then," Andrew L. Shapiro writes, "Congress was asking all Internet users—whether they ran a commercial Web site or just used e-mail or chat rooms for their own benefit—to change the way they used the Internet by changing the architec-

ture of online interaction"; Andrew L. Shapiro *The Control Revolution: How the Internet Is Putting Individuals in Charge and Changing the World We Know* (New York: PublicAffairs, 1999), 70. Also see Marjorie Heins, *Not in Front of the Children* (New York: Hill and Wang, 2001), chapters 7 and 8; Lawrence Lessig, *Code and Other Laws of Cyberspace* (New York: Basic Books, 1999), especially chapter 12; and Sharon Doctor, "The Regulation of Internet," in *Real Law @ Virtual Space: Regulation in Cyberspace*, 2nd ed., ed. Susan J. Drucker and Gary Gumpert, 115–40 (Cresskill, N.J.: Hampton Press, 2005).

4. Christopher D. Hunter, "Filtering the First Amendment," in *Real Law @ Virtual Space*, ed. Drucker and Gumpert, 142; original emphasis.

5. The Children's Internet Protection Act, passed in late 2000, requires schools and libraries to implement filtering software (known as Internet safety policies) on all networked computers in order to maintain federal funds. Without such implementations the use of funding that is available through the Library Services and Technology Act, Title III of the Elementary and Secondary Education Act, and the E-rate program will be withdrawn. Overturning the act in 2002, the U.S. Court of Appeals for the Third Circuit in Philadelphia ruled that filtering software on library terminals was a "blunt instrument" that runs the risk of blocking access to constitutionally protected speech. In June 2003 the Children's Internet Protection Act was upheld by the U.S. Supreme Court. The deadline for implementing Internet filtering software on library-networked computers was July 1, 2004. See the American Library Association home page for information on the history of the CIPA and libraries' responses: www.ala.org. Filtering software, like the following examples, is aimed at networked computers in schools (although most filtering software comes in different versions to "meet the need" of individuals and networks be they schools, libraries, or businesses). Designed for an all-inclusive K-12, Marshal Software's SchoolMarshal (based in West Chester, Ohio) filters content requested by students through a school's computer network based on keywords and sites deemed appropriate by school policy. Blocked activity can be retrieved by school officials. Made up of "MailMarshal" and "WebMarshal," SchoolMarshal is real-time monitoring designed to "take charge of your schools e-mail content and protect your students and faculty from spam, porn and viruses and a wide range of other offensive or inappropriate content"; SchoolMarshal, www.schoolmarshal.com/fw/main/Content_Filters-1592.html (accessed 3 May 2005). SchoolMarshal extends the parental technology of control to place both students and faculty (children and adults) under its segregation of the Web into its rigid categories of "blocked" or "approved."

6. Cyber Sentinel, "What Cyber Sentinel Parental Control Software Does for Your Family," http://www.cybersentinel.com/parental_control_software.html (accessed 2 March 2005).

7. SoftForYou, http://www.softforyou.com (accessed 27 April 2006).

8. SoftForYou, "About Us," http://www.softforyou.com/about.html (accessed 27 April 2006).

9. Hunter, "Filtering the First Amendment," 150.

10. Ibid., 151.

11. In *The Internet Galaxy* (Oxford: Oxford University Press, 2001), Manuel Castells offers three categories for "technologies of control" that attempt to regulate the Internet, which since the 1990s have been debating points for concerns over online privacy, Web censorship, Internet governance, freedom of speech, liberty, and access to information. They are technologies of identification, surveillance, and investigation. Technologies of identification take the form of passwords and "cookies," a text file stored on a user's hard drive that contains information on the user's online activities. For example, cookie files store information about a user's visit to specific Web sites such as user IDs and passwords, while also tracking the number of visits to a site and recording the types of items purchased on a particular Web site. Surveillance technologies, according to Castells, "intercept messages, place markers that allow tracking of communication flows from a specific computer location, and monitor activity around the clock" (172). Surveillance technologies allow their users, and these can range from government officials to local law enforcement, to extract information from a user name. One example that dogged the question of surveillance technology and the right to privacy during the Clinton-Gore administration was the Clipper plan. A result of the National Security Agency's push for a national standard for computer encryption (escrowed encryption standard, or EES), the Clipper chip proposal aimed to provide federal law enforcement agencies with the ability to keep pace with advancing technologies in order to conduct legal (or so it is claimed) surveillance of new mediated communication (the Patriot Act further intensifies debates on civil liberties and state surveillance). The last technology of control that Castells outlines consists of technologies of investigation. These commonly take the form of databases for commercial and governmental use. While all of the control technologies that Castells examines are vital for discussions of freedom online and practices of control, Internet filtering software does not appear to figure in Castells's description. Filters bring an additional regulatory layer to the Internet, one that is located in the self-regulatory hands of end users and the place of the domestic sphere as a habitat for securitization. For a good record of the types of debates on control and the Internet in the 1990s, see Peter Ludlow, ed., *High Noon on the Electronic Frontier: Conceptual Issues in Cyberspace* (Cambridge, Mass.: MIT University Press, 1996); Laura J. Gurak, *Persuasion and Privacy in Cyberspace: The Online Protests over Lotus Marketplace and the Clipper Chip* (New Haven, Conn.: Yale University Press, 1997); and John V. Pavlik, *New Media Technology: Cultural*

and Commercial Perspectives (Boston: Allyn and Bacon Press, 1995). A text that covers Internet governance since the mid-1990s is Drucker and Gumpert, eds., *Real Law @ Virtual Space.*

12. Like the legislation of the Telecommunications Act of 1996, which legally requires television manufactures to include blocking technology in their products designed for the U.S. market, IFS is also legally afforded a guaranteed (not to mention economically enormous) market in the wake of the Children's Internet Protection Act. Equally relevant to the creation of new markets for new media, politicians on both the left and right endorse IFS as a viable solution to the posited dangers of computer networked communications. While Senator John McCain (R-Ariz.), part of the bipartisan group heading up V-chip legislation in the 1990s, introduced early versions of the CIPA, both presidential candidates in 2000 favored market solutions. As Declan McCullagh reported in *Wired News,* Vice President Al Gore endorsed filtering software as "a feature that allows parents to automatically check, with one click, what sites your kids have visited lately. . . ." This is not surprising from Gore considering his euphoria over the V-chip. While governor of Texas, President George W. Bush muttered an oversimplified understanding of filters: "There ought to be filters in public libraries, and filters in public schools, so that if kids get on the Internet, there's not going to be pornography or violence coming in"; www.wired.com/news/print/0,1294,39529,00.html (accessed 10 March 2005).

13. François Fortier, *Virtuality Check: Power Relations and Alternative Strategies in the Information Society* (London: Verso, 2001), 76.

14. Internet service providers like AOL, MSN, Google, and Earthlink, to cite only a few examples, provide content filters so that parents can predetermine the type of content that crosses their screenic threshold. ISPs update and maintain filtering software for their subscribers. The software is run on their servers rather than loaded onto an individual computer in the form of third-party filtering software. Subscribers can select what settings are deemed appropriate for their personal computer and, by extension, their families. AOL utilizes age-based categories like "Kids Only" (recommended for twelve and under), "Young Teen" (thirteen to fifteen), "Mature Teens" (sixteen to seventeen), and "General" (eighteen and up). Google's "SafeSearch filters" offer users three settings to manage their time on online: "Moderate filtering," "Strict filtering," and "No filtering." Many third-party filtering software companies promote their products by arguing that ISP parental controls are ineffective. Integrity Online (Jackson, Mississippi) distinguishes its filtering software from those offered by ISPs. Its "Myth" and "Fact" subscreen explains why: "I have 'parental controls' with my ISP so I don't need a filter." Integrity Online's counterpoint: "Usually offered by big multinational corporations such as AOL Time Warner and Microsoft, 'Parental Control' services are often designed to not offend anyone. While

you may feel good about having them turned on, many customers say they simply don't work"; IntegrityOnline, "Internet Filter Myths," http://www. integrity.com/internetfiltermyths.php (accessed 2 March 2005).

15. Lessig, *Code and Other Laws of Cyberspace*; Lawrence Lessig, *The Future of Ideas* (New York: Vintage Books, 2001); and Shapiro, *The Control Revolution*.

16. Lessig, *The Future of Ideas*, 35.

17. One alternative schema is proposed by J. M. Balkin, Beth Simone Noveck, and Kermit Roosevelt, "Filtering the Internet: A Best Practices Model," Information Society Project at Yale Law School, 15 September 1999, www.law.yale.edu/infosociety. They offer a rating system known as the "Layer Cake Model." It consists of a PICS-compatible layering of first-party basic vocabulary elements, third-party rating templates, and additional third-party ratings superimposed on the second layer to "increase flexibility and ideological diversity." Another, known as "zoning," has been suggested by Lessig in *Code and Other Laws of Cyberspace*. Proposed as an anticensorship solution, the zoning model would require a young person's user information to be housed in a browser. Web sites would be able to recognize a young person's attempt to access content and block his or her access if the content provider deemed the page inappropriate.

18. Seth Finkelstein cited in Jennifer 8. Lee, "Cracking the Code of Online Filtering," *New York Times*, 19 July 2001, sec. G.

19. CyberSitter, http://www.cybersitter.com (accessed 15 March 2005).

20. Jay Munro, "CyberSitter 9.0 Review," *PCMag.com*, 4 August 2004. http://www.pcmag.com/article2/0,1759,1618830,00.asp (accessed 18 February 2005).

21. Categories of blocked URLs based on content are shared as well as modified across IFS companies. Each category is accompanied by a "defined criteria" list that provides the parent with additional descriptions of the specific types of content contained under each heading. The categories used by CyberPatrol are as follows: "Adult/Sexually Explicit," "Chat," "Criminal Skills," "Drugs, Alcohol & Tobacco," "Gambling," "Glamour & Intimate Apparel," "Hacking & Spyware," "Hate Speech," the elusive "Multiple Category Servers," "Remote Proxie," "Sex Education," "Violence," and "Weapons." Many companies make the categories of "Adult/Sexually Explicit" default settings. Netmop.com filters its categories of "Pornography & Recreational Nudity," "Criminal Activity," and "Adult Material" for everyone, even the adults who purchased the software in order not to use the Internet!

22. William J. Mitchell, *E-Topia: "Urban Life, Jim—But Not as We Know It"* (Cambridge, Mass.: MIT University Press, 2000), 43.

23. The organization Peacefire.org conducts ongoing tests of filtering software produced by numerous companies and provides lists of which Web sites are blocked; www.peacefire.org.

24. James Slevin, *The Internet and Society* (Malden, Mass.: Polity Press, 2000), 214.

25. See David R. Johnson, Susan P. Crawford, and John G. Palfrey Jr., "The Accountable Internet: Peer Production of Internet Governance," *Virginia Journal of Law & Technology* 9, 9 (2004): 1–33.

26. Susan Crawford cited in John Schwartz, "Internet Filters Are: [Good] [Bad] [Both]," *New York Times,* 4 July 2004, sec. 4.

27. Marshall McLuhan, *Understanding Media: The Extensions of Man* (New York: Signet, 1964), 200.

28. Lynn Spigel, *Make Room for Television* (Chicago: Chicago University Press, 1992).

29. Jean Baudrillard, *For a Critique of the Political Economy of the Sign,* trans. Charles Levin (St. Louis, Mo.: Telos Press, 1981).

30. Paul Virilio, *The Lost Dimension,* trans. Daniel Moshenberg (New York: Semiotext(e), 1991), 79.

31. Ibid., 79.

32. Ibid., 82. Spigel's research on postwar television culture as well as Raymond Williams's notion of "mobile privatization"—the transference of the outside and inside through home-centered technology—comments on this practice of televisual puncturing; Raymond Williams, *Television: Technology and Cultural Form* (London: Fontana, 1974). However, Virilio's sense of "puncturing" is undone by way of the "virtual window" by Anne Friedberg in *The Virtual Window: From Alberti to Microsoft* (Cambridge, Mass.: MIT Press, 2006). She writes, "the screen—the film screen, the TV screen, the computer screen—is a component piece of architecture, a 'virtual window' that renders the wall permeable to light and 'ventilation' and that dramatically changes the materialities (and—perhaps more radically—the temporalities) built space. A *virtual* window is reliant not on its transparency but on its opacity; its highly mediated modulation of light provides an aperture: not to a reality, but to a delimited *virtuality*" (138).

33. Ibid., 99.

34. Manuel Castells, "High Technology, Economic Restructuring and the Urban-Regional Process in the United States," in *High Technology, Space and Society,* ed. Manuel Castells (London: Sage, 1985), 19.

35. Elaine Lally, *At Home with Computers* (Oxford: Berg, 2002), 51.

36. Marsha F. Cassidy, "Cyberspace Meets Domestic Space: Personal Computers, Women's Work, and the Gendered Territories of the Family Home," *Critical Studies in Media Communication* 18, 1 (2001): 45.

37. When Atari launched its system toward a late-1970s U.S. consumer market, it not only transformed how the television screen could be watched, understood, and interacted with, it also marked the mass introduction of personal computers into the home. The utilization of the television screen as a site for game play has its most direct roots in Ralph Baer's interactive

TV Game Project in 1966 and his "The Brown Box" prototype of 1968. Other television game systems appeared prior to the 2600 Video Computer System, most notably: Magnavox Odyssey 1TL 200 (1972), Videomaster Home T.V. Game (1974), the various Sears Tele-Games versions of *Pong*, Radio Shack TV Scoreboard 60-3051, Coleco Telstar, Atari Pong Fairchild/ Zircon Channel F (all 1976), and Commodore T.V. Game 3000H, Intertron Video, K-Mart S Four Thousand S 4000, Philips Tele-Spiel Las Vegas; all appeared around the same time as the 2600. Not only did Atari begin to capture the popular market, with its nearest competitors being Mattel Intellivision, Bally Astrocade, ColecoVision, and Odyssey 2, it was also one of the earliest home consoles to include the word *computer* in its title, where existing and previous consoles maintained the "television game" moniker.

38. Lally, *At Home with Computers*, 52.

39. Roger Silverstone, "Domesticating the Revolution—Information and Communications Technologies and Everyday Life," in *Management of Information and Communication Technologies*, ed. Robin Mansell (London: Aslib, 1994), 221.

40. Lally, *At Home with Computers*, 62.

41. William J. Mitchell, *City of Bits: Space, Place, and the Infobahn* (Cambridge, Mass.: MIT University Press, 1995), 99.

42. Virilio, *Lost Dimension*, 13.

43. Cass Sunstein, "The First Amendment in Cyberspace," *Yale Law Journal* 104 (1995): 1757, regards filtering software as a form of "insulation from unwelcome material"; cited in Shapiro, *The Control Revolution*, 109.

44. ScreenDoor operates according to a "patented core technology" that supersedes firewalls' capabilities in providing network security; www.palisadesys.com/about_us/coretech.shtml (accessed 7 May 2005).

45. Secure Computing has licensed "Bess" as part of its SmartFilter software. Bess is a content-filtering program for schools and libraries developed by N2H2. Its Web site, www.tribecaexpress.com/N2H2_bess.htm, claims that Bess (whose icon is a golden retriever) "protects" over sixteen million students. From what exactly? Peacefire.org's 1997 test of Bess, during a period in which America was experiencing what Heins, *Not in Front of the Children*, refers to as "filtering fever" on account of the defeat of the CDA, reveals that a number of gay and lesbian sites were being blocked as well as information on prisoners' rights, eating disorders, safe sex, and breast cancer. See Peacefire.org, "BESS, The Internet Retriever Examined," www.peacefire.org/censoreware/BESS/ (accessed 17 February 2005).

46. SecureComputing, "About Secure," www.securecomputing.com/ index.cfm?skey=1 (accessed 3 March 2005).

47. The ability to communicate in real time with "buddies" online can be policed by blocking access to specified contacts or by restricting the actual content of messages shared with peers. Filters vary depending on what type

of IM service one uses (this, of course, stems from competition between ISPs to provide the most "advanced security solutions" available). Subscriber services like AOL allow parents to construct a restricted account for their child's time online. Restricted accounts limit access to Web browsers, chat rooms, and IM. Under the category of "Parental Controls" a parent can predetermine the level of access for their child based on age. For example, AOL's "Kids Only" (twelve and under) disables IM. "Young Teen" (thirteen to fifteen) allows for IM but disallows file exchange such as images or video. "Mature Teen" grants full access to IM while placing certain customized restrictions on Web browsing. Time limitations and designated hours for usage are also determined by Parental Controls. In addition, a child's privacy is public property to parents under the auspices of Parental Controls. Parents can police their child's buddy list by logging on via their child's screen name and password to configure his or her buddy list. Users outside of the AOL service as well as user names unknown to parents or forbidden by parents can also be blocked. Other messaging programs, and these are usually free services, provided by Yahoo, Apple's iChat, and Window's Messenger allow parents to configure their child's IM privacy controls.

48. Johnson, Crawford, and Palfre, "The Accountable Internet," 5. The authors offer a valuable report on the advantages of peer production as a mode of Internet governance. However, in their attempt to enable responsible cyber citizens, their language seems haunted by conservative binaries of "bad" and "good" as well as, at times, furthering a doctrine of harm that is far too often used to mount legislation and fuel moral panics. One example will suffice: "There are bad actors online who do not care what effects their actions have on others. Right now, the costs of being and staying bad online are very low. These bad actors can have disproportionately harmful effects on others" (7).

49. McLuhan, *Understanding Media*, 19.

50. Ibid., 24.

51. Paul Virilio, *Open Sky*, trans. Julie Rose (London: Verso, 1997), 12.

52. Amanda Lenhart, "Report: Protecting Teens Online," Pew Internet and American Life Project, 17 March 2005, http://www.pewinternet.org/ PPF/r/152/report_display.asp (accessed 28 March 2005). Many IFS companies provide their own statistics to demonstrate how well their products protect their users. N2H2, manufacturer of Bess, claims that sixteen million students access the Internet through their filtering architecture. Schools and libraries are huge markets for IFS companies after the federally mandated adoption of filters in the form of the CIPA. The CIPA has created what can be described as a boom for IFS companies. At the time of its passage in 2000, research analyst Brian Burke of IDC estimated the filtering software to a be $90 million market; his statement appears in John Schwartz,

"Protests Arise over Business Aspect of Censoring the Web," *New York Times*, 21 December 2000, sec. C.4.

53. Surfcontrol, www.surfcontrol.com/Default.aspx?id=355&mnuid= 1.4.2.1 (accessed 22 April 2006).

54. Responding to the Kaiser Family Foundation's report on the effectiveness of filters in schools and libraries, "See No Evil: How Internet Filters Affect the Search for Online Health Information" (2002, www.kff.org), which claims that filters in public institutions can effectively block pornography without significantly impeding access to online health information, Judith F. Krug, director of the Office for Intellectual Freedom at the American Library Association, argues that "the importance of the First Amendment is that it provides us with the ability to govern ourselves, because it guarantees that you have the right to access information. The filters undercut that ability"; cited in John Swartz, "Internet Filters Block Many Useful Sites, Study Finds," *New York Times*, 11 December 2002, sec. A28.

55. My reference to the infamous "trick or treat" farce is not that far off the mark from IFS logic. Consider the scenario closely: I am sure that U.S. readers are familiar with the replayed rumor of the nondescript kid (no doubt a friend of your cousin's nephew's brother from back East or down South) who got a razor blade in an apple while out ritually panhandling for candy on Halloween night. The solution (besides eating candy instead of apples)? Rather than ban Halloween outright, like cherry bombs or M80 fireworks during the Fourth of July, it was, in some communities, relocated to a space presumed safer: the mall. In this solution the apparatus of the mall—its policies of conduct, security force, surveillance technology, familiar terrain, close parental supervision, safe candy handed out by retail employees, and presumed security from its well-lit enclosure—will determine who or what could occupy its space. We could say that the hazards from the "unknown," or from "out there," or hazards disguised in the innocent form of an apple could be "filtered" by the overall apparatus designed to protect those inhabitants of its architecture. Inside this space are innocent kids enjoying a safe Halloween night. Outside of this space resides a world where every treat is a potential danger.

56. The expression *forbidden site* can be understood as a moral judgment passed on content. In terms of code, forbidden site is the process of a browser being unable to access a Web site on account of its being flagged as "forbidden" according to a list of URLs housed in an IFS company's database. These data are constantly updated, as companies request that users of their software submit Web sites for evaluation.

57. SurfControl's CyberPatrol employs a real-time activity monitor of the Web activities of children (or employees). Anything from the time of one's visit to a Web page to details of the URL is stored, encrypted, and retrievable by a parent (or employer), who oversees exactly how the Internet

is being explored. As CyberPatrol proudly asserts, its "extensive monitoring and logging tools lift the lid on where users go online . . . and leaves them no where to hide!"; CyberPatrol, "Monitor," http://www.cyberpatrol.com/Default.aspx?id=127&mnuid=2.2 (accessed 7 March 2005).

58. According to *PCMAG.com*'s review of Cybersitter 9.0, one of its strengths is its "good stealth mode" capabilities that keep parents informed of their children's IM activities. "Cybersitter offers a good stealth mode, letting parents filter and monitor kids' activities without their knowledge. Cybersitter can record both sides of IM sessions, as well as log all sites visited and any violations. This information can then be automatically e-mailed to you in a daily activity report"; Jay Munro, "CyberSitter 9.0 Review," *PCMag.com*, 4 August 2004, http://www.pcmag.com/article2/0,1759,1618830,00.asp (accessed 18 February 2005).

59. SpectorSoft, "SpectorPro 5.0," http://www.spectorsoft.com/products/SpectorPro_Windows/index.html (accessed 10 April 2005).

60. Integrity Online, "Web Facts," http://www.integrity.com/filtering_facts.php (accessed 7 March 2005).

61. As of 29 April 2006, Net Nanny's slogan now reads, "Keep Your Kids Safe Online," http://www.netnanny.com/.

62. Netmop, http://www.netnanny.com/ (accessed 3 February 2005).

63. Lessig, *Code and Other Laws of Cyberspace,* 178; my emphasis.

64. Paul Virilio, *The Vision Machine,* trans. Julie Rose (London: BFI Press, 1994), 59.

65. Platform for Internet Content, http://www.w3.org/PICS/ (accessed 8 January 2006).

66. Balkin, Noveck, and Roosevelt, "Filtering the Internet," 12.

67. PICS makes compatibility easy through its PICSRules, also developed by W3C. PICSRules is a programming language for writing filtering protocol. The language functions in accordance to PICS labels and will allow filtering based on those categories.

68. According to the "Label Syntax and Communications Protocols" section of W3C's "Platform for Internet Content Selection Version 1.1" (1996), a label consists of three components: service identifier, label options, and a rating. The service identifier is the URL. Label options provide information of specific properties such as the time that a document was sent. "The rating itself is a set of attribute-value pairs that describe a document along one or more dimensions"; that is, the rating contains the criteria that distinguish the content of a Web page and determine whether or not and in what capacity that a Web site can be accessed by a Web browser; www.w3.org/PICS/labels.html (accessed 9 March 2005).

69. www.w3.org/TR/REC-PICS-services#Rating%20Service (accessed 16 September 2005).

70. By 1997, as Heins, *Not in Front of the Children,* 182, reports, PICS

"offered three ratings systems: RSACi, Net Shepard, and SafeSurf." The Recreational Software Advisory Council (RSACi), to cite an example, utilizes a self-rating system in conjunction with categories like "nudity," "sex," "language," and "violence." By 1999 it had self-rated 125,000 Web sites—no doubt a drop in an ever-expanding ocean. Also, as Geoffrey Nunberg notes, "the architecture of the Internet itself requires filters to block hundreds of thousands of sites that they haven't identified as porn—Google cache sites, for example, and any site that is unlucky enough to be hosted by the same computer that's hosting a porn site"; Geoffrey Nunberg, "Machines Make Moral Judgments, Selectively," *New York Times*, 9 March 2003, sec 4. Since 1997 other rating standards have join PICS: CyberPatrol's CyberList, SafeSurf (which allows for self-rating according to provided criteria), Adequate.com, SurfWatch, and Safe For Kids.

71. Microsoft has adopted the PICS standard for its Internet Explorer in 1997 amid the CDA fervor. Since the late 1990s, PICS has been part and parcel of computer desktops worldwide.

72. A helpful analogy could be films produced to attract a wider audience in the MPAA copyrighted rating of G or PG-13 rather then its R rating. Or a film having to "correct" dialogue or particular scenes in order to then be granted a CARA-approved R rating in order to receive nationwide and local distribution on corporate-owned cinema screens (often housed in malls that have policies against "adult" materials being sold on their premises). Ratings help structure content. They become a template to determine what content can be produced in accordance with age-based restrictions and the MPAA's new text-based descriptors that litter film posters and television trailers with vague phrases like "strong sexuality," "pervasive language," "drug use," "crude sexual humor," and "drinking."

73. Balkin, Noveck, and Roosevelt, "Filtering the Internet," 14–15.

74. Lessig, *Code and Other Laws of Cyberspace*, 177.

75. In 2000 CyberPatrol brought a suit against Eddy L. O. Jansson and Matthew Skala, two activists that hacked CyberPatrol and posted their code-breaking program online. Peacefire.org and the Censorware.net provide information on how to disable filtering software, offer free downloads of circumventor programs, and archive the sites blocked by various filtering software companies. Peacefire.org (maintained by Bennett Haselton) offers its visitors reports on a number of different companies like BESS, CyberPatrol, WebSENSE, Net Nanny, SmartFilter, X-Stop, I-Gear, and CYBERsitter. This information ranges from sites that block to records of testimony and article links on the various companies. These types of actions illustrate what Web sites an IFS company considers to be "harmful" and "dangerous" to its users. CyberPatrol's lawyer Irvin Schwartz does not quite see hacker actions as a type of "liberation" and prefers to play at moral panics when issuing the following statement: "These guys want to give kids

access to Porn"; cited in Lisa Guernsey, "CyberPatrol Sues Hackers Who Broke into Filter Program," *New York Times*, 23 March 2000, sec. G.3.

76. All figures are taken from www.surfcontrol.com. While this figure sounds impressive, it is a mere drop in an ocean of millions of Web sites and billions of Web pages. Seth Finkelstein and Lee Tien, "Blacklisting Bytes," in *Filters & Freedom 2.0*, ed. D. Sobel (Washington, D.C.: Electronic Privacy Information, 2001), 71, describe the impossible task of accurately rating the Internet: "How fast can a person evaluate a Web page? A reasonable overall estimate is one page per minute. One page per minute is 60 pages per hour. That's 480 pages per eight-hour workday. Let's call it 500 pages per workday for ease of calculation. At 200 workdays per year, we have 100,000 pages per work-year. So one person doing only censorware evaluation can only do 0.1 million pages in a year." Heins shares a similar scenario: In 1997 "60 million-plus pages [existed] on the Web, it takes about one minute per page to rate. To rate every existing Web page would take about 60 million minutes—or one million hours—or over 114 years. Using 114 people working 24 hours a day, the job would take a full year. But the bad news is that as soon as everything was rated, the process would have to start all over again, because within a year the Web would change drastically"; Gordon Ross, "Censorship and the Internet," 19 November 1997, cited in Heins, *Not in Front of the Children*, 182.

77. Mark Poster, *The Second Media Age* (Cambridge: Polity Press, 1995), 86.

78. Ibid., 91.

79. As of June 8, 2008, the last time that I accessed FamilyClick.com, its filtering services have been suspended until further notice.

80. On August 1, 2000, a Peacefire.org survey of FamilyClick found the following online articles blocked by its filtering software: "PSYART: A Hyperlink Journal for the Psychological Study of the Arts," "AIDS Day 1997: China Responds to AIDS," and "Gambling and Problem Gambling in Washington State." In addition, the home page for Camp Sussex, a summer camp scheme for low-income children, was blocked on account of the word "sex" in the site's domain name.

81. Monroe E. Price and Stefaan G. Verhulst, *Self-Regulation and the Internet* (The Hague: Kluwer Law International, 2005).

82. In a *New York Times* article, Geoffrey Nunberg, a linguist from Stanford, discusses his involvement in the American Libraries Association's suit against the Children's Internet Protection Act of 2000. As an expert witness, Nunberg testified that his tests of filtering software revealed that they blocked access "to everything from teenage sex advice sites posted by Planned Parenthood and Rutgers University to a dollhouse furniture site, Salon magazine and the home page of the Canadian Discovery Channel"; Nunberg, "Machines Make Moral Judgments, Selectively."

83. Yochai Benkler, "From Consumers to Users: Shifting the Deeper Structures of Regulation," *Federal Communications Law Journal* 52 (2000): 562–63, offers the concepts of multilayers to understand how communications systems are organized. The "physical layer" consists of hardwarelike computers, while the "logical layer" is code, and the "content layer" is made up of media objects and text. Lessig, *The Future of Ideas*, also draws on Benkler's notion of layering to discuss how freedom and control are mixed at different layers of the Internet (23–25).

4. Sanitizing

1. Unknown author cited in Rick Lyman, "Some Video Customers Want Tamer Films, and Entrepreneurs Rush to Comply," *New York Times*, 19 September 2002, sec. E.1.

2. The plaintiffs of the civil action case include Robert Huntsman and Clean Flicks of Colorado, L.L.C. The defendants listed include Steven Soderbergh, Robert Altman, Michael Apted, Taylor Hackford, Curtis Hanson, Norman Jewison, John Landis, Michael Mann, Phillip Noyce, Brad Silberling, Betty Thomas, Irwin Winkler, Martin Scorsese, Steven Spielberg, Robert Redford, and Sydney Pollack. The studios involved include Metro-Goldwyn-Mayer Studios, Inc.; Time Warner Entertainment Co. L.P.; Disney Enterprises Inc.; Dreamworks L.L.C.; Universal City Studios, Inc.; Twentieth Century Fox Film Corp.; and Paramount Pictures Corporation. The companies responsible for edited versions include Video II; Glenn Dickman; J.W.D. Management Corp; Trilogy Studios, Inc.; CleanFlicks; Family Shield Technologies LLC; ClearPlay Inc.; Clean Cut Cinemas; Family Safe Media; Edit My Movies; Family Flix; U.S.A. LLC; and Play It Clean Video. The various suits and countersuits have attracted a great deal of attention. Directors involved have issued statements condemning CleanFlicks for violation of copyright and discrediting artistic license. Michael Apted has voiced concern over the situation that companies like CleanFlicks "are entitled to change anything to suit their own particular will"; Bob Baker, "Are These Videos Rated C for Clean or Compromised? Directors Rail against Firms such as CleanFlicks That Excise Offensive Language and Scenes with Sex of Violence," *Los Angeles Times*, 14 October 2002, sec. E.1. Michael Mann has responded that "there's no polite word for it—it's stealing. It's stealing from the consumers . . . from the copyright holders [studios] and it's certainly stealing from us" (ibid.). For an excellent legal appraisal of the CleanFlicks case, please refer to Scott W. Breedlove, "CleanFlicks v. Hollywood: Intellectual Property Owners Losing Control," *Intellectual Property and Technology Law Journal* 15, 6 (2003): 6–11.

3. Quoted in Baker, "Are These Videos Rated," sec. E.1.

4. Quoted in ibid.

5. Ibid.

6. Ibid.

7. Edited-for-television films contain poorly dubbed voice-overs like when *marmaluka* replaces *motherfucker* for gangster argot in Martin Scorsese's *Goodfellas* (1990), or when tough-talking New York City cop John McClane (Bruce Willis) in *Die Hard* (John McTiernan, 1988) intimidates terrorists with "Yippie-kye-ay, Mister Falcon" rather than "Yippie-kye-ay, Motherfucker" (*f-bomb, flip you, freakin, friggin* have all entered our vocabularies by way of edited films for television).

8. Senator bipartisan cosponsors included Lamar Alexander (R-Tenn.), John Cornyn (R-Tex.), Dianne Feinstein (D-Calif.), and Patrick J. Leahy (D-Vt.). The bill was signed into public law on April 27, 2005.

9. Michael Janofsky, "Utah Shop Offers Popular Videos with the Sex and Violence Excised," *New York Times*, 31 January 2001, sec. A.

10. The heading for this section is Blockbuster Inc.'s first advertising slogan, launched in 1989. James Hay, "Unaided Virtues: The (Neo-)Liberalization of the Domestic Sphere," originally appeared in *Television and New Media* 1, 1 (2000): 53–73. The article has been republished with modification in *Foucault, Cultural Studies, and Governmentality*, ed. Jack Z. Bratich, Jeremy Packer, and Cameron McCarthy (Albany: State University of New York Press, 2003), as: "Unaided Virtues: The (Neo)Liberalization of the Domestic Sphere and the New Architecture of Community." For the sake of consistency and my immediate focus, all references will refer to the 2000 version.

11. "The monitor and remote control," Hay argues, "comprised mutually supporting instruments of self-governing subjects and objects. Furthermore, they brought domestic video and audio systems into a new relation with other household appliances, an ensemble of programmable technologies that could be used in temporally and spatially regulating the household" ("Unaided Virtues," 61). Other household appliances include the expanding RCD, portable telephones, answering machines (becoming more common in the 1980s in the space of the home), washing machines and dryers, microwaves, coffeemakers and other "intelligent" kitchen gadgets, and personal computers. Hay notes that the "monitor" became a common reference to "screen" in the 1980s with computer technology entering the household. In regard to the screen and Hay's use of "monitoring" above, he comes to consider the screen-monitor as "integral to a new regimen for managing a household dependent on programmable, self-governing appliances" ("Unaided Virtues," 61). The long-standing presence of information technology and screens in and *as part of the home* has prompted Tim Putnam, "Beyond the Modern Home: Shifting the Parameters of Residence," in *Mapping the Future: Local Cultures, Global Change*, ed. John Bird, Barry Curtis, Tim Putnam, George Robertson, and Lisa Tickner, 150–68 (London: Routledge,

1993) to conceive of the home itself as a "terminal," while William J. Mitchell, *City of Bits: Space, Place, and the Infobahn* (Cambridge, Mass.: MIT Press, 1995) regards the "display device," like the mantel and fireplace before it, as "the most powerful organizer of domestic spaces and activities" (99). Screens are not neutral apparatuses, spaces, and surfaces for display. In terms of management and the self-governing that Hay speaks of, screens are active in shaping the household and positioning its inhabitants in a delineation of spatial configurations and power relations.

12. Hay, "Unaided Virtues," 69.

13. Aside from the significance of viewer choice and repeatability versus a single viewing and other user-friendly differences between VCRs and film projectors, divergences are most often a result of the space within which one watches. For example, darkness may or may not be a variable in the home. Where the cinema is said to require a docile, immobile spectator, the viewer of video is celebrated for his or her mobility and ability to express control over the images brought into the home. Movement is not restricted by permanent seating or the stern glances of disgruntled viewers. Any restrictions on mobility result from the viewer's choices and his or her privately arranged viewing space rather than public organization and architecture. Lastly, technological differences exist between cinema and television screen sizes that determine the quality of the image.

14. Bill Whittington, "Home Theater: Mastering the Exhibition Experience," *Spectator* 18, 2: (1998): 76.

15. Timothy Corrigan, *A Cinema without Walls: Movies and Culture after Vietnam* (New Brunswick, N.J.: Rutgers University Press, 1991), 1.

16. Within the context of television viewing and home theater systems, control is often expressed as the viewer's ability to personally manage broadcast scheduling. To cite an example of how the VCR can affect broadcast, Sean Cubitt, *Time Shift: On Video Culture* (London: Routledge, 1991) has remarked how the functionality of a VCR allows its users to "disturb the diegetic hold of broadcast, the chance to watch in bite-size chunks, and therefore multiply the available programme formats" (78). This depiction recalls the initial appeal of the VCR: primarily the ability to record broadcasts and its playback features. Complementing this commonly held account is Corrigan's sentiment that during the playback of a prerecorded videocassette, the viewing situation is "a selected experience and subject to the choices and decisions of the spectator—to stop it, replay parts of it, to speed through sections of it" (28). As such, with the emphasis on viewer decision making, it comes as no surprise that academic scholarship on the VCR has encouraged the response that its capabilities liberate and free users from the domination of broadcast television scheduling and the inconvenient travels outside of the household to a cinema. With the advent of home video, Douglas Gomery, *Shared Pleasures: A History of Movie Presentation in the United*

States (London: British Film Institution, 1992) claims, "no one is dependent on the desires of a theatre owner or television station programmer" (276). Alongside studies dedicated to film and television, theorists of interactive media have also commented on how the VCR permits viewers (once thought passive and inert) to exert a considerable amount of control over their viewing choices. Examining media fandom, Henry Jenkins, *Textual Poachers: Television Fans and Participatory Cultures* (London: Routledge, 1992) writes, "videotape expands control over the programs, allowing us to view as often or in whatever context desired" (71). And as Mark Poster, *Mode of Information* (Chicago: University of Chicago Press, 1991) observes, "the VCR provides the ability to reproduce information cheaply, quickly and easily. It puts the viewer in control of the images he or she views" (48).

17. Barbara Klinger, "The New Media Aristocrats: Home Theater and the Domestic Film Experience," *The Velvet Light Trap* 42 (1998): 10.

18. Nikolas Rose, *Powers of Freedom: Reframing Political Thought* (Cambridge: Cambridge University Press, 1999), 247.

19. Ibid., 249.

20. Hay, "Unaided Virtues," 67.

21. Cited on Blockbuster Inc. "Ratings Defined," http://www.blockbuster.com/catalog/DisplayMPAADetails 2006 (accessed 6 March 2006).

22. See Jon Lewis, *Hollywood v. Hard Core*, chapter 7; and Stephen Vaughn, *Freedom and Entertainment*, chapter 8, for sustained engagements with the NC-17 rating.

23. At the request of Viacom, Blockbuster left the conglomerate in October 2004.

24. Gail DeGeorge, *The Making of a Blockbuster: How Wayne Huizenga Built a Sports and Entertainment Empire from Trash, Grit, and Videotape* (New York: John Wiley and Sons, 1996), 189.

25. Greg Clarkin, "Fast Forward," *Marketing and Media Decisions* 3 (1990): 59.

26. See "About Blockbuster," 2006, http://www.blockbuster.com/corporate/displayAboutBlockbusterDetails.action?articleId=1085770 (accessed 7 January 2006), for a time line of the company's history; and Thomas K. Arnold, "Blockbuster 20th Anniversary," *Hollywood Reporter,* 24 May 2005, http://www.hollywoodreporter.com/thr/television/feature_display.jsp (accessed 21 June 2005), for an additional overview of Blockbuster's various ventures over the course of its twenty years in operation.

27. Blockbuster is a friend, a neighbor, part of "The Neighborhood"—a telephone calling plan—built by MCI, circa 2002. Blockbuster is not *just* a store. Its services—ranging from KIDPRINT (video identification for children) to BLOCKBUSTER AWARDS, from the BLOCKBUSTER ENTERTAINMENT AWARDS to BLOCKBUSTER TICKET—demonstrate

that the walls of the store do not restrict. Children—"We're big believers in kids as customers," says Marva Cathie, Blockbuster's vice president for advertising—are targeted through Radio Disney and in-school Channel One. Tie-ins also include the MTV Movie Awards (also owned by Viacom) and the American Film Institute (AFI). Blockbuster's relationship with Hollywood studios has made it the "voice" of the AFI in the retail market. Blockbuster also supports a number of "anchor programs" through local affiliations with the Boys & Girls Clubs of America, the NAACP's ACT-SO Program, and the LULAC's National Education Service Center. As its Web site states, Blockbuster is most interested in supporting nonprofit groups/ projects that have a family/children focus and will donate to independent film or video productions.

28. Naomi Klein, *No Logo: No Space, No Choice, No Jobs* (New York: Picador, 2002) offers a resourceful discussion of how corporate conglomeration manages media content in relation to retailers like Blockbuster. While anti-Blockbuster advocates online contend that "America's Favorite Video Store" does indeed edit certain films that were previously rated by the MPAA for its own "family" market, Blockbuster Inc. denies this practice. When asked whether Blockbuster would stock CleanFlicks' reedited DVDs, its spokesperson Blake Lugash stated that Blockbuster would not carry these DVDs and added that "we don't edit or censor any of the films we carry in our store and we try to carry the theatrical version"; cited in Xeni Jardin, "Film Moguls: Let Sex, Gore Stay," *Wired News,* August 28, 2002, http://www.wired.com/news/technology/0,1282,54759,00.html (accessed 25 July 2003).

29. Some discrepancy exists about when the first store was actually opened. In 2002, Blockbuster's "IN REEL TIME: A Historical Look at the Growth of BLOCKBUSTER" on its home page listed 1985 as the year of its first store, whereas its 2006 version states 1986. Clarkin, "Fast Forward," claims that "Blockbuster began with one store in 1985, grew to 415 by the end of 1988 . . ." (57). Again the time line on the 2006 Web page contradicts this account. At the end of 1988, the same year that Blockbuster relocated its headquarters from Dallas to Fort Lauderdale, Florida, it boasted only two hundred stores. To cause further confusion, the 2002 time line has 1988 ending with four hundred stores. Financed through his earnings in the petroleum industry, the first store was opened by David Cook in Dallas, October 19, 1985. Wayne Huizenga purchased a 60 percent stake in the new company in 1987, and Cook departed soon after. The "Company Overview" page at blockbuster.com declares 1985 to be the year that the company was founded, and the current home page no longer provides a time line for company growth; http://www.blockbuster.com/corporate/ companyOverview (accessed 7 June 2008).

30. Companies that Blockbuster has acquired over the years include Erols

Video Inc., Major Video, Movies-To-Go, Video Library, Ritz Video (UK), WJB Video LTD., Video Factory Inc., Xtra-vision (Ireland), Video Flicks (Australia), Super Club Entertainment, and Christianshavn Video (Denmark). In December 2004 Blockbuster Inc. attempted a hostile takeover of its biggest U.S. competitor, Hollywood Video. In early January 2005, Hollywood Video was bought out by its smaller competitor Movie Gallery, thus denying Blockbuster Inc. full acquisition and avoiding possible prosecution under antitrust laws.

31. DeGeorge, *The Making of a Blockbuster,* 126.

32. "Blockbuster Online Changes Pricing," 2006, http://www.b2i.us/profiles/investor/ResLibraryView.asp?BzID=553&ResLibraryID=11076& Category=27 (accessed 7 March 2006).

33. Blockbuster launched its "End of Late Fees" slogan on January 1, 2005. The new policy allows renters to have a DVD or game for one week without paying any fees. If kept out beyond the allotted no-late-fees period, the full price of the DVD or game is automatically charged to a customer's credit card. Attorney General Peter C. Harvey of New Jersey filed suit against Blockbuster Inc. shortly after its new campaign, charging that it failed to disclose the automatic sales price after the rental period and that Blockbuster was violating New Jersey's Consumer Fraud Act and Merchandise Advertising Regulations. See "Attorney General Sues Blockbuster," press release, Office of the Attorney General Online, 2005, http://www.state.nj.us/lps/newsreleases05/pr20050218a.html (accessed 31 March 2005).

34. One way that Blockbuster asserts its "family agenda" is through buying out video chains and immediately liquidating their libraries. Used videos or DVDs are sold at reduced prices, which one could argue allows collectors to increase their own personal media libraries, and removed permanently from the holdings. Thus, other potential renters are denied access to specific titles if they do not fit with Blockbuster's holdings policies.

35. Bruce C. Klopefenstein, "The Diffusion of the VCR in the United States," in *The VCR Age: Home Video and Mass Communication,* ed. Mark R. Levy (London: Sage 1989), claims that 52 percent of U.S. households owned a VCR by the end of 1987. By spring 1988 that number rose to 65 percent. In the beginning of the 1990s that number moved to 70 percent; see Janet Wasko, *Hollywood in the Information Age* (Cambridge: Polity, 1994). Accompanying unit sales, prerecorded videocassettes also began to emerge as a prosperous industry. The initial rise began in 1983 when figures charting the U.S. market illustrated 11.0 million cassettes sold; 1987 saw this number multiplied by seven for 72.0 million in sales; see Michael Weiss, *Home Video: Producing for the Home Market* (self-published, 1986).

36. The new enterprise of the "video store" became a transitory nonplace where "renters" (not spectators) roam the shelves seeking a "new release," converse over selections ("have you seen . . . ?"), socialize, contest

late fees, read the backs of videocassette box covers, inquire about a title with employees ("that video has been flying out of the store this week," as Blockbuster employees are trained to respond), rent a tape, DVD, or video game, or go home empty-handed on account of lack of availability ("it was rented," or "it's out but due back tomorrow"—more Blockbuster customer management etiquette) or limited stock (too many of those "hot new releases" that Blockbuster prides itself on obtaining). The slogans for meeting customer needs were borrowed from Blockbuster's *Employee Material Handbook* (2002), removed from store premises.

37. See Daniel Moret, "The New Nickelodeons: A Political Economy of the Home Video Industry with Particular Emphasis on Video Software Retailers," unpublished master's thesis, University of Oregon, March 1991. Cited in Wasko, *Hollywood in the Information Age*, 1994.

38. Gomery, *Shared Pleasures*, 289.

39. Wasko, *Hollywood in the Information Age*, 149.

40. DeGeorge, *The Making of a Blockbuster*, 92.

41. Ibid., 92.

42. The accusation of sleaze was an umbrella term that failed to acknowledge that many video stores did not stock X-rated materials or went to great lengths, usually at personal expense, to safeguard X-rated titles from the roaming eyes of potential renters: a heterogeneous group that even included Blockbuster's preferred profitable object—the family.

43. Michel Foucault, "The Eye of Power," in *Michel Foucault Power/ Knowledge: Selected Interviews and Other Writings 1972–1977*, ed. Colin Gordon (New York: Harvester Wheatsheaf, 1980), 153.

44. Dennis Sharp, *The Picture Palace and Other Buildings for the Movies* (New York: Praeger Publications, 1969) employs the term *morality lighting* to account for the increasing lack of darkness in interior cinema spaces as they enter into a new history of design in the 1920s. He writes, "the common practice of showing films in complete darkness was also questioned by designers and promoters and some experiments took place with daylight and artificial light projection. Immediately after the First World War most picture houses used soft amber or rose-tinted lamps for low-level illumination (known as 'morality lighting') throughout performances" (54). While ornamental and service lighting continues to eradicate total darkness in today's cinemas, Blockbuster offers only an extreme high level of illumination, where mood is given over to security.

45. Erik Calonius, "Meet the King of Video," *Fortune*, June 1990, 208.

46. Gomery, *Shared Pleasures*, 282.

47. DeGeorge, *The Making of a Blockbuster*, 110.

48. Uniformed staff remain a visible feature of the cinema experience. In the 1920s Samuel "Roxy" L. Rothafel hired a retired Marine Corps colonel, Howard H. Kipp, as morale officer to train his cinema staff. Dressed in

quasi-military uniforms, they adhered to a strict dress code, etiquette, and discipline in the service of visiting patrons and in maintaining excellence in the service of the Roxy Theatre. See Ben M. Hall, *The Best Remaining Seats: The Story of the Golden Age of the Movie Palace* (New York: Bramhall House, 1957). Blockbuster's uniform is one of corporate leisure, the equivalent to a "Docker's Friday" look. Its employees don unobtrusive khaki trousers and button-down light-blue shirts or wear company knit collar shirts embroidered with the Blockbuster logo.

49. Rental media contain information beyond film content. Tapes, in the period that Hay studies, and discs today are bar-coded to enable quick processing. A brief description of the title is listed. An MPAA and Blockbuster description is included to better inform viewers as to the suitability of their choice. This surface is invaluable for Blockbuster's sanitizing effect. It is informative, unobtrusive, and banal: a surface standardized for quick consumption and instant information gathering. In addition, customer information is stored in a database to monitor viewer preference, rental status, and whether restrictions—age, for example—are placed on an account. In 2001 the database was estimated at fifty-two million with three million customers visiting a Blockbuster each day, according to its home page. The Blockbuster database is not regarded as an invasion of privacy but rather as a service rendered through willing participation. Each transaction is recorded via bar code scan upon checkout. Profiled customers are sent mailings to promote new releases. Customers are profiled based on taste preferences, preferences restricted to Blockbuster's product range. At Blockbuster, we are the summation of our choices. Our choices are Blockbuster's business.

50. Tom Gruber, cited in Greg Clarkin, "Fast Forward," 57. Management experience from non-media-based entertainment companies is common to Blockbuster. Bill Fields (CEO, 1996–97) was from Wal-Mart, the current CEO, John Antioco, was with 7-Eleven and Taco Bell prior to Blockbuster. Forty-nine-cent tacos are the model for Blockbuster's à la carte home cinema.

51. "Family Viewing Guide," BlockBuster.com, 2002, http://www.blockbuster.com//bb/familyviewingguide/0,7784,,00.html (accessed 9 December 2002).

52. This was an off-the-cuff remark about the restricted access to *Crash*. The statement "You don't have to watch" is hardly unique to Cronenberg and is common parlance in debates on film censorship.

53. DVD players were first introduced in the United States in 1997. Prices of DVD players fell substantially between 1997 and 2004, and this may account for the rapid growth and acceptance of DVD players (some of which enter the home as computer drives or video game systems) within the domestic setting. The Consumer Electronics Association (2006) reports that the average price for a DVD player was $489.97 in their debut year,

while by 2004 prices as low as $108.60 were reported. In conjunction with the growth of DVD players, the availability of DVD titles has grown tremendously. Anne Friedberg, "CD and DVD," in *The New Media Book*, ed. Dan Harries (London: British Film Institution, 2002) claims that "in 1997, in the US, 900 titles were available on DVD; in 1998, 3,000. By the end of 2000 there were over 10,000 titles available on DVD in the US . . ." (38).

54. *Family Entertainment and Copyright Act of 2005*, U.S. Cong., Senate, 109th Congress, S. 167: SEC. 201 (B).

55. *Sony Corp. of America v. Universal City Studies, Inc.*, commonly referred to as the "Betamax Case," was a Supreme Court decision that declared copy recording of a television broadcast via a time-shifting device like a videocassette recorder was protected by the doctrine of fair use and not a violation of copyright law. Equally, manufacturers of such technology were not held liable for a consumer's usage in the privacy of the home.

56. *Family Entertainment and Copyright Act of 2005*, 202A 3.11.

57. Rick Lyman, "Hollywood Balks at High-Tech Sanitizers; Some Video Customers Want Tamer Films, and Entrepreneurs Rush to Comply," *New York Times*, 19 September 2002, sec. E.1.

58. Breck Rice, "Interview with Charles Osgood," *The Osgood File*, CBS Radio Network, 11 November 2002.

59. U.S. Cong., House, Judiciary Subcommittee on Courts, the Internet, and Intellectual Property; Derivative and Moral Rights, Movie Filtering Technology, Congressional Testimony, 20 May 2004. Statement of Bill Aho, ClearPlay Inc.

60. Cited in Benny Evangelista, "House Passes Piracy Measure: Film Industry Wins Some, Loses Other Battles in Congress," *San Francisco Chronicle*, 20 April 2005, sec. C.

61. The early RCA DRC232N DVD player with ClearPlay content-filtering software comes with one hundred filters preloaded. With this particular model, filters first have to be downloaded via a networked computer and then burned onto a CD to transfer to the DVD player. This process must occur for every DVD beyond the preloaded filters. ClearPlay's new ClearPlay DVD player with USB eliminates the need for a CD burner and allows for easier filter upload through the use of a flash drive, and the MaxPlay modem player comes preloaded with one thousand filters, and its memory can hold up to two thousand. With the built-in modem, filters are downloaded directly to the DVD player.

62. The 2006 annual subscription for access to all ClearPlay filters costs $79.00, and a monthly subscription is $7.95.

63. Keith Merrill, "Cleaning Up the Movies," *Meridian: The Place Where Latter-day Saints Gather*, 2002, http://www.meridianmagazine.com/arts/020604clean.html (accessed 7 January 2006).

64. David Pogue, "Add 'Cut' and 'Bleep' to a DVD's Options," *New York Times*, 27 May 2004, sec. G.

65. CleanFlicks, "What Makes CleanFlicks Unique among Online DVD Rental Services," http://www.cleanflicks.com/lovDetail.php?detailID=10 (accessed 31 March 2007).

66. Nervous over the repercussions of CleanFlicks' suit against the Directors Guild of America and several of its affiliated directors, Albertsons, the United States' second largest grocery-store chain, ceased to carry Clean-Flicks DVDs. Prior to Albertsons' decision, the retail chain proved to be a major outlet for sanitized versions.

67. CleanFlicks, "What Is a CleanFlicks Edited DVD?" http://www.cleanflicks.com/lovDetail.php?detailID=5 (accessed 25 April 2005). Family Flix (out of Provo, Utah, and now renamed Faith and Family Flix, "FFF") no longer reedits Hollywood copyrighted films for its customers. Similar to CleanFlicks' services, Family Flix provides films, sports, documentaries, and television content that conforms to the company's ideas of faith-based family entertainment. It regards its services as providing an alternative to online rental companies like Netflix and Blockbuster and encourages its customers to boycott these businesses. The company also draws a striking analogy between its online rental services and national security. "FFF has vowed to do what we can to help protect and nurture the family. Just like men and women in the military everyday put their lives at risk to protect our physical well-being, shouldn't we put as much effort into protecting our spiritual/moral well-being?" http://www.faithandfamilyflix.com/about.php (accessed 4 June 2008). Prior to the outcome of *Clean Flicks v. Steven Soderbergh*, Family Flix's operations worked as follows. In order to acquire a "Family Friendly" version of *Million Dollar Baby* (Clint Eastwood, 2004), for example, the customer was required to send their own prepurchased copy to Family Flix so that an edited backup copy could be prepared for $12.50 plus shipping and handling. (This is the "send and edit" option. Family Flix also offered a "purchase and send" option, which did not require the sender to post their original copy.) The edited version was burnt onto a DVD-R, and customers received their original copy and their new Family Flix edited version (also rated by Family Flix to provide extra caution). However, upon its return the original copy would no longer be playable. Its inability to play was a further precautionary measure employed by Family Flix. While great strides were taken to clearly mark the unedited MPAA-rated Hollywood DVD to distinguish it from the recently edited DVD-R (now marked "Family-Friendly"), "many families," Family Flix explains, "send the original DVD to be edited and request the original to be rendered useless because they do not want curiosity of children or themselves getting the best of them." Rendering the original DVD unplayable implies that neither

parent nor child can be trusted and thus the parent must allow Family Flix's "Family-Friendly" version to replace the original copy through its destruction. In this instance, choice can be read as replacement. In addition, Family Flix provided extensive editing guidelines should customers require descriptive details of the content removed from a particular title. While simulated sex and nudity are common themes edited out of Hollywood features by various sanitizing companies and software, Family Flix also removed magazine pictures, drawings, posters, and portrait paintings that were deemed to be of a pornographic nature. Close-ups of "private parts" as well as "distasteful animal behavior" (the example Family Flix provides is a "dog sniffing privates") were removed from reedited versions. Language was policed thoroughly. The expression "Oh my God" was considered an "inappropriate reference to a Deity," and like major swear words, these phrases were deleted from the existing context. Deletions could also include the word *dork* from children's titles. The notion of "correct usage" of specific words that support Family Flix's ideology of family were left intact. For example, the expression *bastard* was considered acceptable language when used to describe "an illegitimate child." Lastly, entire groups (either self-identified or depicted as such) coming under the auspices of Family Flix's "Non-Traditional Family Values"—these include homosexuality and lesbianism along with perversion and cohabitation—were also regarded as unsafe or inappropriate for viewers and excised from the original DVD release.

68. Cited in Janofsky, "Utah Shop Offers Popular Videos," E.1. Ray Lines entered the business of "film sanitizing" when a neighbor, knowing of Mr. Lines's editing skills as a television sportscaster in South Dakota, asked "if he would edit out scenes in *Titanic* that showed actors nude" (ibid., 1). As the story goes, word got around, and additional requests came in. CleanFlicks' first stores opened in 2000, and by 2002 seventy-six outlets were operating in eighteen states. CleanFlicks charges new dealers a $5,000 operating fee and $14,000 for its start-up inventory of edited media. In 2001 CleanFlicks offered just over one hundred Hollywood films at its chain of rental stores. As of 2006 that number had increased to seven hundred edited copies available for purchase or rental, with new titles premiering regularly.

69. Henry Jenkins, "*Quentin Tarantino's Star Wars?* Digital Cinema, Media Convergence, and Participatory Culture," in *Rethinking Media Change: The Aesthetics of Transition*, ed. David Thorburn and Henry Jenkins (Cambridge, Mass.: MIT Press, 2003), 281–312, 288.

70. Ibid., 289.

71. Additional short versions (or "fucking" short versions as they are known) where all dialogue has been ripped from popular Hollywood films except the use of the word *fuck* include *Pulp Fiction, Die Hard, Jay and Silent Bob Strike Back, Snatch, The Departed,* and *The Big Lebowski.*

72. Jane M. Gaines, *Fire and Desire: Mixed-Race Movies in the Silent Era* (Chicago: University of Chicago Press, 2001), 230.

73. Ibid., 232.

74. The Dove Foundation. "Our Mission," http://www.dove.org/ (accessed 31 March 2007).

75. A nonprofit organization based in Grand Rapids, Michigan, Dove believes that since the film ratings restructuring in the late 1960s, the majority of Hollywood-produced films range in the R-rated category. According to Dove's home page, MPAA "ratings don't protect our children from exposure to movies that glorify and encourage negative behavior." Dove Foundation, http://www.dove.org/Frames.asp?URL=partners/families.htm (accessed 2 April 2006).

76. Not all of the Dove Foundation's "Dove Worldview" reviews are this condemning. For example, the synopsis for the ClearPlay filtered version of *Four Brothers* (John Singleton, 2005) describes the brothers' actions as seeking "revenge for the death of the woman who brought them together, made them brothers and taught them the value of family." Whereas the "Dove Worldview" reminds those that seek its expertise in their secured viewing affairs that the actions of the brothers are not wholly justified: "They begin a search for the killers and of course in the process they overstep the boundaries and take over what should be the police investigation." Debbie Satala, "Review: *Four Brothers*—Filtered," Dove Foundation home page, http://www.dove.org/reviews/default.asp (accessed 1 May 2006).

77. David Lukens, "Review: *A History of Violence*," Dove Foundation home page, http://www.dove.org/reviews/default.asp (accessed 1 April 2006).

78. Dove's "Content Descriptions" provide reasons for why *A History of Violence* is "not approved." In the categories of sex and violence the film is purported to contain "way too much and way too graphic. Soft porn." Dove reviewers take the time to cite how many times certain expletives are used in the film. *A History of Violence* looks like this to Dove reviewers: "2 slang for woman's vagina; slang for man's penis; SOB-2; s-cking 1; f-word-12; s-word-8; good L; JC; J 4; GD-5" (L = Lord, J = Jesus, JC = Jesus Christ, GD = Goddamn). The film is also not approved because of elements of nudity: "woman reveals her crotch to her husband." Dove does not provide a review for CleanFlicks' version of *A History of Violence*. However, we can get an idea of how it might be reviewed by looking at other examples. Filtered content provided by ClearPlay filter settings that warrants the "Not Approved" rating by Dove includes nudity: "Guy in boxers" (*Batman Begins*, Christopher Nolan, 2005); occult: "Witchcraft and spells. Incantations and hexes" (*Bewitched*, Nora Ephron, 2005); nudity: "Woman in shower—viewer can see shoulders" (*The Hitchhiker's Guide to the Galaxy*, Garth Jennings,

2005); sex: "gay bar, scenes of homosexuality, wife swapping" (*Kinsey,* Bill Condon, 2004); sex: "kissing" (*The Island,* Michael Bay, 2005). Reedited DVDs like those offered by CleanFlicks are all approved because any *potentially* offensive material has already being deleted.

79. Gaines, *Fire and Desire,* 231.

80. Most of the derisive edits in the *CleanFlicks version* involve the presence of Edie, either her body, language, or actions.

81. Gaines, *Fire and Desire,* 226.

5. Cleaning

1. Measures used to police cinema during the early twentieth century did not rely on editing techniques. The prominent pair of scissors regularly associated with the cut of censorship did not become an actuality until much later in the form of national self-regulation. At the turn of the past century, the seemingly recalcitrant object of cinema was largely policed through direct physical and municipal responses. The physical removal of films (*Dolorita's Passion Dance* of 1894, for example) considered morally objectionable by outraged patrons, state officials, or moral reformers watching over popular entertainment was perhaps the only response possible at that time. Measures most employed to regulate film exhibition prior to the establishment of formal review associations included the removal of specific films, the closing down of spaces for exhibition, and unofficial age restraints. Keep them out, close them down, or get it out were the prevailing sets of actions used to police cinema. Films at the turn of the century mostly consisted of one shot to show the captured movements. Editing was still in its extreme infancy, not yet a staple of filmmaking let alone conceived of as a method for censoring films in the name of public morality. The arrival of narrative film, recognized to begin with *The Great Train Robbery* (1909), enabled the production of longer films and utilized editing to convey a story over a period of time. The coming of narrative coupled with the growing prominence of permanent structures for film exhibition prompted further regulatory actions. For example, New York City's Mayor George McClellan closed all city nickelodeons on Christmas Eve 1908, and the outcome of *Block v. Chicago* (1909) upheld police inspection and licensing of all films exhibited within the city of Chicago. In that same year a local-level attempt at prior restraint—films were to be previewed by a committee prior to exhibition in New York City—became the National Board of Censorship of Motion Pictures. In 1915 (the same year that *Birth of a Nation* was released) the board was renamed the National Board of Review. Its task, like the local committee's before it, was to preview films prior to public release in order to "protect" U.S. audiences from matters considered potentially troublesome by securing ideals of decency and morality through the me-

dium of film. Film itself becomes the primary object of inspection (not the cinema) and surface on which regulatory measures are carried out. It was not until the 1920s that the "Hays Office," officially known as the Motion Picture Producers and Distributors Association of America led by Will H. Hays, prescribed a set of guidelines to promote its policy of self-regulation. Under self-regulation, studios were asked to submit scripts to the Hays Office for review. Prior to release of the finished film, the Hays Office advised studios whether or not their materials were morally appropriate according to its 1927 "Don'ts and Be Carefuls" list of suspect themes and practices. These and other cautionary measures solidified self-regulation in the form of the 1930 Production Code.

2. Laurent Bouzereau, *Cutting Room Floor: Movie Scenes Which Never Made It to the Screen* (New York: Citadel Press, 1994); Tom Dewe Mathews, *Censored* (London: Chatto and Windus, 1994); Murray Schumach, *The Face on the Cutting Room Floor: The Story of Movie and Television Censorship* (New York: William Morrow and Company, 1964); and Baxter Phillips, *Cut: The Unseen Cinema* (New York: Bounty Books, 1975). Signifiers of the "cut" also appear in the form of the red cross-out to indicate which individual frames must be deleted. Annette Kuhn, *Cinema, Censorship, and Sexuality, 1909–1925* (London: Routledge, 1988); and Gerald Gardner, *The Censorship Papers: Movie Censorship Letters from the Hays Office 1934 to 1968* (New York: Dodd, Mead and Company, 1987) both adorn their book covers with this image.

3. Bouzereau, *Cutting Room Floor,* x.

4. Lev Manovich, "What Is Digital Cinema?" in *The Digital Dialectic: New Essays on New Media,* ed. Peter Lunenfeld (Cambridge, Mass.: MIT Press, 1999), 179–80. Manovich's article is expanded into his final chapter in *The Language of New Media* (Cambridge, Mass.: MIT University Press, 2001).

5. Jay David Bolter and Richard Grusin, *Remediation: Understanding New Media* (Cambridge: MIT Press, 1999), 154.

6. Andrew Darley, *Visual Digital Culture: Surface Play and Spectacle in New Media Genres* (London: Routledge, 2000), 18–19.

7. Michele Pierson, *Special Effects: Still in Search of Wonder* (New York: Columbia Press, 2002), 141.

8. Sean Cubitt, *The Cinema Effect* (Cambridge, Mass.: MIT University Press, 2004).

9. Tom Gunning, "The Cinema of Attractions: Early Film, Its Spectator and the Avant-Garde," in *Early Cinema: Space, Frame, Narrative,* ed. Thomas Elasesser, 56–62 (London: BFI Press, 1990).

10. Angela Ndalianis, "Special Effects, Morphing Magic, and the 1990s Cinema of Attractions," in *Meta-Morphing: Visual Transformation and the Culture of Quick-Change,* ed. Vivian Sobchack, 251–71 (Minneapolis:

University of Minnesota Press, 2000). Contemporary films reliant on and promoted on account of digital technologies are said to mark a return to the principles that structured the infancy of cinema: in the simplest terms, showing over telling. For many, these principles are encapsulated by Tom Gunning's term for the epoch before 1906–07: the cinema of attractions. Unlike narrative-driven films that would eventually come to predicate realism on the effacement of the medium by investing believability and authenticity on a film's fictional structure, formal conventions, and an investment in an actor's performance, the cinema of attractions predicated its performance on its ability to display and exhibit images in an astonishing yet convincing manner. "Early audiences," Gunning writes, "went to exhibitions to see machines demonstrated (the newest technological wonder, following in the wake of such widely exhibited machines and marvels as X-rays or, earlier, the phonograph), rather than to view films" ("The Cinema of Attractions," 58). These same principles and practices, modes of extending vision in new ways and onto new surfaces, and the elaboration of the medium's persuasive potential resting hand in hand with its extraordinary capabilities are, by recent accounts like Ndalianis, Bukatman, Bolter and Grusin, Cubitt, Pierson, Darley, and McQuire, just to name a few, the attraction of special effects–driven digital cinema. The connection is not lost on Gunning, as he himself cites Spielberg, Lucas, and Coppola as inheritors of the spectacular cinema.

11. Ndalianis, "Special Effects, Morphing Magic," 258.

12. Pierson, *Special Effects,* 124.

13. Scott Bukatman, "The Artificial Infinite: On Special Effects and the Sublime," in *Visual Display: Culture beyond Appearances,* ed. Lynne Cooke and Peter Wollen (New York: New Press, 1998), 265.

14. Responding to the outrage over the posthumous rating requirements from the MPAA, Terry Semel, cochair of Warner Brothers, issued the following statement on the studio's compliance: "We're not in the NC-17 business. When one looks at 'Eyes Wide Shut' perhaps there was not a huge difference between what would be an R, what would be an NC-17. But NC-17 is a whole industry. It includes triple X-rated porno films. So to us that's just not a business that we're in. Never have been." Cited in Bernard Weinraub, "Critics Assail Ratings Board over 'Eyes,'" *New York Times,* 28 July 1999, sec. E. We can only guess if Kubrick would have pulled the film's release in the way that he did *A Clockwork Orange* (1971) in the United Kingdom. Had Warner Brothers fought to legitimize the MPAA's NC-17 rating and refused its suggestions for its "voluntary" process, we can also wonder if Kubrick's last film would have succeeded in opening up this debate in a way that *Showgirls* (Paul Verhoeven, 1995) could not.

15. Jon Lewis, *Hollywood v. Hard Core: How the Struggle over Censor-*

ship Saved the Modern Film Industry (New York: New York University Press, 2000), 1.

16. Ibid., 2.

17. Nicholas Mirzoeff, *Watching Babylon: The War in Iraq and Global Visual Culture* (London: Routledge, 2005).

18. Ibid., 16.

19. Ibid., 17.

20. Bukatman, "The Artificial Infinite," 265.

21. Cubitt, *The Cinema Effect,* 258.

22. Warren Buckland, "Between Science Fact and Science Fiction: Spielberg's Digital Dinosaurs, Possible Worlds, and the New Aesthetic Realism." *Screen* 40, 2 (1999): 177–92, 184.

23. Manovich, "What Is Digital Cinema?" 192.

24. Walter Benjamin, "The Work of Art in the Age of Mechanical Reproduction," in *Illuminations,* ed. Hannah Arendt, trans. Harry Zohn, 211–44 (London: Fontana Press, 1973).

25. A post on LiveJournal.com queries the decision: "I'm a little confused as to why large breasts are considered non-G-rated, while smaller breasts are fine for G. Are they trying to say that large-breasted women shouldn't be around children?" Secularkangaroo, "Today in Bizarre Censorship News: Digital Boob Reduction," 2 June 2003, http://www.livejournal.com/users/jwz/206726.html (7 July 2003).

26. Sander L. Gilman, *Making the Body Beautiful: A Cultural History of Aesthetic Surgery* (Princeton, N.J.: Princeton University Press, 1999).

27. Mike Ward reviews the 2002 rerelease against the Reagan-Bush context of the original. See his "Peace Frog," *PopMatters,* 4 April 2002, http://www.popmatters.com/film/reviews/e/et.shtml (19 June 2002).

28. Scott McQuire, "Impact Aesthetics: Back to the Future in Digital Cinema?" *Screen* 6, 2 (2000): 41–61.

29. Ward, "Peace Frog," 2002.

30. Buckland, "Between Science Fact and Fiction," 184.

31. Lev Manovich, "Old Media as New Media: Cinema," in *The New Media Book,* ed. Dan Harries, 209–18 (London: BFI Press, 2002), 212.

32. John Corbett, *Extended Play: Sounding Off from John Cage to Dr. Funkenstein* (Durham, N.C.: Duke University Press, 1994), 69.

33. Omayra Zaragoza Cruz, "Let's Talk @!#?%!# Politics," *PopMatters,* 6 October 2004, http://www.popmatters.com/columns/cruz/041006.shtml (7 October 2004) offers an account of Latino/a actor's commentary at the 2004 Latin Grammy Award and network censor's management of Spanish language.

34. Rebecca Marks, spokesperson for NBC, which aired a live benefit concert for Hurricane Katrina relief in October 2005, claimed that the person in

charge of NBC's tape-delay procedure was instructed for profanity and proceeded to "apologize" for the network's lack of censorship. Olivia Madison,
"Rap Artist Kanye West Censored on NBC," *Freemuse*, 27 October 2005,
http://www.freemuse.org/sw10987.asp (accessed 29 October 2005).

35. Judith Butler, *Excitable Speech: A Politics of the Performative* (London: Routledge, 1997).

36. Events in the history of music censorship briefly referenced here are
synoptically chronicled in Eric Nuzum, *Parental Advisory: Music Censorship in America* (New York: Perennial 2001), and further discussions with
an eye toward global cases of music censorship can be found in the collection edited by Marie Korpe, *Shoot the Singer! Music Censorship Today*
(London: Zed Books, 2004).

37. Wal-Mart is not the only retailer to have adopted this position; it just
happens to be the largest and most influential chain for music distribution
in the United States. Other retailers that have adopted a no "Parental Warning" policy include Camelot Music and Video, Sears, J.C. Penney, and Disc
Jockey; see Marjorie Heins, *Sex, Sin, and Blasphemy: A Guide to America's
Censorship Wars* (New York: New Press, 1998). Many retailers dependent
on shopping mall space must abide by mall policy that restricts what types
of products can be sold in its leased structure. Also, other retailers opted to
continue to stock labeled CDs but restrict sales based on age: "Trans World,
Tower, Musicland, Waterloo, Record Bar, or Sound Exchange declared that
despite the absence of legislation they would not sell these records to minors, requiring proof of age from their customers and making their employees responsible if records were found to have been sold to minors." Claude
Chastagner, "The Parent's Music Resource Center: From Information to
Censorship," *Popular Music* 18, 2 (1999): 179–92, 188.

38. Cited in Geoff Boucher and Jordan Raphael, "Pop Beat: Cleanups of
CDs Don't Clean Up; Edited Versions of Controversial Songs Have Failed to
Become a Hit with Consumers, Critics of the Music Industry or Insiders,"
Los Angeles Times 9 December 2000, sec. F.1.

39. Corbett, *Extended Play*, 72.

40. Redesign and redirect tactics such as Ice-T's were not limited to hip-
hop artists. The Dead Kennedys orchestrated a similar gesture on their
Frankenschrist (1985) when they included the following warning: "The inside fold-out to this record cover is a work of art by H. R. Giger that some
people may find shocking, repulsive, and offensive. Life can be that way
sometimes."

41. Corbett, *Extended Play*, 72.

42. Despite the extensive rewriting of "Purple Pills," in the form of
"Purple Hills," the FCC fined Colorado Springs radio station KKMG-FM
(based on the complaint of a single listener) $7,000 for airing an edited clean
version. The FCC claimed that even in this form the song "contains un-

mistakable offensive sexual references." In this isolated instance, the clean version fails to guarantee distribution. For coverage on the case, see Fred Goodman, "The FCC Takes On Eminem," *Rolling Stone,* July 2001, 14.

43. Baz Dreisinger, "Doo-wop Hip-hop Despite Blips: She Done Him Wrong. Now the Airwaves Are Full of Eamon's Anguished Cries, Minus the Expletives," *Los Angeles Times,* 28 March 2004, sec. E.28.

44. Boucher and Raphael, "Pop Beats," F.1.

45. Neil Strauss, "Recording Industry's Strictest Censor Is Itself." *New York Times,* 1 August 2000, sec. A.

46. Ibid., A.1. ·

47. Skip Miller, cited in "Wu-Tang Readies 'Clean' Version of Album," *Billboard* 12 March 1994, 14.

48. Ibid., 14.

49. Butler, *Excitable Speech,* 133.

50. Michel Foucault, afterward to *Michel Foucault: Beyond Structuralism and Hermeneutics,* 2nd ed., by Hubert L. Dreyfus and Paul Rabinow (Chicago: University of Chicago Press, 1982), 221.

6. Patching

1. Senator Hilary Rodham Clinton cited in "Senators Fight Hidden Sex in 'Grand Theft Auto,'" *New York Times,* 15 July 2005.

2. I am referring to anti-gaming advocate and Christian conservative Jack Thompson, who has dedicated his legal career to prosecuting "obscenity" in rap music and "pornography" in video game content (namely the *Grand Theft Auto* series and *Bully*). The Florida Bar began disbarment proceedings against Thompson for professional misconduct in 2007. On June 4, 2008, Miami-Dade Circuit Judge Dava Tunis recommended disbarment for a ten-year minimum.

3. Senator Clinton states in her letter to the Federal Trade Commission that "we should all be deeply disturbed that a game which now permits the simulation of lewd sexual acts in an interactive format with highly realistic graphics has fallen into the hands of young people across the country"; cited in Steven Bodzin and Alex Pham, "Modified Video Game Spurs Clinton Protest," *Los Angeles Times,* 15 July 2005. According to the ESRB, this should not be the case given that restrictions on sales are already in place on account of *GTA: San Andreas*'s original rating of M for mature, intended for gamers over the age of seventeen. "Fallen into the hands" seems to suggest that no restrictions existed prior to Senator Clinton's proposed legislation to fine retailers $5,000 for selling M and AO games to youths. The proposed bill is titled "The Family Entertainment Protection Act" and is sponsored by Senators Clinton, Joe Lieberman, and Evan Bayh. Opposition to Senator Clinton's proposal has been voiced by Bo Andersen, president of

the Video Software Dealers Association, who claims that Clinton's "proposal is politically savvy but will do nothing to help parents make informed choices about the video games their children play. In fact, by turning the voluntary video game ratings system into a cudgel of government censorship, Senator Clinton's proposal ironically would likely lead to the abandonment of the ratings system"; cited in "Senators Fight Hidden Sex in 'Grand Theft Auto,'" *New York Times,* 15 July 2005. According to Senator Clinton's recommendation, retailers who sell games to underage buyers could be found guilty of a federal misdemeanor and thus provide governmental enforcement of the voluntary workings of the ESRB.

4. Bodzin and Pham, "Modified Video Game Spurs Clinton Protest."

5. Michael White, "Take-Two Has Profit on Sales of 'Grand Theft Auto' (Update2)"; http://www.bloomberg.com/apps/news?pid=20601103&sid=a8UnDNWDmL2w&refer=us (accessed 5 June 2008).

6. Congressman Joe Baca of California is a founder and cochair of the Congressional Sex and Violence in the Media Caucus. He, along with Representative Frank Wolf (R-Va.) and Representative Tom Osborne (R-Neb.) are pressuring the ESRB to tighten its certification criteria in the wake of *GTA: San Andreas* and attempting to make the policing of video game content a federal issue by enlisting the assistance of the Federal Trade Commission to investigate existing video ratings.

7. All statistical information taken from "Industry Facts," Entertainment Software Association, 2008, http://www.theesa.com/facts/index.asp (accessed 10 June 2008).

8. Mystique is best known for its infamous 1982 release *Custer's Revenge,* where part of the game play requires that players rape Native American females.

9. On May 7, 2008, another bipartisan bill aimed at carding minors who purchase console games rated "Adults Only" and "Mature" was introduced in the U.S. House of Representatives. Sponsored by Representatives Jim Matheson (D-Utah) and Lee Terry (R-Neb.), the new legislation, known as "The Video Games Enforcement Act," would require retailers to check a purchaser's I.D. before selling a game and would impose fines ($5,000) for retailers who do not comply; http://www.gamepolitics.com/2008/05/07/in-wake-of-gta-iv-launch-video-game-legislation-proposed-in-congress (accessed 8 May 2008). Gamepolitics.com provides its visitors with a "Legislation Tracker" to monitor new legislation aimed at restricting access to games. Similar legislation has been defeated in various federal courts of appeal on the grounds of First Amendment violations. Governor Arnold Schwarzenegger (Calif.) supported legislation in October 2005 that would make sales of Adult Only and Mature games to minors illegal. In August 2007 a U.S. district court overturned the law.

10. Figures cited in Associated Press, "Parents Search for Family-Friendly Games," *New York Times,* 10 January 2005.

11. See "Enforcement," Entertainment Software Rating Board, 2006, http://www.esrb.org/ratings/enforcement.jsp (accessed 19 May 2006).

12. The Federal Trade Commission published a report in 2002 that gave "video stores the highest marks of any industry segment for controlling children's access to entertainment"; cited in American Society of Association Executives, "Video Retailers Promote Parental Control Involvement," *Association Management,* March 2002, 26. Information on the Video Software Dealers Association's "Pledge to Parents" program can be found at VSDA,"VSDA Pledge to Parents Program," http://www.idealink.org/Resource.phx/vsda/benefits/parents/pledge.htx (accessed 9 June 2006).

13. Cited in Bodzin and Pham, "Modified Video Game Spurs Clinton Protest."

14. Cited in Alex Pham, "Hidden Sex Scenes Spark Furor over Video Game," *Los Angeles Times,* 21 July 2005. http://www.latimes.com/technology/consumer/gamers/la-fi-sexgame21jul21,1,2936817.story?page=1&coll=la-business-games (accessed 25 July 2005).

15. Ibid.

16. Tor Torsen, "Confirmed: Sex Minigram in PS2 San Andreas," *GameSpot News,* 15 July 2005, http://www.gamespot.com/news/2005/07/15/news_6129301.html (accessed 1 June 2006).

17. Ibid. This charge of "pornography" was transformed into a pending bill in the Washington State Legislature that rather than target sexually explicit content, legislates a causal relation between games and real-life events. HB 2178, "Relating to Violent Video and Computer Games," of the Committee on Juvenile Justice and Family Law, neatly sidesteps the debate on sexually explicit material in *GTA: San Andreas* to establish a causal relation between game content and "real-life" actions in the name of protecting law enforcement from the "effects" of violent content. HB 2178's brief reads as follows: "Provides that a person may maintain an action for personal injury or wrongful death against a manufacturer or retailer of violent video or computer games if the manufacturer or retailer has distributed, sold, or rented a violent video or computer game to a person under the age of seventeen and the game was a factor in creating conditions that assisted or injury or death to another person"; "Bill Information: HB 2178—2005–06," Washington State Legislature, 2006, http://apps.leg.wa.gov/billinfo/Summary.aspx?bill=2178&year=2005 (accessed 19 May 2006).

18. Joe Baca, "Rep. Joe Baca Questions Accuracy of Video Game Ratings," www.house.gov/apps/list/press/ca43_baca/videogameratingssystem.html (accessed 3 May 2006).

19. Exempt from congressional debate on sexual content in video games

is the "Nude Raider" patch. The downloadable patch is the result of hackers who hacked the *Tomb Raider* game engine to alter Lara Croft's appearance. Her iconic shorts and top were removed and replaced with nude textures. Boots and gun belt remain. The Nude Raider patch has sparked heated discussions and petitions within the gaming community as many feel such a patch undermines the integrity of the Croft character, especially as too few female avatars exist in games. Such concern by actual gamers demonstrates that matters of "nudity" and sexual portrayals in games are not limited to the rhetoric of protecting children but also resonate within a larger political and social sphere. See Anne-Marie Schleiner, "Game Reconstruction Workshop: Demolishing and Evolving PC Games and Gamer Culture," in *Handbook of Computer Game Studies,* ed. Joost Raessens and Jeffrey Goldstein (Cambridge, Mass.: MIT Press, 2005), 405–14.

20. Hillary Rodham Clinton, "Children and Families," http://clinton. senate.gov/news/statements/details.cfm?id=233740 (accessed 8 June 2006).

21. Ibid.

22. Ibid.

23. It is more likely that added expenses incurred to produce multirated games as well as a predictable surplus of "clean" games that prove unpopular with gamers may deter such an enterprise.

24. "PS3 Parental Controls Outlined," *PS3 Today,* 25 October 2005, http://www.ps3today.com/Blogs/News/hqs/blr_805.aspx (accessed 9 June 2006).

25. Microsoft, "Microsoft Xbox 360 Family Settings Help Create a Safer Gaming Environment," 16 March 2006, http://www.microsoft.com/athome/ security/children/xbox_360_family_settings.mspx (accessed 9 June 2006).

26. Ibid.

27. Apple.com, "Family: For a Kid-Safe Computer," 2007, http://www. apple.com/macosx/features/family/ (accessed 30 April 2007).

28. See Peter Kafka, "iPorn?" *Forbes,* 4 November 2005, http://www. forbes.com/2005/11/03ipod-porn-digital-cx_pk_1104ip (accessed 21 December 2005).

29. For the various features of Firefly Mobile's kid phone, see "Detailed Specifications," http://www.fireflymobile.com/phone/specs.php (accessed 11 November 2005).

30. Steven Barrie-Anthony, "Cellphones: Just a Leash for Children?" *Los Angeles Times,* 21 June 2006, http://www.latimes.com/technology/ la-et-phonetrackers21jun21,1,4106095.story (accessed 21 June 2006).

31. Appleinsider, "Exposed: iPhone 2.0's Parental Controls, Redesigned Calculator"; http://www.appleinsider.com/articles/08/03/13/exposed_ iphone_2_0s_parental_controls_advanced_calculator.html (accessed 10 June 2008).

32. Family Safe Media's "iShield" purports to block Internet porn through its image recognition software.

33. Jon Sorenson, quoted in C. Medford, "New York Pans Google Video," *Red Herring*, 13 June 2006, http://www.redherring.com/Article.aspx?a=17209&hed=New%20York%20Pans%20Google%20Video (accessed 17 June 2007).

34. Jim Griffiths, quoted in R. Thomas Umstead, "Playboy Preaches Control," *Multichannel News*, 22 May 2006, http://www.multichannel.com/article/CA6336423.html (accessed 17 June 2006).

35. Takeparentalcontrol.org, http://www.takeparentalcontrol.org/images/tpcmain.htm (accessed 18 June 2006).

Index

Raiford Guins is assistant professor of digital cultural studies in the Department of Comparative Literary and Cultural Studies and Consortium for Digital Arts, Culture, and Technology (cDACT) at SUNY Stony Brook. He is a founding principal editor for *Journal of Visual Culture*.